RESHAPING
FAMILY
RELATIONSHIPS

RESHAPING FAMILY RELATIONSHIPS

The Symbolic Therapy of Carl Whitaker

By
Gary Connell, Ph.D.
St. Vincent Family Medicine Center
Erie, Pennsylvania

Tammy Mitten, Ph.D.
Private Practice
Erie, Pennsylvania

William Bumberry, Ph.D.
St. John's Mercy Medical Center
St. Louis, Missouri

BRUNNER/MAZEL
· Taylor & Francis Group ·

USA	Publishing Office:	BRUNNER/MAZEL
		A member of the Taylor & Francis Group
		325 Chestnut Street
		Philadelphia, PA 19106
		Tel: (215) 625-8900
		Fax: (215) 625-2940
	Distribution Center:	BRUNNER/MAZEL
		A member of the Taylor & Francis Group
		47 Runway Road
		Levittown, PA 19057
		Tel: (215) 269-0400
		Fax: (215) 269-0363
UK		BRUNNER/MAZEL
		A member of the Taylor & Francis Group
		1 Gunpowder Square
		London EC4A 3DE
		Tel: +44 171 583 0490
		Fax: +44 171 583 0581

RESHAPING FAMILY RELATIONSHIPS: The Symbolic Therapy of Carl Whitaker

1 2 3 4 5 6 7 8 9 0

Printed by Edwards Brothers, 1998.

A CIP catalog record for this book is available from the British Library.
ⓔ The paper in this publication meets the requirements of the ANSI Standard Z39.48-1984 (Permanence of Paper).

Library of Congress Cataloging-in-Publication Data

Connell, Gary.
    Reshaping family relationships : the symbolic therapy of Carl
Whitaker / by Gary Connell, Tammy Mitten, William Bumberry.
      p.   cm.
    Includes bibliographical references and index.
    ISBN 0-87630-878-7 (hardcover : alk. paper)
    1. Family psychotherapy. 2. Whitaker, Carl A.   I. Mitten, Tammy.
II. Bumberry, William M., 1951-   . III. Title.
RC488.5.C636   1998
616.89'156—dc21

98-38283
CIP

ISBN 0-87630-878-7 (cloth)

This book is dedicated to the loving memory of Ruth V. Connell.

Contents

Preface

Dr. Carl Whitaker was a master therapist. He was an intuitive genius and a preeminent clinician of our time. He had a rare capacity to make contact with families. He found slivers of himself in them. He shared his impressions with families in a way that was illuminating and challenging. Intuition was his methodology, his clinical hunch his forte. There is no disputing his clinical presence and his profound impact on the field of family therapy.

Time with Carl was an exhilarating experience. He was a man with an energetic presence. He gave freely of himself, loved having his ideas challenged, and was willing to mentor the serious student. His brilliance was blinding, his outrageousness shocking, his personal warmth enormous. Salvador Minuchin (1982) commented on Carl's clinical impact as follows: "By the end of therapy, every family member has been touched by Whitaker's distorting magic. Each member feels challenged, misunderstood, accepted, rejected or insulted. But he has been put in contact with a less familiar part of himself."

Carl believed that an overemphasis on theory and technique would negate creativity, dull intuition, and ultimately destroy the personhood of the therapist. Consistent with the belief that "nothing worth learning could be taught," Carl gravitated to an apprenticeship model to training. The training and mentoring experience included co-therapy and the sharing of his therapy experiences through endless case discussions. It was a highly personal, clinically potent approach to training. Being drawn into Carl's world meant focusing on understanding the therapy experience, whether writing, talking about cases, or doing therapy consultations. Carl's world was intimately involved with understanding families.

The evolution of the ideas and underlying theoretical tenets of symbolic-experiential family therapy was clinically derived. They emerged from massive clinical experience. Terms such as the battle for structure and the battle for initiative were added to the family therapy literature. The personhood of the therapist, the therapist's use of self, and the usefulness of craziness became generally accepted clinical constructs. A therapy pattern developed that had obvious clinical utility but lacked an organizing framework or coherent unifying theory.

As a model, symbolic-experiential therapy has a solid group of proponents. Despite Carl's widespread recognition, relatively few clinicians identify themselves as symbolic-experiential family therapists. One problem with the model has been its idiosyncratic language. The apprenticeship model is an extraordinary model for learning therapy; however, it tends to insulate clinicians who think alike. It is similar to the shared language developed by twins. They clearly understand each other's communication, while outsiders struggle to comprehend the dialogue. In the case of symbolic-experiential therapy, followers of the theory understand the subtleties of the technique, while outsiders are confused and apprehensive. The goal of this book is to expand the language of symbolic-experiential therapy, to make the theory and techniques more accessible to clinicians interested in family therapy. We have attempted to concretize the model, and we discuss techniques frequently used by symbolic-experiential therapists. Throughout the book, we incorporate dialogue taken from audiotaped consultations and personal communication between Gary Connell and Carl from 1988 to 1992. Quoted dialogue comes from these audiotapes unless cited otherwise.

Acknowledgments

This book could not have been completed without the mentoring and inspiration of Carl A. Whitaker, MD. Throughout the years he provided guidance, encouragement, and stimulating discussion about the symbolic-experiential approach to working with families. Carl was provocative in his approach to both therapy and mentoring and tireless in his efforts in the field of family therapy. His energy and enthusiasm were limitless. A special thanks goes to his wife, Muriel, who is a remarkable, caring human being.

We would like to take this opportunity to thank our families for their support, commitment to our dream, and nurturance throughout the project. They cheered us on when we needed it most. A special thanks to Christian and Jennifer Connell for their typing, formatting, and editing of the manuscript. Thank goodness Christian can work magic with the computer.

We'd also like to thank Fred Piercy, Ph.D., and Sidney Moon, Ph.D., Purdue University, for their guidance with the research on which the six-stage model is based. A final thanks goes to Richard Cogley, MD, Corporate Leader for Medical Affairs Saint Vincent Health Center, who provided the initial impetus for the project through his encouragement and helpfulness.

Introduction

Although Carl's work is considered brilliant, creative, and innovative, his techniques are commonly viewed as being beyond the reach of the average clinician. Some have thought his therapeutic successes reflect his personal charisma rather than a clearly formulated, internally consistent, replicable approach to therapy. This book offers a model for understanding the process of change in family therapy from a symbolic-experiential perspective. It provides a vivid picture of symbolic-experiential therapy highlighted by clinical vignettes of the work of Whitaker as well as the authors. Clinical material and case discussion illustrate each component of the approach.

This model is based on a research project conducted by Gary Connell and Tammy Mitten in which grounded theory methods were used to identify the core variables of symbolic-experiential therapy. An extensive review of the literature, coding of videotapes, and interviews with experts who trained with Dr. Whitaker generated the material for this book. This research-based conceptual model gives shape to the "tacit knowledge" and clinical wisdom underlying Whitaker's work. The model not only identifies the various stages of the therapy process but clearly isolates the types of interventions that are typical of each stage.

The six stages of therapy that constitute the core variables of symbolic-experiential therapy are (a) generating a relational point of view, (b) creating a therapeutic alliance, (c) stimulating a symbolic context, (d) activating stress to fuel change, (e) catalyzing change through symbolic experiences, and (f) termination.

This perspective is a new lens for examining, organizing, and using the central ideas and theoretical tenets sprinkled throughout Dr. Whitaker's many contributions to our field. Building on his previous works, this book presents a more rigorous analysis and integrated conceptualization of symbolic-experiential therapy. Carl's accumulated wisdom is reconfigured and presented in a fashion easily accessible to the average clinician.

This volume presents a blend of theoretical and philosophical positions that naturally flow into the treatment process and the therapeutic techniques that follow. Clinical vignettes, case histories, and treatment strategies bring the conceptual framework to life.

Chapter 1: Symbolic-Experiential Family Therapy

This chapter provides an introduction to symbolic-experiential family therapy, emphasizing the philosophical understructure of this approach to treatment. The significance of the symbol world is addressed, with particular emphasis on its relevance to day-to-day living.

Chapter 2: Evolution of the Model: Carl Whitaker's Journey

This chapter chronicles Carl Whitaker's professional journey. As we revisit the path he walked, we highlight significant learning experiences.

Chapter 3: Personal Beliefs of the Therapist

This chapter explores the centrality of the person of the therapist to the therapeutic process. We explain our working assumptions about people, relationships, change, and therapy. Their belief systems are the guiding framework that enables clinicians to organize their work. Critical issues such as therapists' capacity to tolerate ambiguity, contain their own anxiety, and maintain a differentiated position are examined. The importance of the professional role structure the therapist embraces is also explored. This professional posture is another filter that guides a therapist's actions. It determines what data to attend to and what to ignore, when to intervene and when to wait, what techniques to use, and when therapy has been completed.

Chapter 4: Family Relationships

In addition to clarifying one's ideas and beliefs about therapy, it is essential to be cognizant of one's automatic assumptions about people, families, relationships, and normality. Our mind-set regarding these issues profoundly colors the therapy process, all too often without our conscious consent. This complex matrix of beliefs, values, prejudices, and biases must be acknowledged and embraced if its unintended impact is to be minimized. This chapter invites the reader to explore his or her covert belief systems and to appreciate how they affect all we see and do. Assumptions regarding marriage, gender, parent/child relationships, and three-generational dynamics, as well as our beliefs regarding the "human condition," are examined.

Chapter 5: Generating an Interpersonal Context

While we live in a culture that values individualism over the relational world, this approach focuses on creating an interpersonal point of view. We want family members to experience the power of their connections and recognize their natural interdependence. A central goal of this phase of therapy is to move beyond the isolating perspective of one identified patient and a healthy family to a more integrated set. When families have a difficult time making this shift, the therapist's goal is to create an experience that counters isolationism and enhances a sense of mutuality. Commonly used techniques include expanding the symptom by creating multiple scapegoats, discovering cross-generational influences, redefining pathology, and dealing with repetition compulsion.

Chapter 6: Creating a Therapeutic Alliance

Once the family has shifted into a relational set and developed an appreciation for its identity as a unit, the therapist must establish a position in relation to them. The therapist must join the family without being seduced into thinking he or she can be one of them. The process of joining and distancing will continue throughout the therapy. The therapeutic alliance is a relational set between the family and the therapist whereby the therapist enters the system, engages the family in a catalytic fashion, and then pulls out. The family then decides how to respond. They must take ownership for what they do and what happens next. Commonly used interventions include joining or connecting with the family's experience, adopting their language, and parallel play.

Chapter 7: Stimulating a Symbolic Context

Once the family and the therapist have settled into a working alliance, the therapist begins to shift from the content of the family's life to attending to the symbolic significance of their stories. While the family focuses on the "facts," the therapist listens to what's underneath. The therapist relates to the symbolic world in order to facilitate primary process relating and cut beyond the limitations of socially sanctioned "rational" relating. Stimulating a symbolic context is a way of bypassing the family's defenses and circumventing the types of impasses that prevent growth. The following techniques are useful in creating a symbolic context: exploring symbolic bits and fragments, expanding fantasies, and using play, humor, and absurdity.

Chapter 8: Activating Stress Within the System

When a family is in pain, they want relief; they want to feel better. Unfortunately, merely wanting to emerge from the misery is not enough. A certain level of desperation is required. This chapter examines ways in which the therapist can increase the family's level of productive anxiety. The goal is to push them to the point where they're willing to do what it takes to change. Techniques described in this chapter include active waiting, challenging roles, deviation amplification, and establishing differences.

Chapter 9: Creating Symbolic Experience Through Associative Communication

This chapter addresses the core phase of the treatment process. While creating a symbolic context and activating anxiety are necessary, they are not sufficient to ensure actual change. Unless the family has an experience that infiltrates their infrastructure and enlarges the way they perceive life, there will be no significant, lasting change. The therapist must access and intervene in the family's symbol world in order to expand their living. By creating a context for new experiences, the therapist can help the family transcend their established way of relating and discover a new way of being with each other. During this phase, the therapist is free to be more spontaneous. The level of personal investment is elevated, and the focus is on generating symbolic experiences in the present. Therapeutic interventions aimed at providing this opportunity include telling stories; sharing free associations, fantasies, visual images, and metaphors; creating symbolic experiences; and using roles.

Chapter 10: Termination: Moving Out and Moving On

As symbolic shifts take root and the family begins to emerge as an open, creative unit, it becomes clear that they can function effectively without the therapist. The therapy loses some of its intensity. The therapeutic task then is to help the family face this issue and make a decision. Suggesting that they're not quite ready to leave is a serious error at this point in the therapy. They need the freedom to make a decision, with our support as a backdrop. Letting them know you respect their right to decide is crucial. Techniques that are typical of this phase include making the covert overt, highlighting changes and competencies, reversing roles, and letting the family know you'll survive.

Chapter 11: Consultation

With the model now clarified, this chapter serves to integrate each step of the process via a full-length case study. The reader will get more of a feel for the flow of the therapy and the continuity of the evolving process of change.

Chapter 1

Symbolic-Experiential Family Therapy

To understand complex processes, one needs a map. To cross the United States by car, to understand chemistry or mathematics equations, a map is essential. In like manner, family therapy is a complex process and needs a model to outline the trip.—Carl Whitaker

Psychotherapy is a symbolic project. We believe that if therapy is to have a lasting impact, it must become a symbolic experience. Symbolic-experiential therapy focuses on unique family symbols that deter growth. As therapists, we help our clients realize that their initiative fuels the process of growth. Merely arriving at our office does not guarantee change. The journey is theirs, traveled by their footsteps. They pay the price and exert the effort. This is intentional, for the gains and losses are theirs, not ours. Anything we do to obscure this fundamental fact is countertherapeutic.

Carl Whitaker often told the story of a police officer who was on the scene as a man was about to commit suicide. As the distraught man was about to jump from the bridge, plunging to a certain death, the policeman spontaneously reacted.

Officer: Hey you! Stop right there! Don't move! You can't do that!

Man: What do you mean, I can't?

Officer: What about your wife?

Man: Who cares.

Officer: But your kids need you!

Man: So what.

Officer: Your parents will be devastated!

Man: Big deal.

1

[In a moment of frustration, the policeman draws his gun and aims at the man]

Officer: You S.O.B., don't jump or I'll shoot you!

[So the man climbed down from the bridge]

Carl referred to this as the best example of symbolic therapy he'd ever encountered. The policeman was fully in the moment. His response had that odd quality of being both sincere and absurd. It broke through the man's certainty about wanting to die. It contaminated his fantasy of controlling his own destiny, solving his problems, punishing those who neglected him, and finally being appreciated. Being shot by the policeman, a stranger who had suddenly become invested in him, didn't fit with his agenda. It ruined the dark purity of his plan. The tragic, romantic feel of his fantasy was gone. Once disrupted, he couldn't get it back. The decision to come down from the bridge and go on living now made sense.

It is our belief that experience, rather than understanding or insight, is the real impetus to meaningful change. While our intellect can try to put words to experience, mere intellectual understanding doesn't usually produce change. Experience is nonrational. It's subjective, not based on fact or logic. It occupies a different domain than the world of cognition. If therapy is not symbolic, if it strives only to educate and problem solve, if it pushes social adaptation over individual creativity, the outcome will be limited.

The transformation from caterpillar to butterfly involves a sense of disorientation that calls into question a family's certainties. It casts a sense of doubt, however slight, on all they hold dear, all they considered sacrosanct. It creates the need to review their basics, to look at life anew. If this process fails to occur, the family's behavior will not change. Life will continue on automatic pilot.

THE SYMBOL WORLD

The goal of symbolic-experiential therapy is to provide an experience that flips the family's way of thinking. It must contaminate their way of perceiving reality and project them into a different way of interpreting and embracing life. As they "look over the top" and transcend their pre-existing set, everything changes. They can't resort to the old template. It no longer makes sense.

Carl Whitaker did not believe that it was important for the client to understand the symbolic experience. For example, it was not important for a client who had difficulty expressing anger to gain insight as to how internalized anger related to his childhood experiences. It was important for the therapist to provide experiences in which the client could express anger within the therapeutic relationship and discover that he or she needn't experience rejection or completely fall apart. Providing experiences within the context of an interpersonal relationship facilitates deeper levels of change within the infrastructure of a system.

The predicament in dealing with families is discovering how to create a symbolic experience. What kind of experience changes the family's internal computer? What differences do these experiences make? In discussing the complexity of creating a symbolic experience, Carl referred to a symbolic experience he had as a way of understanding this difficult change process. He shared that, prior to a presentation he was giving, he had prepared a talk about his mother. He had outlined in his mind what he would say and had become anxious anticipating the types of questions the audience might ask. However, the session didn't go at all as planned. The therapist hosting the presentation asked him few questions about his mother and was overly attentive to the information Carl offered on the subject. Then, prior to ending, the therapist inquired, "Did you ever think your father might be the problem?" This shocked Carl. He had never considered the possibility. This was a symbolic experience for Carl.

Another experience that was symbolic for Carl involved a time when he visited a university early in his career. He addressed the entire medical community, including spouses and other attendees. He was to talk on communication. He started off by telling them "You know, they told me to talk on communication, but I don't believe in it. I think it's a ridiculous subject, but they told me to talk about it anyway. I can't talk about anything else and because I'm talking, you have to sit there and listen and you can't do anything else." At this point, one of the residents got up and walked out. Carl responded by saying, "The hell with you, too." Carl wasn't sure if this was a symbolic experience for the audience, but it certainly was for him. He had found a way to get out of his professional role and relate in the more genuine and personal way he loved. Granted, there may have been a better way to do it, but it was an experience Carl never forgot.

Carl once said, "I think symbolic experiences are often mysterious." He referred to a time he spent half a day with the famous Nobel laureate, Elie Wiesel. He admitted he had no recollection of what the man said or what had happened. Carl revealed, "I think he could have said the ABC's and it would have been a powerful experience for me. He was such an enigma that I became more of myself in spite of myself. In trying to expand to meet him, I became more of who I was. That's a symbolic experience." Symbolic experiences shatter a family's gestalt. We can all recall symbolic moments in our lives. It's as if we're driving along, almost in a trancelike state, when a sharp curve or sudden turn in the road takes us in a completely different direction. The experience becomes imprinted in a way that we never forget.

Symbols are the unconscious accumulated residue of experience. Symbolic experiences constitute the best and worst moments, moments that have an impact and make us who we are. Symbols give meaning to family life. They represent such events as being born, loving, living, intimacy, and death. We pass them on intergenerationally through family stories, rituals, and myths.

Symbols hold meanings that words alone cannot capture. Carl said, "Symbols are more than words. It's the smile or frown that's behind the words that infers something." A mother's raised eyebrow or a certain tone in a father's voice can symbolize an entire experience. It's not the raised eyebrow or vocal tone, it's what they signify that's so meaningful. It's the picture they represent that carries extra weight. The message is instinctive. It does not need decoding.

Our experience of living comes through all of our senses on a moment-to-moment basis. As we begin to process this sensory information, we automatically strive to make sense of it. We give it meaning. We organize life around a core of internal symbolic representations that lend meaning and significance to our sensory experiences. As sensory data move beyond the perceptual realm and into the world of psychological meaning, they pass through a number of templates. We filter these data from our life experiences to create our symbol world. Each symbol represents a construct that is of significance to us. Together these symbols form a gestalt that speaks to who we are and what we believe. They are the guides to our living. They are the set of subjective perspectives that constitute our "belief system." Like the editorial page in a newspaper, our belief system can be as idiosyncratic as it is compelling.

The richness or poverty of our symbol world determines our subjective experience of living. How we feel moment to moment, how we hang onto the past, and how we anticipate the future are tied to the constructs and symbols that organize our experiences. Our internal reality defines our experience. Symbols may be either positive or negative.

THE UNIVERSAL, CULTURAL, AND FAMILY TEMPLATES

At the most generic, pervasive level, the template of the human condition connects us all. By virtue of birth we are blessed, as well as cursed, in grappling with the universal themes of fear, anger, sexuality, and death. Loneliness, fears of being abandoned or engulfed, primitive insecurities, and infantile dependencies reside in us all, as do homicidal, suicidal, and incestuous impulses. These are some of the basic ingredients that bubble below the surface. They organize our perceptions and affect everything we do.

Every culture organizes around the issue of how to handle the cauldron of human impulses. The values of the group shape and modulate the primitive expression of these impulses. As a culture, we influence and at times even control the perceptions of our members. For example, men are encouraged to ignore fear (the hero), deny death (immortality and the idolization of youth), and openly express anger and sexuality. They value needing no one and always being in charge. Women are asked to play a different role. They're encouraged to be self-sacrificing and responsive to the needs of others. While they are not discouraged from outwardly expressing anger, expression of fear, insecurity, and self-doubt is more acceptable. Despite the feminist movement, our culture's images of the ideal man and ideal woman continue to be worlds apart.

Beyond the culturally sanctioned model, each family subgroup further shapes and molds its members. This is the finishing school. The family finely tunes and programs its members on how to actually live in their culture. The family translates values into daily social living. Each family emphasizes certain themes to the relative exclusion of others. It's the family's archetype for dealing with the impulse world. It's analogous to a psychological family coat of arms.

These cultural and familial templates determine how we deal with the universal impulses that reside within. Some families view anger as positive and promote its expression in an aggressive approach to life. Others consider it dangerous, childish, or even sadistic. Another family may consider fear to be something that fully legitimizes avoiding certain behaviors, while others rigidly adhere to the belief that one must directly confront one's fears until they are conquered. Some view sexuality, sensuality, and eroticism as natural and important aspects of being human, while others reject them as sinful. Each family stamps its members with its spin on these universal themes. Few of us could articulate with any degree of accuracy a full listing of the actual filters or templates that organize our living. We discover them in our living, not in our words or in our thinking about living. They may take root from traumatic events, as well as innocuous, irrelevant comments or actions.

Let us give an example of how a seemingly trivial exchange can create a powerful symbolic template. John, a 29-year-old young man in therapy, was enchanted by the imagery of Kahlil Gibron's poetry, yet rarely dated and remained oddly cynical about the prospects of a loving relationship in his own life. One day, while casually discussing his parents' marriage, John smiled and began to chuckle. "You know, my dad never says much about his experience of the marriage. When I was 18 he came up to me and jokingly said, 'John, you're a man now. I have one bit of advice for you. If you ever find yourself getting serious about marriage, see me first.' We both had a good laugh. That's it. Never another word. Strange it would come to me now."

This is a nice example of the way the symbol world operates. With his father's words superimposed over the poetry of Gibron, a unique filter was created in which John wanted to believe in "happily ever after." He hoped for a soulmate, yet was mindful of his father's chilling caution. Cynicism seemed a natural compromise.

Paying attention to how families actually live together, not how they describe living together, reveals these templates. Observing how they connect, as well as how they operate autonomously, is critical. Family rituals are also revealing. The rituals of daily living, as well as those for special occasions, are telling. How a family approaches mealtimes—who participates, who doesn't, who serves who, how they handle various tasks—speaks volumes about who they are. The family's way of handling birthdays, anniversaries, and holidays sheds light on a domain sometimes only dimly viewed.

THE THERAPY WORLD

If the symbol world is the collection of internal representations that organize and give shape to experience, the therapy world is the expansion of this realm when it becomes constricting. The goal is to get in and challenge the family's way of relating and living. It involves contaminating the narrowness that has become comfortable or, at least, familiar. We want to break the trance and restimulate the family's humanness.

In the following clinical vignette, Dr. Milton Miller, former chairman of the Department of Psychiatry at the University of Wisconsin, recalls his initial exposure to the work of Carl Whitaker (personal communication, September 1997).

> I remember so well the first Carl Whitaker family interview that I observed. Carl had come as a visiting professor to Wisconsin, largely on an invitation from Carl Rogers, who was on the Wisconsin faculty at that time. The "patient," a young, icy paranoid boy of 18, was burning holes in his arms with a cigarette while his sophisticated professional parents talked in pleasantries about the cool summers of Martha's Vineyard. Carl, his shoes off, naïve, rambling, incomprehensible, told stories about fishing with nightcrawlers. He said he liked to squish them in his fingers before putting them on the hook. As he talked on, he took hold of the dad's hands, rubbed them, until they were red, then reached out and put his hand on the boy's shoulder and told him, "That's the craziest way of getting warm I ever saw. Put the cigarette away." In the moment of uncertainty as to what would happen next, Carl was firmly massaging the boy's shoulders as they began to quiver and pulsate with his sudden sobs. When Carl also began to cry, even the most intellectual of the professors in the audience covered their faces while coughing in order to remove an unprofessional tear.

Carl gave us all something. He laid it on the line with the patient, the family, and the 20 doctors and professors who were watching. In the presence of a crowd of hanging judges, Carl bared his neck (Miller, 1982).

This consultation is vintage Carl Whitaker. The family presented with a constricted, hardened symbol world. They organized themselves around being professional, composed, and in control of their emotions. They were cool, calm, and collected, at least on the surface. This family ethos created a distinctive distance, a sense of detachment that left the son isolated and desperate.

As the family chatted while the son continued to sear holes in his arm, Carl broke set and became personal. He spoke in graphic sensory detail, hoping to counteract their sterility. He rubbed Dad's hands until they were red, hoping to help him feel. Perhaps if they suddenly burst into flames, like two pieces of kindling wood, he would come to know something of his son's pain. Carl violated the family norm by making contact. He challenged the prevailing family set by attending to the symbolic implications of the son's actions and offering himself as a person who cared, as someone who was willing to get involved. His willingness to engage, to invest himself in the moment, countered the family's frozen facade. The physical touch of massage and the emotional vulnerability of tears broke their social protocol. There was an experience, in the moment, that couldn't be ignored or denied. Carl broke the spell and penetrated the family's icy sophistication.

This capacity, the ability to go counter to the family set, to penetrate the infrastructure of their central belief system, is a hallmark of Carl's work. The feel of his work is clearly "personal," not political or merely professional. The process of therapy breaks social protocol; it goes beyond political correctness and gets personal. It connects to the center of the "human condition." It does not settle for the peripheral. The experience finds its way into the family's symbol world, reverberates, and then catches onto something. Suddenly they discover something is different; they've changed! The shade is lifted. Living takes on a new hue. A transformation has begun.

THE PROCESS OF SYMBOLIC-EXPERIENTIAL THERAPY

Families typically seek treatment when their efforts to self-correct have failed. While there may be a general consensus about the goal of getting along better or communicating more, each family member typically has a different spin on the correct solution. They each have a different idea about what is necessary to solve the problem. As they go about the process of implementing their preferred solutions, power dynamics emerge. Members start to feel discounted and ignored, and the seeds of an impasse take root. Add some time and repetition and a full-blown impasse evolves. As each family member remains loyal to her or his point of view, the impasse deepens and hardens. The phone rings in your office.

In preparing to meet with the family, it's important to understand that, no matter how crazy it seems, they're doing what makes sense to them. They're acting in accordance with their underlying beliefs. Our working hypothesis is that their symbol world, the internal representational system that organizes their perspective, has become too narrow, too constricting. Rather than continuing to take in new information, they have become stagnant. They merely recycle the data. No new information is added to the mix. There is no flexibility or capacity to adapt.

Families enter therapy with a clear but often narrow view of the problem. They have tried numerous solutions; they just haven't been able to resolve their issues. The family comes to therapy hoping we'll make the unit operate as it should. They're looking for a hired gun to subdue the bad guys and restore order. While this is a great fantasy, it fails to recognize the all-too-obvious fact that therapists, no matter how well intended, are often just shooting blanks. Symbolic-experiential therapy helps the family access their inner wisdom. It helps them become their own guru, not find someone else to tell them how to live.

The therapeutic journey begins with trepidation. The family's guard is up as they mobilize for the quest. The experience of psychotherapy is foreign to most families. They are not sure of this stranger in their midst. There is often a deep split in the family regarding the definition of their problems and what they need to do about them.

Change is stressful. It's triggered by desperation and fueled by anxiety. Human beings are creatures of habit. Throughout the course of history, we have demonstrated, over and over, that we crave security and shrink from the unknown. We prefer safety, yet need to be vulnerable. Our lives are predictable, but uncertainty leads to new discovery. Worst of all, we tenaciously cling to the fantasy that someone will rescue us if we can hold on long enough.

The failure to integrate the dichotomies of life is the real villain. It interferes with our living, our sense of aliveness. As therapists, we strive to help our clients trust their collective voice. We want them to trust the wisdom of their own experience. This is the task before our clients.

It is imperative to recognize that anxiety fosters growth. Dissatisfactions with the status quo and motivation are central to change. Families become complacent when stuck or locked into a chronic impasse. They feel hopeless and helpless about their ability to live differently. Being unhappy or dissatisfied with their life, the flaws of their partner, or the failings of their children is not enough. Insight does not produce long-lasting change. Real change is predicated on the gut-wrenching, soul-shaking desperation that wells up within us. It clambers for expression. In its natural state, it begins as a sense of panic. As the inevitability of the journey settles in, a sense of resolve emerges. An air of determination supplants fear. The therapist's job is to help the family connect with their underlying anxiety and discover the desperation within that will fuel their journey.

We, as therapists, don't have all of the answers. We draw from our knowledge, experience, and history. We are skilled in relationships and believe strongly in the potential for growth. If we're clear about our limitations and human enough to connect intimately, we may be useful in helping families discover their resources.

The beginning of therapy is a deprogramming maneuver. The family is stuck, locked in with no sense of how to break free. We see them as a teetering Humpty-Dumpty, much in need of a fall. We want to break their mind-set and open the possibility of new configurations. We want to nudge them off the wall. Through overloading the system and inducing confusion, there's a chance they might put themselves back together again, better than before!

SUMMARY

Symbolic-experiential therapy emphasizes the emotional versus cognitive domain. We focus on how a family experiences life, not what they think about family problems. We want to access the symbolic infrastructure of the family. We want to know what issues are affectively loaded and develop a sense of how the family's experiences have created symbolic meaning around events such as birth, life, and death. We want to cut to the core, go underground to the symbolic realm. What are the family's fears, dreams, and fantasies? How are these communicated and passed on intergenerationally? What are the family's stories, myths, and rituals?

The goal of symbolic-experiential therapy is to enrich and expand the family's symbolic world. Carl believed that the goal of therapy is to create a symbolic experience that flips the family's way of thinking about itself. Carl provided symbolic experiences to expand and enrich the constricted symbolic world of the family.

Carl had an uncanny way of intruding because he dared to be human. By taking off his shoes during an interview, playing with children, rubbing the shoulders of a sobbing adolescent, or sharing his own experiences of life on a dairy farm, he broke through the family's rigid social facade. Carl was quick to make contact. Once inside the system, he stayed only long enough to heat things up. He was just as skilled at getting out, leaving the family's living to them. His ongoing joining and distancing maneuvers were brilliant. His stories resonate with us when we greet each new family.

Chapter 2

Evolution of the Model:
Carl Whitaker's Journey

We put people in the hospital because they have delusions.... But if I have a delusion they call it a theory.—Carl Whitaker

Carl Whitaker leaves a profound professional legacy to the field of family therapy. His numerous contributions have shaped our understanding of how to work with families in distress. Carl believed, above all, in personal investment in the process of therapy. Other than being personally invested in the therapy process, Carl was not quite sure himself why his therapy worked. He told a story about his work with a 10-year-old boy who refused to talk and adamantly stared into space the entire session. Therapy consisted of opening the door every week to let the boy in, sitting for an hour while the boy stood, and then opening the door to let the boy out. After 10 sessions, the teacher called to say she was amazed at the remarkable change in the boy. He no longer burned the curtains or engaged in other disruptive behaviors. The teacher exclaimed, "I don't know how you did it." Carl revealed, "I didn't tell her. It was a professional secret because I didn't know how I did it either" (Whitaker, 1976, p. 193).

Another recollection involved his work with an 8-year-old boy who had not spoken since age 2. Carl saw the boy over a 6-month period. Each session, the boy remained silent. The two of them tossed a football back and forth. Carl would talk and the boy would listen. Finally, feeling frustrated, Carl told the boy's mother he couldn't help and terminated the sessions. Three weeks later, the mother called to say the boy had started to talk. Whenever Carl thought he had the answer to what made therapy work, he discovered he could not replicate the process in exactly the same way. He indicated that each interaction was experienced differently, "so my dynamic theories are always up for suspicion" (Whitaker, 1973, p. 4).

During the last two decades of his career, Carl endured the status of being elevated (or is it relegated?) to guru status. While never auditioning for the role, he went about the business of being as fully human as possible, regardless of the setting or the demands of others. Whether in a therapy session, professional workshop, or personal conversation, Carl Whitaker was first and foremost himself. The thread that connected Carl's experiences of living, both personally and professionally, was the effort to live with integrity. He didn't hold himself as a model for others to emulate. He didn't mask his flaws. He didn't succumb to image. Carl merely went about the process of living, and as he lived he grew.

Spending time with Carl Whitaker, whether in the therapy room, at a professional workshop, or over a meal, was an enriching experience. Rubbing shoulders with him, walking in his footsteps taught others something about living, about the process of being more human. We learned without being taught. Time with Carl had the exhilarating impact of freeing one to be more and more oneself. It permitted one to face long-denied aspects of oneself that were too painful to notice and to discover corners of oneself that were long suppressed. Being in his presence was catalyzing.

Carl's consultations had the same impact on the families he encountered. To the observer, it was like watching a multileveled, intimate drama unfold: sometimes tragic, sometimes comedic; at times serious, at others absurd. Carl was clearly the director of this improvisational experience that not only revealed the family's underlying story but simultaneously challenged its confining certainty.

While each story is unique, the process becomes familiar. As Carl joined with each family member, he was looking for a contact, trying to find a way in. As he made it past their social facade and the anxiety-reducing initial presentation, the family's interior world and their inner experiences became more available. The tone became personal, not merely social. When family members' primitive affect surfaced, it was deeply emotional. While it was difficult to find words to capture the experience, it was easy to recognize the power.

According to Dr. Milton Miller, one of Carl's colleagues, "It's always safest in a human encounter if nothing happens. But with Carl there were few nonevents. People may love him or hate him, but something happens. He's unwilling to pretend to go through the motions. It is as if he lives by the principle that the perfunctory kiss is the worst perversion" (personal communication, September 1997).

In addition to his capacity to invest and his willingness to push for an actual experience, Carl was also renowned for his ability to stay cool under fire. Another story from Dr. Miller captures the essence of Carl's imperturbability.

> There was a time when an irate paranoid man said, "Whitaker, I'll get you. And you'll never know when it's coming. Someday when you turn the corner your fat belly will run into a shiv. Or you'll open your car door and a bomb will go off or you'll be standing at a urinal peeing and a steel club will hit your head. What do you say to that, Whitaker?" Carl said, "You helped me. Up till now, all I had to

worry about at the urinal was getting my shoe wet or meeting the wrong kind of people. You've given me something else to think about.''

When Carl worked, his words, his demeanor, his interventions all seemed so natural, so spontaneous. It was easy to remain oblivious to the years of training, experimentation, and struggle that guided the moment. Although there is no doubt that Carl was a brilliant man and a creative, intuitive clinician, we forget that his ideas and beliefs evolved over six decades of investment and dedication.

This chapter provides a review of Carl's professional evolution with the goal of illustrating how the basic tenets underlying symbolic-experiential therapy were formulated. Many criticized Carl's work, believing that his methods were atheoretical. Even those who studied with Carl often described him as a clinician, failing to notice the contributions he made to theory and our understanding of the therapy process.

However, if one reviews Carl's work, it becomes evident that he often alluded to the role of theory and research in relation to practice. One can track theoretical concepts, noting how they were refined and expanded over time. It also becomes apparent that he wrestled with the idea of how to study symbolic-experiential therapy. What is lacking in the literature, however, is an organizing framework. Carl did not leave us with a well-integrated, coherent theory that neatly ties together his ideas. This is not surprising. When Carl worked with families, he shared thoughts, fantasies, and free associations in relation to their living. He refrained from providing the family with directives or telling them how to live. They were free to take what he said and make of it what they wanted. In a similar way, we are left to make sense out of what he left behind.

THE EARLY YEARS (1938–1944)

Carl received his medical degree in 1936 and his master's in psychology in 1941 from Syracuse University. After entering medical school with the intention of becoming an obstetrician, he elected to spend a year working in the university psychiatric hospital following his OB-GYN residency. There he had one of the most profound experiences of his professional life. While spending his time on the inpatient units, Carl was first exposed to, fascinated with, and captured by the courage and complexity of the patients. Their willingness to expose the richness of their inner world gave Carl the courage to make contact with his own internal reality. As he quickly "fell in love" with schizophrenia, the thought of returning to obstetrics faded. In 1940 Carl accepted a child psychiatry internship in Louisville, Kentucky. There he was exposed to the magical world of play therapy. He recalled spending months on the floor with children, watching them talk about their families with toys, and found their honest replay of death, birth, jealousy, hatred, and sexuality to be quite humbling (Whitaker, 1976). This experience had a profound impact on Carl's emerging professional identity. He learned the importance of nonverbal communication and how to relate to children through play. He came to appreciate the power of the symbol world and to value process over outcome. This was also his initial exposure to the relevance of his internal feelings and associations to the therapy process. There was no hiding from the kids. Faking it didn't cut it. Logic and rationalizations didn't work. Carl learned to be honest. He learned to be present. Throughout his career, this intense experience with children affected his work. Carl used play to lower defenses, engage clients in a nonthreatening way, and access primary process.

Carl's work with delinquent adolescents also shaped his unique brand of therapy. From 1941 through 1944, he worked at Ormsby Village, a residential treatment program for delinquents. There he experimented with different ways of reaching and relating to rebellious adolescents. Early in his career, Carl focused on the interpersonal relationship between the therapist and client as the most crucial ingredient in therapy. During the interview, whether playing checkers, exchanging stories, or sitting in silence, Carl believed it was the process of relating to each other, not the actual content, that was important. Carl suggested that, when working with delinquents, the therapist's job was to develop an intense friendship, a real relationship that would provide the patient with the skills necessary to make friends and tolerate closeness. Even then Carl was convinced that experiential learning, not intellectual understanding, was central to change.

Working with delinquent adolescents made him acutely aware of the fact that therapists had to be both caring and tough (Whitaker, 1944). While his capacity to care allowed him to make contact and get in, the ability to be tough enabled him to set limits and challenge the adolescent's view of the world. He normalized adolescent rebelliousness, believing that we all harbor aggressive impulses. At the same time, he confronted them with the fact they had reached the edge and were now running the risk of foolishly ruining their lives. As Carl and the patient grappled with each other, the distinction between impulse and action would surface. While suicidal, homicidal, and aggressive impulses are "normal," acting impulsively on them only leads to "cutting your own throat." The issue then became how to be smarter, how to stay out of institutions and make it in the social world without selling out and giving up on one's individual identity. Carl's fundamental sense of caring and investment often permitted even the most alienated, frightened adolescents to stop posturing and engage in real person-to-person contact. Despite the contact, despite the investment, Carl respected the fact that ultimately the adolescent had to make the final decisions about how to live.

THE MIDDLE YEARS (1944–1964)

Carl's next move took him to Oak Ridge, Tennessee. This was in the mid-1940s, during the tumultuous years of World War II. Oak Ridge, a self-contained community of nearly 75,000 people, was organized around the production of plutonium for nuclear bombs. Life was colored with a sense of secrecy and mystery. Carl accepted a psychiatry position at Oak Ridge Hospital in a department with a grueling workload. He typically saw 20 patients a day, back to back, for half-hour sessions, as well as participating in running an acute inpatient service.

The combination of a demanding pace and a challenging population, including returning war veterans suffering from acute psychotic episodes, made the position scary and at times overwhelming. This stress led Carl to realize he needed a professional partner, someone to share experiences and communicate with, in order to survive. When Dr. John Warkentin joined the staff, he and Carl formed a professional partnership that was life sustaining. Together they focused on developing therapy methods aimed at increasing the intensity of the interpersonal relationship between therapist and client. In an effort to make personal contact, they experimented with seemingly outrageous approaches. They went through phases in which bottle feeding and arm wrestling/slapping games (being nurturing and tough) with patients became standard procedure. At times they would be intensely confrontive, at others they would fall asleep during sessions, often sharing their dreams upon waking. While unconventional and unorthodox on the surface, there was a profound message underlying these interactions. They reflected a level of personal investment in the client and in the therapy process. The therapist was no longer a blank screen; the clients were off the couch. Carl was able to transcend the traditional detached role of the therapist and engage personally. In so doing he created a powerful understructure of caring.

This intensely personal and professional bond with John Warkentin was synergistic and enhanced their courage and creativity. It led Carl, quite naturally, to discovering the value of co-therapy as both an antidote to burnout and a pathway to more potent treatment. Carl and John began to routinely consult with each other, to rely on one another in a jam, and to do clinical work together. One of Carl's favorite examples of the importance of a partner occurred during the first session with a veteran recently back from the South Pacific. Midway through the interview, Carl became terrified that this battle-tested veteran was going to come across the room and kill him on the spot. Carl excused himself, crossed the hall, interrupted one of John's sessions, and brought him into the session for a spontaneous consultation. As Carl described his fear, John made eye contact with the patient and said, "You know, I don't blame you. There have been times when I wanted to kill Carl myself" (Whitaker, 1976, p. 18). John then turned and exited without another word. This brief contact not only defused the patient but also relaxed Carl. He didn't feel so alone, so vulnerable.

As time passed, the two men's investment in each other increased. They did more co-therapy. The experience of working as co-therapists led to their discovery of the therapeutic power of the *we* element. The patient had more to relate to, struggle with, and transfer onto. The therapists had a newfound freedom to rely on unconscious processes. One could nod off to sleep and then share his dreams and associations or engage the client in a wrestling match while the other manned the gates, signaling or taking over if need be.

Carl's work with schizophrenics added another important ingredient to his therapy. He spoke of schizophrenia as a disease of abnormal integrity. By this he meant that schizophrenics were simply too brutally honest. The problem was that they were unaffected by socialization. They let it "all hang out" at times when society demanded restraint. Carl revered schizophrenics' willingness to honor and live by their own internal experiences rather than capitulating to cultural requirements. Carl believed the typical socially adapted person was basically duplicitous, living a lie, betraying him- or herself just to fit in. Schizophrenics, while remaining fiercely loyal to their internal world, were terribly naive about the power of the culture. Carl insisted that schizophrenics were not crazy but were merely "being stupid" by openly flaunting social convention. He identified with the schizophrenic's craziness, believing that we are all schizophrenic in the middle of the night, but most of us wake up and call it dreaming.

In 1946, Carl accepted a position at Emory University in Atlanta as chairman of the Department of Psychiatry. During this time, his clinical focus remained largely on individual therapy with schizophrenics. This was also the period when he became more solidly convinced of the clinical value of co-therapy. The ideas that germinated at Oak Ridge now took root. Two therapists and one patient created a therapeutic team with considerable power and fewer blind spots. In addition to more obviously symbolizing the original parenting couple and intensifying the transference implications, this also offered some sanctuary to the therapists. There was now a therapeutic "we" that was crucial to avoiding burnout.

In 1948, Dr. Tom Malone joined the department. He and Carl focused on exploring the process of psychotherapy. Several years later, they published their controversial ideas in *The Roots of Psychotherapy* (1953). They emphasized play, spontaneity, and the therapist's reliance on his or her own creative process. The book provided the first detailed description of how to activate the symbolic infrastructure and intervene in symbolic processes with patients. It challenged prevailing methods of psychoanalysis. While the authors incorporated many concepts of psychoanalytic theory into their work, they disagreed with the psychoanalyst's view of the therapist's role in treatment. In comparison with the psychoanalyst, who functions as a "blank screen," Whitaker and Malone portrayed the therapist as being more personally invested in the therapy process. The therapy process was organized around experience, not insight. Rather than making interpretations, the authors stressed the need for the therapist to rely on the use of self to create actual experiences in the therapy session that would augment or fill in missing developmental experiences. Therapy shifted from talking about life in the past to living life in the present.

While many of Whitaker and Malone's ideas are not controversial today, they were considered radical, even heretical, in the 1950s. One of their central contributions was to introduce a number of new techniques to the therapy world while cautioning against an overreliance on technique. They believed that techniques were a "double-edged sword." The use of techniques by a mature therapist could enhance the power of the treatment; when in the hands of an inexperienced or immature clinician, however, the same techniques would seem superficial and deter progress. The purpose of techniques was to increase the level of affect between the therapy participants. When they became a hideout or a way for the therapist to alleviate his or her anxiety, they were countertherapeutic. Techniques such as jointly developing and expanding fantasies and sharing free associations, dreams, or physical sensations were introduced. They even went so far as to suggest that the therapeutic techniques we develop and use say more about the character of the therapist than about the needs of the patient.

The controversial nature of *The Roots of Psychotherapy* created tremendous professional debate, some of which was respectful, some acrimonious. When paired with medical school politics, it led to Carl and a number of his colleagues leaving Emory in 1956 and forming a private practice, the Atlanta Psychiatric Clinic. He referred to this association as a "professional cuddle group." The group met on a regular basis to discuss cases, write about their ideas, and provide mutual support. Throughout his writings, Carl stressed the need for all therapists to have such a group to prevent burnout and facilitate ongoing professional development. The survival of the therapist became one of the identifying characteristics of his work.

In the mid-1950s, Carl and John again went against the grain, this time by experimenting with couples therapy. This was a time when couples were not seen conjointly. While it was perfectly acceptable for both partners to be in their own individual therapy, the idea of exposing them to each other during a therapy hour was unorthodox. When the presenting complaint seemed relational, Carl began inviting both partners to attend. He discovered that although one spouse presented with overt symptomatology, the level of dysfunction seemed equal in both spouses (Whitaker, 1958). He conceptualized their interlocking dynamics to be a result of projected unresolved issues related to their own family of origin. Carl found it helpful to identify repetitive interactional patterns and break up interlocking transferences. He was talking about and working with triangles before it was fashionable.

Assumptions About Marriage

As he continued working with couples, Carl developed a number of assumptions about couples therapy that have survived the test of time (Whitaker, Greenberg, & Greenberg, 1979). His core assumptions included the following:

1   Marriage itself is a third entity. In every couples session, there are three patients: the husband, the wife, and, most important, the marriage.
2   'The power of the marriage is greater than the positive and negative summation of the two people in it'' (Whitaker, 1965b). The experience

of the "we" is what makes marriage rewarding and at times threatening. The natural struggle of maintaining one's identity while yearning
for togetherness is compelling. It provides the bilateral impetus to
change and adapt to one another.

3   Pairing is not random. Partners choose each other on the basis of a
    myriad of conscious and unconscious needs and motives. Both have
    secret goals and wishes, including the desire to be made whole. There
    is also a profound wisdom in the match, if only we have the courage
    to find and face it.

4   There are two aspects of marriage, the legal commitment and the emo-
    tional commitment. They are distinct, yet interconnected.

5   Long-term marriages must experience and resolve a series of normal,
    predictable impasses. The resolution of these crisis points is vital to the
    continuing growth of the relationship.

Just as Carl helped shape our thinking about the role of the therapist in
therapy, his early work with couples contributed to a new way of viewing
interpersonal relationships that added to the evolution of systems theory. As he
became more and more fascinated with the power of interpersonal relationships,
he was no longer interested in altering intrapsychic dynamics.

Carl's ongoing experience with intensive co-therapy with individual schizophrenics further fueled his move toward a systemic perspective. He became
increasingly aware that, when sent home after finally emerging from a psychotic
experience, the institutionalized schizophrenic would regress, and the symptom
cluster would recur within weeks of the patient returning to the family. This led
to the decision to shift away from working with individuals and to begin working
with the family unit.

Carl incorporated more and more systems concepts into his thinking. He
became particularly enamored with the power of nuclear and extended families.
As he continued to work with families, Carl eventually refused to begin therapy
without the entire family being present. While considered unnecessarily demanding by some, Carl viewed it as merely being respectful of the family's
power. During this time, Carl identified new concepts based on his observations
of families in therapy. He introduced the concept of "acting out" on the part
of the family, as well as the therapist. This led to a series of articles that defined
acting out as any behavior diminishing the level of affective investment in the
therapy. He also contributed core papers concerning the use of aggression and
the usefulness of "craziness" as crucial ingredients of the therapy process.

Philosophical Assumptions of the Model

In responding to the ongoing controversy generated by their groundbreaking
work, Carl and his colleagues continued to define and refine their model. They
began to call their approach experiential or nonrational (as opposed to irrational)
therapy. Their focus was clearly on the power and intensity of emotions, feelings,

and primary process experiences rather than on the cognitive/intellectual realm. Experiential therapy emerged from three core philosophical assumptions (Malone, Whitaker, Warkentin, & Felder, 1961).

1   Pathology reflects an effort to grow, an attempt to come alive and be a person, not merely a social robot. It does not represent a disease or deficit.
2   Every human being, every family, has an enormous potential for growth. Unless interfered with, we naturally pursue that potential.
3   We are healthy to the extent we exercise our freedom to make choices in our living.

Goals of Therapy

Whitaker and Malone (1953) also more clearly articulated the therapeutic objectives or goals of experiential or nonrational therapy.

1   Personal growth, or a greater congruity between inner potential and what a person actually became, how he or she actually lived.
2   Symptom relief as a byproduct of personal growth, not as a direct goal.
3   Greater freedom of choice, the willingness to follow one's own beliefs.
4   Character development, resulting in the breakup of repetitive compulsions, and an increased capacity to live with anxiety.
5   Resolution of underlying dependencies, accepting the fact of aloneness and being free to pursue connectedness, and learning to enjoy both.
6   The capacity to experience an ever-broadening range of affect.
7   Increased spontaneity and creativity in living.

THE MADISON YEARS (1965–1982)

In 1965, Carl accepted a faculty position in the Department of Psychiatry at the University of Wisconsin. He was hired by Dr. Milt Miller into a department with an existential ethos and an openness to innovation. It was during this time that he developed and refined the style of family therapy for which he has been so widely recognized.

In order to facilitate the learning process of the psychiatric residents, Carl invited them to join him as co-therapists. This gave them the opportunity for profound learning experiences without direct instruction. The shared encounter made it easier to grasp abstract experiential concepts that were difficult to translate into words. In the process, new ideas emerged, new concepts took root.

In addition to working with the residents, Carl consulted with or conducted co-therapy with faculty and students. His extensive collaboration and co-therapy partnership with Dr. David Keith greatly enriched the evolution of the approach. The writing of the *Family Crucible* (1978) with Dr. Augustus Napier further clarified and popularized Carl's approach to working with families. Times had changed. Carl's work, once considered sacrilegious, was in its ascendancy. The approach was now called symbolic-experiential family therapy.

Over the years, out of this extensive experience with families, a pattern began to emerge. The therapy process, while in many ways unique with each family, began to reveal some consistencies. By the mid-1970s, a predictable clinical pattern had been established.

Stages of Therapy

In the 1970s, Carl provided a blueprint for conducting family therapy (Whitaker, 1974). He referred to the various stages of therapy as the battle for structure, the battle for initiative, midphase, and termination. Every family case, regardless of presenting problems, had to first resolve the politics of the therapist-family therapeutic relationship before therapy could proceed. Carl believed the initial struggle, the battle for structure, centered around the need for the therapist to establish his or her administrative power with the family. In response to his or her reverence for the family's power, Carl felt the therapist had to demonstrate his or her strength. It was a way of letting them know you had the courage it would take to be of use to them. While this could take many forms, it typically began over the issue of who would attend. Carl typically insisted that all family members come to the initial session.

From the first meeting, the emphasis was on establishing the family as the patient, not accepting their offering of a single scapegoat as the real problem. The effort was to more evenly distribute the anxiety to all family members. This led to less isolation of the original scapegoat, invited them all to become patients, and created more of a "sense of the whole." Sessions typically began with a sustained effort to engage the more peripheral parent, most often the father. The mother, considered the real powerhouse of the family, was addressed only after Dad and the kids had been asked to open up. The final family member to be addressed was the identified patient.

Once the therapist's administrative power was established, he or she stepped back, refusing to lead. As the therapist sat in silence waiting for the family to move forward and take responsibility for the session, the family's anxiety increased. Members often sought direction by asking "Well, what should we talk about today?" or "What else do you want to know about us?" By refusing to take the reins, Carl forced the family to be in the present and deal with the issue of taking the lead in the session. This battle for initiative, as it was called, was a time for getting the family to realize that if any change was to occur, it would be fueled by their energy. While the therapist could be a competent coach, the family members had to play the game. Carl further emphasized the idea that while he was willing to participate or assist in the process of therapy, his territory ended as they left the office. While he was part of the therapy, their living was wholly and uniquely theirs.

If the battle for structure was about the integrity of the therapist, the battle for initiative reflected the integrity of the family. Once both were established and a working alliance had been forged, the core or midphase of the therapy emerged. This was the time for breaking patterns, escaping ruts, and developing more intimate relationships. The therapist's emphasis was on catalyzing change and promoting growth, his or her own as well as the family's. During this phase, the therapist became increasingly autonomous, sharing free associative fantasies, visual images, and slivers of his or her own pathology. The therapist might disclose experiencing the couple as ''stubborn as two mules'' or guess they were most comfortable ''living back to back.'' The therapist might suggest it appeared that Mom was married to the children and Dad was in love with his tractor. Communicating by inference, innuendo, and associative thinking was the style. This seemed to catapult the family into a more open, flexible, spontaneous framework. They became more creative, more adaptive in dealing with the impossibilities of life.

As the family became a more powerful team, their sense of urgency began to wane. The intensity of the sessions and the level of affect diminished. This signified the beginning of the termination phase. Comments about the inconvenience of coordinating schedules or a missed baseball game could quite easily lead the therapist to ask the obvious question: ''Are you ready to quit?''

As the family discussed this topic, it was important for the therapist not to contaminate their process. Their decision deserved respect. Consistent with the philosophical posture underlying each phase of treatment, the family had to take full responsibility for their living. The therapist had to be careful not to dull their growth edge by suggesting that a few more sessions would help or even asking if they weren't being a bit precipitous in their decision. Having a real life and a professional cuddle group was considered central to the therapist's capacity to terminate therapy without blurring boundaries.

By the late 1970s, Carl's methods were clinically valid, experientially based, and philosophically consistent. For Carl, this was a congruent, integrated, full-person approach. He was finally reaching the rarefied clinical ground of transcending technique. It was a time of enormous creativity and personal growth. Carl had become more than merely a therapist; he was now a human being who was naturally therapeutic.

THE LATER YEARS (1982–1995)

In 1982, at the age of 70, Carl retired from the faculty of the University of Wisconsin. While this marked the end of a special period in his professional life, it signaled the beginning of yet another phase. There was a resurgence of Carl's creativity. Much like other seminal thinkers, he was interested in integrating and unifying his approach.

Following his retirement, the world of professional workshops became a focal point for his creativity. With audiences ranging from a handful to hundreds,

Carl would take the stage, share his thoughts, conduct live consultation interviews, and generally expose his ideas to a new professional group. Rather than being constricted or encumbered by the audience, Carl was more alive, more creative, more activated. He explained it by saying that he became a patient to the audience. Their interest and investment allowed Carl to be more open and spontaneous.

Carl's personal integration and professional synthesis of his ideas led him to continue to write. He collaborated in the writing of *From Psyche to System* (Neil & Kniskern, 1982), a collection of his earliest essays that provided numerous case examples of his methods. He also coauthored *Dancing with the Family* (Whitaker & Bumberry, 1988), which was accompanied by a videotape depicting clinical vignettes of his attempts to intervene in the symbolic world of the family. His final book, *Midnight Musings of a Family Therapist* (Whitaker, 1989), was an autobiography describing his life and his beliefs about families and therapy.

Carl referred to his work as an intuitive approach to treating families. Symbolic-experiential therapy is growth oriented, and it is based not on intellectual understanding but on interaction and metaphorical language (Keith, 1982). Carl evaded those who tried to operationalize his therapy by responding to questions about his methods with metaphors and stories. He believed that nothing worth learning could be taught. It had to be experienced.

Carl is not the only founding therapist who has not fully operationalized his work. Milton Erickson and Virginia Satir, like Whitaker, resisted intellectual explanations of their methods. Erickson's stories, metaphors, and attempts to "pull the contextual rug from under" (O'Hanlon, 1989) those who studied with him made it difficult for others to operationalize and replicate his techniques. Satir only gave general descriptions of what she did and was appalled by Bandler and Grindler's attempt to do a "left brain analysis" of her work (Simon, 1989, p. 41). Erickson, Satir, and Whitaker relied on their own idiosyncratic creativity to symbolically communicate with families in ways that produced change. Each went about it in a different way. All three had difficulty verbalizing what they actually did and refused to be specific about their methods.

Spradley (1979) suggests that much knowledge is "tacit knowledge" that remains outside of awareness. This may explain why "many expert therapists are not conceptualizers. They often know what to do but when asked why, they can only invent reasons" (Haley, 1988, p. 365). This was probably the case with Carl. In the chapters to follow, we attempt to access this "tacit knowledge" while being careful not to rigidly operationalize the approach.

SUMMARY

While Carl's work may have appeared whimsical on the surface, it's important to remember that the concepts and theories underlying his interventions evolved over more than six decades. The reader can track how the basic tenets of the

approach were formulated by reviewing the vast literature on symbolic-experiential therapy, which spans from the 1940s to the 1990s.

Like many other master therapists, such as Milton Erickson and Virginia
Satir, Carl was not much interested in operationalizing his work. He relied on
intuition, spontaneity, and his own creativity as catalysts. He didn't stop to think
about what he did. The key ingredients of his therapy were probably beyond his
conscious awareness.

However, through close observation of videotaped sessions, an extensive
review of the literature, and interviews with experts, we have isolated what we
believe are the key components of Carl's work. While each encounter was
unique, there was a consistency to Carl's "madness." Clearly discernible patterns become visible, and these patterns delineate the process of symbolic
change. We believe Carl's methods can be replicated and adapted to the reader's
clinical practice. We outline these patterns in a six-stage model of symbolic-
experiential therapy presented in Chapters 5–10.

Carl's most significant contribution to the field was his belief that the interpersonal relationship was the primary ingredient in therapy. The children he
worked with early in his career captured his heart and engaged him in a world
of fantasy from which he never emerged. From this experience, he became aware
of the power of play and the creative unconscious, which he relied on throughout
his career to lower defenses and access primary process relating. His struggles
with adolescents made him more acutely aware of his own suicidal, homicidal,
and aggressive impulses. He normalized these feelings, referred to them as
universal, and believed that, under the surface, they connected us all. He also
developed the capacity to be both tender and tough, caring enough to be confrontive and more than willing to take the client/family on as a way to push for
change. He redefined pathology as an effort to grow. All of these experiences
contributed to the evolution of symbolic-experiential therapy, a growth-oriented
interpersonal approach that focuses more on experiential learning than on symptom reduction.

Although Carl became a bit more explicit in terms of describing his methods
in the late 1960s, he cautioned against overreliance on technique. He admitted
to his own use of techniques and expressed a desire to one day surpass the use
of them: "Techniques or tactics which I as a therapist employ deliberately protect
me and make me less personal. I am in hopes one day I will not only be past
the endless innovations but past the use of them as such" (Warkentin & Whitaker, 1964, p. 3).

It was at the end of the decade that Carl began to achieve his long-term
professional goal of surpassing techniques. The evolution of his ideas and the
integration of wide-ranging experiences resulted in a free-flowing style of therapy. In the early 1970s, he described his work as a "mixture of all previous
stylistic patterns" (Whitaker, 1972, p. 15). Perhaps it was this ability to transcend technique that resulted in his becoming a master in the field of family
therapy.

Carl's ideas evolved over the years through his work with various colleagues. He encouraged his students to challenge his methods and theories. As a result, Carl's therapy model was significantly shaped by Drs. Warkentin, Malone, Napier, and Keith, changing form as each became invested in the symbolic-experiential process. Carl's involvement in the training process paralleled his work with families. He joined with colleagues in a collaborative effort to identify concepts underlying the approach. He then disengaged himself and encouraged students/colleagues to extrapolate from his work. Perhaps this is why his approach is so difficult to operationalize. His theories and methods were in a constant state of flux, shaped and modified by others.

Chapter 3

Personal Beliefs of the Therapist

My theory is that all theories are bad except for preliminary game playing with ourselves until we get the courage to give up theories and just live.—Carl Whitaker

The symbolic-experiential model of family therapy evolved primarily from the personhood of Carl Whitaker. Similarly, a therapist's personal history and world view color each family session. The core ingredient of therapy is the therapist's humanness, not rehearsed techniques and strategies. As Betz and Whitehorn (1975) noted, the dynamics of psychotherapy reside in the person of the therapist. Therapeutic ideas and interventions come alive only when filtered through the personhood of the therapist. Life experiences, values, and patterns of relating to people significantly influence one's approach to therapy. Some of us relate primarily on an affective level, while others prefer logic, with less emotional upheaval. We learn these differences in early childhood. Our families teach us values and patterns of interaction. This early imprinting remains with us and influences our therapy style.

While the model we present provides a map, the reader obviously needs to adapt it to fit his or her own therapeutic belief system. Decisions regarding which direction to go in therapy, how hard to push families, and how to respond to unpredictable situations are based on the therapist's discretion. The therapist interweaves personal beliefs, assumptions, and biases into the therapy experience. A seasoned therapist, like any experienced wilderness guide, knows that intuition and judgment are often more useful than technical information found on a map.

While every therapist has a unique perspective on life, there are a number of ideas and beliefs that are common to those who embrace a symbolic-experiential orientation. These form a core "belief system" that guides the therapy process.

This belief system affects how one views people, how one assesses familial relationships, and how one makes decisions regarding the use of therapeutic interventions. In the subsequent sections, we describe our most common beliefs. We hope they will serve as a catalyst for you to reflect on your own belief system.

ALTRUISM IS NOT THE ORGANIZING THEME FOR THERAPY

A core facet of the symbolic-experiential belief system is for the therapist to keep himself or herself first in importance by remaining cognizant of personal growth and limitations. In other words, the therapist needs to hold his or her own psychological, emotional, and spiritual growth in high regard. Carl often said, "You must come first in your world." Every encounter with a family is demanding. We respond to these demands by using our inner resources. This can leave us drained and depleted at times. While empathy and compassion are essential attributes for any therapist, it's vital to retain enough self-love for personal preservation. Burnout is a direct function of giving to a family at your own expense. It may appear caring on the surface, but at a deeper level it models a lack of self-care. The familiar instructions of airline cabin attendants can serve as a warning for therapists: "In the unlikely event the cabin depressurizes, an air mask will drop in front of you. Place the mask over your mouth and nose and secure the strap behind your head. For those of you traveling with children, be sure to secure your own mask first before assisting your child." In other words, if you don't take care of yourself first, you'll be of little help to anyone else!

We challenge the idea of altruism as an organizing theme for the therapy process. The core axiom of our belief system is for the therapist to stay alive. The therapist preserves the capacity to be useful to others by avoiding burnout. Carl avoided burnout by attending to his own growth, thereby remaining creative in his efforts to interact personally and professionally with families. His capacity to be real and his willingness to become involved were central to his personality and his therapy. It is essential for therapists to nurture themselves in their own families and in their encounters with colleagues. A professional "cuddle" group and a loving family are crucial for the difficult task of being a family therapist.

SIMILARITIES AND DIFFERENCES

Another organizing element of our belief system is the conviction that people are more similar than different. The common denominator of being human is the opportunity to learn from one another. Long ago Carl gave up on the delusion of the "healthy therapist and the sick patient," believing that this stance undermined the therapeutic process. Rather than supporting this unhealthy dichotomy, we're able to recognize ourselves in the families we see, to find the suicidal corner of our own psyche or face the long-disguised homicidal impulses we've nurtured. This permits us to see the family as human beings, not as those who are less fortunate. This belief helps us step down from our pedestal and communicate on a more personal level. Carl humorously pointed out to the clients he saw, "Don't worry, if I haven't already seen it in me, I'd never recognize it in you." None of us are problem free!

The fact that we are all more similar than different affects how we look at pathology. There was a time when Carl looked for pathology in himself and, consequently, in others. In his later years, he became more intrigued with health and growth. The basic assumption is that we all seek growth. He contemplated ways to promote health in himself and in the families he saw for therapy.

THERE'S NO SUCH THING AS AN INDIVIDUAL

Despite our culture's myth of the rugged individual—the self-made man and the independent woman—it's important to remember that we all grow and develop in relation to others. Carl often said he didn't believe in individuals: "We're all just fragments of families." We emerge from and continue to live in an interpersonal context throughout the life cycle. Who we become is a collage of our past relationships. While we continue on our individual paths of development, we remain forever connected through childhood experiences and family life.

It's important for the family in therapy to realize that the therapist is more interested in them as a group—in their collective "we"—than as individuals. We want to know how families approach, connect, and respond to each other in their daily living rather than focusing on individual experiences. Early on, we view presenting problems as a ticket of admission to be expanded within an interpersonal context. We encourage family members to view themselves interpersonally. Through their collaborative efforts, the family has the power to change.

FAMILIES ARE NOT FRAGILE

It's popular to call families dysfunctional and blame them for the ills of society, but one thing is certain: Families are not fragile. There's no need to treat a family as if it's made of fine china. It won't break. Families are robust and powerful. The complexity of each family's unique interactions serves as a safety net, offering resilience in times of stress. For example, when Dad becomes ill 4 years after the death of his wife, 15-year-old Sally takes over as the family's caretaker. She mothers Dad, her older brother, and the two younger children. Ben, the white knight, takes on two jobs, forgoing his after-school activities. The family bounces back. This resiliency provides the momentum for growth. Carl marveled at the ability of some families to bounce back rather than be defeated by their misfortune.

Carl and John Warkentin told an old story that is still pertinent. It's a tale of a maiden who had a cat named Emily. The maiden found the cat as a kitten.

It was like a person to her. She was very cautious with Emily and would walk her on the front lawn when needed, but she never allowed the cat in the alley. Emily was a virgin, and the maiden knew it. One day the iceman made his rounds in the neighborhood, and, as luck would have it, the maiden became better acquainted with him. Soon after, they were married. When it was time for them to leave for their honeymoon, Emily was a major problem. The neighbors who had grown fond of the cat agreed to take care of her in the manner she was accustomed to. Three days after the newlyweds' departure, the maiden wired her neighbors a telegram reading "Let Emily out!" When working with families, Carl believed it was more fun to "let the cat out" than keep it sheltered.

Carl could be blunt when communicating with a family. He believed that families paid for his authenticity, even if, at times, his conversation was stinging. His intent was to push the family's sense of desperation and collaboration. He respected the family's strength as a group so much that he allowed himself to be more open and direct.

PAIN IS NOT THE ENEMY

Our culture mandates us to help people feel better. It is naïve to think we can accomplish this by avoiding conflict or numbing a family's pain. Carl believed that pain and stress make us stronger. His intent was not to make families feel better; on the contrary, he purposely activated stress to ignite the system and get things moving. Stress, anxiety, and even pain are part of being alive, part of being human. If channeled productively, stress triggers growth. As therapists, we don't want to cut off the family's circulation. Instead, we want to explore and find ways to productively channel stress. We believe that desperation, rather than a mere wish for something to occur, is the motivation required to fuel change.

A symbolic-experiential therapist must tolerate intense emotions without panic. It's important to fight the desire to overact and control the session as a way of diminishing anxiety. The work belongs to the family. While we can help charter their course, the family needs to struggle as a unit, to sink or swim. To intervene prematurely may calm things for the moment and may even soothe our own anxiety, but it deprives the family of the momentum necessary for growth.

FAMILIES MAKE SENSE

No matter how dysfunctional a family may appear on the surface, the situation makes sense when the family is seen as a whole. They have a finely tuned style of living, interacting, and grappling with each other. This doesn't mean the family's way of living is healthy, effective, or even enjoyable. However, it makes sense when perceived from the family's world view.

Sometimes alternative lifestyles are difficult for an outsider to comprehend. For example, a therapist told a story of a couple that came to him for help,

complaining of marital conflict. As the session began, the husband announced that he and his wife were both involved in affairs outside the marriage. His real problem was that his lover saw his wife as controlling. As a result, she wanted little to do with him. This increased conflict between the spouses ultimately brought them to therapy. The therapist wondered at the beginning of the session how to help them. He listened to their story. Midway through the session, it became evident to him that the couple was not serious about working on the marriage. Their real concern was how to maintain the integrity of the family unit for the sake of the children, despite their unusual living arrangement. The therapist could support their efforts in this endeavor even if, on the surface, he did not understand their lifestyle.

FAMILY ROLE ASSIGNMENTS ARE POWERFUL

Family systems develop role assignments that keep them stable. These designated roles serve a useful purpose much of the time; for instance, they facilitate bonding. However, they have the potential to limit our possibilities by narrowing the definition of who we are. For example, it can be rewarding to hear ''You're such an angel, just like your Aunt Norma,'' but how then does an angel learn to assert herself or deal with unacceptable qualities? Compartmentalization is the ultimate damage stemming from a rigid role structure. We become limited to a few stereotyped characteristics.

In a marriage, family role assignments can become powerful weapons. For example, Kady, a 37-year-old mother of two, is viewed by her 53-year-old husband, Bob, as being just like her sister, who is having extramarital affairs. Bob badgers Kady about this every time she goes out alone or becomes too independent. By focusing on her, he doesn't have to deal with his insecurities about their age difference or with his fear of intimacy. He needs only to continually remind her of her similarities to her sister. In therapy, we provide opportunities for family members to step out of rigid roles that consume them. Our intent is to facilitate more genuine interpersonal relatedness, where people are free to be themselves.

THE THERAPIST IS ALWAYS AN OUTSIDER

Regardless of how much you care about the family, to be effective you must recognize that you're an outsider in the family's world. The family's relationship with each other is always more important than their relationship with the therapist. The family is a self-contained unit, an intimate group with a shared past, present, and future. They're ''real'' people talking about their real life together. The therapist's role is professional, that of a coach, not a player. While the coach is certainly invested in the game and wants the team to do well, he makes it clear that he won't step onto the field as a player. The therapist may put the

family through drills and conduct strategy sessions; however, the therapist refuses to play for them. The therapist's job is to maximize the family's collective potential while being careful not to be seduced into playing the game.

The therapist's recognition that he or she is an outsider is crucial to getting the process off to a productive start. From an outside position, the therapist is able to poke and prod, to give directions and call plays for the family in ways an insider could never get away with. The assumption is that an outsider's caring about the family lacks the affective voltage of the family's responses to each other. Since the therapist doesn't know them, they can dismiss her or his advice. The saying "One kiss from your mother is worth a thousand from a blind date" captures the essence of this belief.

The middle phase of therapy is challenging. While the therapist becomes more personally invested in the process, he or she must maintain the status of coach, as the players become more skilled in their interactions. The outcome is the family's responsibility, despite the therapist's hopes for the group. For example, a middle-aged couple sought therapy to resolve commitment issues. The therapist enjoyed the couple and hoped for a reconciliation. When the couple reached a decision to separate, the therapist was disappointed and wondered whether he had done all he could to help them. It's important to remember that the ultimate decision for living is not the therapist's.

The *empty nest* is an analogy for termination. The termination phase elicits feelings similar to those experienced by parents when their first child is ready to leave home. Launching children is an anxious, ambivalent process. As parents, we reassure children of our confidence in them and our ability to tolerate the loss. This frees them to embark on the inevitable journey of learning to follow their own intuition and face the consequences of their life decisions. Carl likened the role of therapist to that of foster parent. A contractual agreement governs the relationship. It is time limited. Carl cautioned therapists not to impose their own value system on the family: "You can't make a Jewish family into an Italian family or an Irish Catholic family into a Protestant one."

THE ABSURDITY OF LIFE

Gaining an appreciation for the fundamental absurdity of life is essential to the process of living spontaneously and playfully. At a surface level, we insist that life is logical, reasonable, and fair. We like to believe that if we play according to the rules, justice will prevail; we'll get what we deserve. At some level we cling to this notion, no matter how it differs from our actual experience.

The symbolic-experiential model promotes the idea of facing life on its own terms, of dealing with "what is." In reality, we don't always get what we deserve, and life isn't always fair. We look beyond the predictable, programmable aspects of living and delve below the surface. The approach focuses on the affective, intuitive, primary process level of living that is fluid and wholly unpredictable. At its core, life is unpredictable. Living can be absurd. Insisting

that it be rational only amplifies that absurdity. Rather than analyzing the past, we focus on the here-and-now experience of the therapy encounter. Being in the present permits us to experience and enjoy the daily ironies of living.

INDIVIDUATION AND BELONGING ARE COMPLEMENTARY

The concepts of individuation and belonging have been portrayed as inherently adversarial. Typically, the belief is that one is attainable only at the expense of the other. For example, we think of adolescence as a time of moving away from the family or refer to marital separation as a way to "find yourself." Individuating is not an escape from belonging. Belonging need not be an engulfing, confining, or restricting experience. We believe that it's possible to integrate these processes. In other words, we think of individuation and belonging as complementary in nature. You cannot truly belong unless you can detach. Individuation and belonging represent a natural dialectic. The more connected you are, the freer you are to venture out and find yourself. The more secure you feel as an individual, the freer you are to be involved in relationships with others, to belong without fear of engulfment or enslavement.

MARRIAGE: INSPIRATION OR INSANITY?

Carl often told the story of a time, during therapy with a couple, when he asked, "So why did the two of you decide to get married?" The couple looked at each other, smiled, and responded simultaneously, "Temporary insanity!" While love may be blind and being "in love" can make you crazy, the decision to get married is not haphazard. There's a bilateral selection that is reminiscent of the life-forming complexity and symmetry of the double helix pattern of the DNA molecule. The intricate process of mate selection goes beyond the surface-level "blind love" that proposes we wed in the belief that somehow our needs will be magically met. It transcends the adolescent sense of entitlement that lures us all. Unconsciously, we seek out others with characteristics that complement our own and challenge our growth. It is the search for our "better half." Our selection of a mate, at an almost mystical level, presents us with the opportunity to grow. If we invest ourselves fully in marriage, we will inevitably come face to face with our greatest fears and our sharpest growth edge. Whether we tremble at the fear of being abandoned or cringe at the possibility of being engulfed, we will have the opportunity to face our personal demons. Marriage is a natural vehicle for growth. We shouldn't lose sight of the fact that marriage, while at times maddening, is also life affirming.

PROCESS VERSUS PROGRESS

As therapists, we focus more on process than progress. We're more interested in how the family relates to each other and grapples with a variety of life issues

than we are in trying to find solutions for specific problems. You would rather teach the family how to fish than give them a fish for their evening meal. By focusing on the *how* of their relationships, we hope to make them a better team.

Another way of conceptualizing the idea of process versus progress is to consider the therapist's experience of the session. The therapist and family share equally in the relationship; it is not a matter of cause and effect. If the flow of the interaction is meaningful and the process alive for the therapist, odds are good the family has also benefited from the encounter. If the hour is boring and the interaction repetitive for the therapist, the experience is probably dissatisfying for the family. Consciousness of mutuality and reciprocity are natural ingredients in relationships. They encourage more intimacy.

THERAPIST AS FOSTER PARENT

When assuming a foster parent role, it's important to be aware of your limitations. For example, you are clearly not able to fill the role of a biological parent. The pervasive bond that comes from a shared biology is missing. While you may care about the family, you are playing a role. Therapy does not continue long enough to become real life. You are not engaging with the promise of a lifelong psychosocial bonding. Carl believed the role of foster parent best described the therapist's function. You are actually entering into a contractual agreement in which the conditions are clear and on which, at the beginning, everyone agrees. Both you and the family have rights, including the prerogative of unilaterally discontinuing the relationship. It's not a lifetime commitment.

The foster parent takes responsibility for setting limits and structuring the relationship in hopes that a positive connection will occur. Negotiating the foster parent-foster child relationship colors the initial phase of therapy. Carl referred to the following dialogue as a way of exemplifying the foster parent role:

> The foster mother says, "Well, here we are young fellow. I am going to make believe I'm your mother but I'm not. This is just the way I earn my living. I didn't know you were coming and I don't know who you are because the judge didn't say a thing about you. While you're here you can do almost whatever you want, but let me tell you about the rules in my home. You can't light a bonfire in the middle of the living room. You can eat anything in the refrigerator, if you don't take so much that we don't have enough for supper. You can telephone your mother, the judge, or anybody else, and if you want, you can cuss me out. I usually won't mind but if you get too rough with me I may lose my temper and then you'd better be careful. Oh, don't ever get in the middle of a fight between me and my husband because we'll both clobber you. Don't forget, I love my own kids more than I could love you because you are my make-believe kid and I'm your make-believe mother. You can run away if you want to and I won't chase you. Of course, if you do, I'll have to call the judge because he pays me to take care of you. If they catch you and want to bring you back that would probably be all right. Finally, it would be nice if we got to care about each other because it would be fun to

have somebody here I enjoy. We don't have to, though; you can stay mad at me, but I do hope we can have a nice time.''

If the initial phase is successful, the foster parent and child move ahead together. If not, the contract can be voided. If the child chooses to run away or the foster parent doesn't feel up to the task, they have a way out.

BEWARE OF THE GURU

Since the very mention of the word *parent* suggests hierarchy, with one generation being above and responsible for the other, we'd like to offer a note of caution. Once we've completed the administrative function of setting the conditions for the therapy regarding who will attend, the time to meet, and so forth, we work hard to demystify the family's perception of ''therapist as guru.'' Our goal is to help the family find themselves and learn self-sufficiency. It's a mistake to let them cast us in the role of a guru. Sheldon Kopp (1976) captured this dilemma: ''If you have a hero, look again. You have diminished yourself in some way.'' It's our responsibility to burst the family's fantasy of the therapist's goodness, wisdom, and unconditional love. If idolization is present, the temptation is for them to wait for us to fix them. This stance devalues their integrity. We must actively disrupt this mind-set.

The only problem more damaging than the deification of the therapist by the family is the therapist's assumption of the same delusion. While this professional folie à deux can be comfortable for everyone at the beginning of therapy, it inevitably leads to disaster. Our comfort with ''helping,'' with showing them the way, discredits the family. Family members incorporate the message that they should value someone else's voice over their own rather than following their inner wisdom.

While one of Carl's favorite sayings was ''Nothing worth learning can be taught,'' it's not that he didn't believe in learning. Families learn and grow every day. However, Carl believed that real learning is more apt to occur when no one is trying to teach. When there is no teacher in the classroom giving directions, the family must go about the daunting but necessary task of making their own decisions. Experience is our most profound teacher.

THE THERAPIST'S USE OF SELF

The therapist's use of self is captured by the phrase ''the only you I know is me.'' Despite the many tools, techniques, and strategies that fill our professional journals, the therapy process evolves from our personhood, from who we are as people. Our personal experiences and professional belief system color all we see. We can't separate ourselves from the therapy experience because we're part of it. Unlike the psychoanalyst who reflects back only a blank screen, we invite the family momentarily into our world, engaging in more of a shared encounter.

We are then in a position to feed back to the family our experience of them, sharing our internal reactions to the process and free associations that may have relevance for their life.

In the initial phase of therapy, the therapist listens to and identifies with the family's pain. This sort of identification, whether it relates to social awkwardness, primitive impulses, or basic fears of inadequacy, establishes a genuine connection based on the therapist's and family's humanness. It conveys a sense of compassion that deepens the therapy process.

As the therapy progresses, the therapist's self-disclosure becomes a central part of the experience. Self-disclosure often expands the openness of the group. As the therapist shares slivers of his or her own emotional issues, the family has the freedom to access large, often crucial areas of life that have been extruded or sealed off. The therapist's self-disclosure is contagious. As the family watches the therapist forging his or her path, guided by personal values, they discover the courage to follow their own beliefs.

The following clinical vignette provides an example of a therapist's spontaneous use of self. Midway through the fifth therapy hour, the therapist became concerned with the family's comfort in listening to their son. Phil, the 21-year-old suicidal black sheep, spoke of how horrible he was for having violent impulses, both toward himself and others. The therapist, struck by the loneliness and isolation he felt as Phil spoke, responded instinctively.

Therapist: I just had the craziest thought as you were sitting there berating yourself to the silent applause of the family. The more you sounded like a black sheep, the more I imagined your brother [25-year-old David] as a white knight. I began to get worried about him. You know white knights need to act heroic no matter how they feel inside. How about it, Dave? Do you have any awareness of your covert murderousness?

[Dave, who is normally quite articulate and quick to respond, sits in an uncomfortable silence for a moment and then begins]

David: I don't know. I've always handled my problems privately. Sometimes I do talk about them, but only after I've fixed them. I guess there's nothing I feel comfortable sharing right now.

Therapist: You know, when I was about your age, maybe a bit younger, I had the craziest experience. I got into a scrape during a ballgame. It turned into a real melee. Everyone became involved, fists were flying. Right there in the midst of it all, I had this flash that I should have been over in Vietnam fighting. It was a terrifying thought. I worried that I would have been too cold-blooded. The thought of it scared me. I think I'm over it now. But I do believe everyone has things like that inside of them.

David: I don't think my parents could handle it if they knew how violent I feel sometimes.

Therapist: Maybe it would help Phil get over his suicidality. Maybe he wouldn't feel like such a freak in this super-nice, competent family. [turns to Phil] Can you even imagine Dave getting enraged, losing control, being violent?

Phil: No. I find it hard to believe. I can't believe he's saying this now. He's always handled things so perfectly.

Therapist: So, can you help him out, Dave? I assume we're all potentially violent. Suicide and homicide are inside each of us. It's just a matter of being in the wrong place at the right time.

David: Well, my girlfriend is really the only one who knows about my temper. I've never hit her, but sometimes I scare myself. I can get pretty mean. I lash out verbally.

Therapist: Well, that's love for you. Welcome to the human race.

As the session continued, the parents discussed embarrassing episodes of anger and violence filed away long before. Mom was able to reveal an early adult experience of suicide, while Dad spoke of his intermittent periods of despair, hopelessness, and suicidal ideation. Phil was surprised, even shocked. At least he was no longer alone.

By paying attention to and sharing an internal association about violence, the therapist unlocked memories the family had tried to forget. As a result of the family's denial of violence in their psyches, Phil was isolated when he experienced suicidal impulses. He feared asking for help. Fortunately, his efforts were unsuccessful. Perhaps the family's courage to finally expose their hidden impulses served as an inoculation for all.

It's important, however, to be aware of the potential pitfalls related to the use of self-disclosure. "Know thyself" is perhaps the central axiom. While sharing ideas, stories, spontaneous associations, and personal revelations is part of the therapy process, it's critical to remember that you're in role. You're fulfilling a professional function. The therapist's chair is not a place to seek help with unresolved family-of-origin or relationship issues. It's not an arena for gratifying your dependency needs, fulfilling your grandiosity, or engaging in any sort of uncontrolled regression.

BECOMING A FAMILY THERAPIST

Carl believed that there were three phases involved in becoming a family therapist. The initial phase, learning about family therapy, comprises the academic task of reading about theory, grappling to understand how families work, and observing the clinical work of others. The second stage involves doing family therapy. This is the process of actually getting your feet wet by working with families. It's best to begin this process accompanied by a supervisor, or mentor, as a co-therapist. This phase can occupy anywhere from a few years to a lifetime.

New learning occurs with each family we see. Finally, as your accumulating experience and personal maturity converge into some sort of professional integrity, you reach the level of being a family therapist. At this point, the therapy flows from your personhood. Techniques become secondary. You comfortably rely on intuition rather than on strategies. You're more free to be in the moment. This final stage is clearly the one at which self-disclosure is most appropriate; it's best to proceed with caution at earlier stages.

THERAPY FOR THE THERAPIST

Carl believed that before we can be worthwhile family therapists, we need to experience the depth of our craziness by participating in our own therapy. We believe that a therapist who has never been in therapy is practicing in bad faith. Carl felt that such a therapist was a fake. Family therapists need not only face their craziness; they must deal with unresolved issues in their family of origin as well. Some of us are fearful of confronting mothers in therapy because we continue to feel overpowered by our own mothers. Others of us have difficulty engaging fathers in therapy because we never learned to connect with our own fathers. Supervision and therapy can help us overcome blind spots. It takes courage to deliberately expose the inner workings of one's family. However, we believe that, without this experience, one cannot truly learn how to be a family therapist.

SUMMARY

The symbolic-experiential model emphasizes the personal values, biases, and beliefs of the therapist as central to the process of therapy. Foremost, it holds that the therapist must come first in his or her world. The therapist must not take over for the family. We must refuse to work harder than the family. While we remain emotionally available to the system, we're careful not to take on the role of guru.

We view ourselves as more similar to than different from the families we see in therapy. Sharing fragments of our world is a way of joining. If Mom reminds us of ''Aunt Janie'' and we can't see past her endearing qualities, we don't hesitate to share it. When Dad has difficulty gaining his composure after talking about losing his brother in the Vietnam War, we express our feelings. It's all part of the process. The family is entitled to our experience of them. They are then free to do what they want with our disclosures.

We believe that families are resilient and can tolerate our pushing the system. Stress and anxiety aren't viewed as culprits but as fuel necessary for growth. We believe that families make sense within the context of their living. Although their rigid role structure may appear absurd on the surface, role assignments keep the family stable.

We believe that, no matter how connected we feel to the family, we are always outsiders. We don't need to understand the family completely or become one of them to change their patterns of functioning. Therapy is a profound experience that should not continue long enough to become real life.

We focus on the interconnectedness of the family rather than on individual members. We attend to process rather than progress, believing that regardless of content, the process of interaction remains the same. It doesn't matter if a couple argues about money, the children, or sex; it's the interpersonal interaction that's problematic. The husband's need to control or the wife's tendency to interrupt prevents understanding, intimacy, and resolution. We focus more on how they interact and experience each other than what they are talking about.

In subsequent chapters of this book, we present a model for facilitating symbolic change in families. It represents one way of organizing Carl's work and takes a closer look at some of the key components underlying his approach. However, we do not present it as the only way to organize symbolic-experiential therapy. Instead, we hope that you'll adopt it to fit your own personal style and belief system. We hope that you have fun and savor the experience.

Chapter 4

Family Relationships

Love can only increase in proportion to hatred, sensitivity in proportion to toughness, togetherness in proportion to separateness, depth in proportion to humility.—Carl Whitaker

Families are central to people's growth and development. This tenet provides the framework for the theory and techniques of symbolic-experiential therapy. Family life is the stage at which our sense of self and capacity for intimacy develop. We experiment with relationships, roles, and interpersonal interactions with parents, siblings, extended family, and peers. During childhood, we absorb basic lessons of who we are and how we fit with others. Our values, strength, and security take root in the context of our families. Our expectations of ourselves and others unfold as we experiment with an array of emotions and attachments. Family relationships set the foundation for all future relationships. The pervasive, primitive power of the family is undeniable. Despite their enormous potential, not all families provide the optimal ingredients for secure development.

It is crucial that therapists not only have a solid sense of themselves personally and professionally but also fully understand the complexities of the families they see in therapy. They must attend to an individual's uniqueness while capturing the potency of his or her interdependence. We are strong believers in systems thinking. It is equally important to understand the societal pressures exerted on family development. We live in complicated times, and numerous demands are placed on individual family members. Technology, media, financial strain, personal expectations, and time constraints complicate family life. The symbolic-experiential approach to therapy emerges from a view of families rooted in health and vitality rather than pathology and limitations. We believe that every person has a powerful drive toward growth and an innate capacity to fulfill that potential. Therapy focuses on building a solid infrastructure while enhancing the strength and creativity of the family as it progresses through life.

39

THE HEALTHY FAMILY

The healthy family is an ever-changing, evolving organism. It's in a perpetual process of evolution—never static, always expanding. Relationships fluctuate as the family develops an identity and consensual ways of operating. Individual personalities influence family living, in addition to outside forces such social contacts, schools, churches, and so forth. We are bombarded daily by what appears to be the norm for family life. We compare ourselves with this fantasy ideal of the "normal" family. These ideals should serve as benchmarks for plotting our course rather than as disappointing reminders of our shortcomings. Nowhere do we learn the explicit rules for developing a healthy family environment. If we are lucky, we muddle through.

The concept of the family life cycle is useful in understanding the normal developmental process families encounter. Family life becomes increasingly complex as we respond to life events. Biological markers such as births, deaths, and illnesses have a profound impact on family members and familial relationships. Social decisions to marry or divorce or to geographically separate from or return to one's family of origin can deeply influence the experience of living. Academic success or failure, job loss or promotion, and financial security or instability all color the journey. Positive life events create stress on the family with added change and renegotiation of the status quo. Although families are similar in their life course, they all write their own scripts. Their unique stories speak for themselves.

Developmental phases are critical to life transitions. Each new stage of development requires mastery of complex tasks for each family member and the group as a whole. These tasks are inherent to their particular phase of life. Successful mastery of these tasks is essential for the family to continue to grow emotionally. For example, families with children find themselves juggling roles and schedules to meet the rapidly changing needs of the youngsters. Parents wonder whether they are doing all they can to ensure their children's optimum development. Likewise, children influence the lives of their parents through reciprocal interaction, from sleep deprivation and irritability to the indescribable joys of seeing them master new skills. The family responds to the needs of adult members in other stages of development while organizing much of family life around the needs of children. It is essential for the couple to spend time alone to solidify their bond while managing the expectations of daily life. Teenagers further complicate the family as they vacillate between independence and the safety of the family unit. As parents struggle with the issues of middle age and their parents begin to deal with their own mortality, the family bounces and careens down the path of living.

The process of living is challenging, at times traumatic. Stress is unavoidable. According to Napier (1988), almost all growth is fueled by the "imperative of unhappiness." The process of struggling together is essential. This being the case, there is ample opportunity for growth in most families. Perhaps the most distinctive trait of a healthy family is the capacity to productively address its cumulative stress. Intellectually, it's impossible to prepare yourself for family life. There is a complicity to family relationships that can be learned only through experience. Families do not fit neatly into categories, despite facing similar obstacles to development.

Despite all of the odds, healthy families learn to deal with stress in a productive fashion. To put it simply, healthy families are *adaptive*. The rules and roles that guide them operate in the service of the family's adaptability. Healthy families evolve and shift with the changing demands of their situation. While not abandoning their beliefs or betraying their values, they're capable of taking in and responding to new information. New experiences expand the family computer. The accumulation of such experiences upgrades family wisdom, blending the old with the new as additional challenges are faced.

Healthy families come in all shapes and sizes, from two-parent households to single-parent units, blended families, and other nontraditional forms. All family groups are capable of providing security and nurturing. As family members struggle individually and collectively with the unfolding challenges of life, they become more energized, more fully human.

In healthy families, there is a clear separation of generations. The hierarchy implicit in this separation indicates that the parents and children are not equals in terms of power, authority, and responsibility. The parents are in charge. They provide an environment in which their children can flourish. This framework is not based on the idea of parents exerting dominance over their children; rather, it is predicated on the notion that strength and caring provide a sense of security, a safety net that enables children to face the world with confidence. The children are then free to experience their childhood without the added burden of responsibility for the adult generation. It's the parent's responsibility to set the tone for family life by providing an emotional environment that considers everyone's needs.

The healthy family has the capacity to play, to celebrate life. For example, when her mother is tired, 4-year-old Samantha can play "as if" she were Mommy, covering her mother with a blanket and asking what she'd like her to "cook up" in her play kitchen. Play is a great buffer for stress. The playful "as if" quality of family life is a safe haven from the outside world and its demands. When 7-year-old Johnny is bossed around by the neighborhood kids, he can come home and pretend he's a drill sergeant ordering Dad to get up for the Saturday morning camping trip. This sort of freedom is crucial in permitting kids to experiment with power, control, and influence. They're free to try on a variety of roles and behaviors. It's a way they can flex their muscles, test their competencies, and discover new aspects of themselves. Younger children are free to play at being older, to experience being in charge of the family without shouldering the day-to-day pressures. They can experiment with being both mother and father as they develop skills in nurturing. Teenagers are free to experiment with leaving home and testing their own wings without real-world risks. Parents can regress by being playful and silly without feeling weak. Grand-parents can return to their youth and enjoy their grandchildren without concern or angst about the future.

Healthy families do not have rigid roles and relationships. Any member can take on differing roles. The family enjoys the process of rotating alliances and shifting triangles based on the task before them. The husband-wife relationship is primary and is the basis for all other family relationships. It is not necessary to exert the primacy of this relationship. Dad and the kids can go skiing and are free to connect without Mom feeling left out. Mom can take the younger kids to a movie, or the older ones to dinner, without Dad getting jealous. The women can team up against the men without anyone being offended. Being free to side with someone, then pull out and enter into a different alliance is crucial to learning about healthy boundaries. These boundaries are fluid, not rigidly fixed.

Healthy families develop an openness to the ideas and experiences of each family member. In other words, healthy families can tolerate individual differ-ences. This has little to do with family members agreeing with each other. It's really about respecting the right to have ideas and experiences that may differ from family norms. Family members can respect differing opinions without needing to agree with each other's perspective. They can talk about sex, politics, and religion without fear of being cut off or shut down. Family members cele-brate differences as they learn from each other. They're capable of having strong ideas and opinions while retaining the ability to adjust when other family mem-bers don't fall in line. For example, a mother with a young daughter wanted to raise her to compete athletically with boys. Despite her best efforts, she ended up with a frilly girl interested in other things. The mother laughed as she said, "I hadn't considered I'd be the one who would change." Despite their differ-ences, this mother-daughter relationship thrived as they explored new territory together.

As the family continues to progress through various developmental stages, it opens its doors to outsiders. These individuals add to rather than detract from the family. Each member feels free to invite friends into the family, confident they will be accepted and enjoyed, not viewed with suspicion. During this stage, parents are sending their children into the outside world of school, day care, and so forth. This is an anxious time for parents, because they begin to receive feedback from others about their child-rearing skills. Will Susie be as capable as her peers? Can Chris follow the rules in the classroom? How will Mike do at sports? We secretly wonder whether we have done an adequate job in prepar-ing our children for the rigors of the world.

This whole process of "becoming" involves the struggle of being an individ-ual in the midst of the family group. Belonging and individuating exist in tandem, as opposing but synergistically connected poles of family existence. They evolve together in an expansive rather than competitive process. Once the family accepts the legitimacy of each individual's right to leave the nest and develop his or her own uniqueness, all are equally free to return and revel in their connection while celebrating their individuality. The sense of belonging is much more rewarding when it's a volitional choice rather than an obligation.

Families are multigenerational units. In healthy families, the nuclear family is connected to the extended family but not controlled by it. The family can explore the past and still be free to be in the present. Parents and grandparents can discuss the horrors as well as the joys of raising children without either generation feeling put down or disregarded. Grandparents can share ideas without feeling insulted when their children ignore their advice. They can revere the past, experience the present, and look forward to the future. As the family story expands, all members enjoy the process.

The accumulation of shared life experiences, good and bad, adds to the family's joint history, creating a lasting bond. The evolving family history is a creative, compelling force. Through sharing family stories, continuing family rituals, passing on heirlooms, and revisiting photo albums, children become acquainted with their past. Sharing family anecdotes and recalling long-forgotten events create memories that cement the family together. Families provide a history rich in emotions, relationships, and connections both to the past and the future. The family tapestry is rich in color and texture.

MARRIAGE

Marriage is one of the most significant relationships an individual can experience. The strength of this relationship provides the foundation of the family. Marriage can be heaven or hell and is usually both. It brings out the best and the worst in spouses as they struggle to resolve their similarities and differences.

Our culture has done a horrible thing to marriage. First, we went too far into the image of belongingness. This perspective was popular through the 1950s. The image of marriage was based on the idea that marriage was fundamentally a "losing of self" to the other. Marriage consisted of a homogenized "we" that led to a form of closeness resembling fusion. Marriage was two organisms joined at the hip, connected for life with little opportunity for growth and evolution. The problem with fusion is that individual identities are subjugated. This type of marriage offered stability and security but little intimacy. The marriage of the 1950s devalued women by limiting their options for development. Men assumed dominance with rigidly defined gender roles. Few couples aspired to peer relationships. The cultural and societal values of the times contributed to the picture of marriage.

By the late 1960s, another distortion had gained prominence. This time we went too far in the direction of individuating. Marriage was a way to get personal needs met, a means of self-gratification. The "me generation" was rebelling against the chains of their parents. It was a time of free love, self-indulgence, and fear of commitment, and it spawned social experiments such as open marriage. Although different in appearance, it was no more successful than the previous model of marriage. Intimacy remained elusive. The pendulum had swung to the opposite extreme.

Although diametrically different on the surface, these models shared a crucial component. They failed to recognize the importance of marriage being a home for both the "we" and the two "I's." This dialectical quality of marriage was overlooked. We now know that marriage is not about one or the other. Marriage is a way to connect with another human being, to truly engage, without losing oneself. While this sounds simple, today's epidemic divorce rates and sobering number of "stable but miserable" marriages reveal the difficulty involved.

Marriage is a blending of two foreign cultures, a mixing of the raw ingredients of family A and family B. It's an effort to merge two groups with different values, beliefs, and traditions. Interestingly, couples often are unaware of the depth of their differences until after their wedding. In a healthy marriage, the couple accomplishes the challenging task of establishing a home environment that is both similar to and distinctly different from their families of origin. This is quite a feat since these two families have a vested interest, with the subtle or not so subtle directive to replicate themselves. Too many couples seem to organize their living around this loyalty struggle. Healthy marriages move beyond the patterns of the past in order to flourish. The spouses must give themselves permission to choose the aspects of their own families that fit their emerging family style.

Another realization early in marriage is the mistaken fantasy that the mere act of exchanging wedding vows guarantees a life of intimacy and euphoria. The fairy tale ending of the prince and princess riding off into the sunset to live "happily ever after" implies that the couple will attain nirvana through marriage. This myth is destructive in that it sets unrealistic expectations of intimacy. There is disappointment when, at the end of the rainbow, instead of gold we come face to face with our spouse's imperfections. Those traits we found so lovable during the dating period now drive us crazy. Intolerance rears its ugly head. Viewing the wedding ceremony as an endpoint rather than the beginning of the journey is deceiving. While healthy, growing marriages frequently begin with the same distortions as those that fail, there's something different about them. Couples in healthy marriages recognize early on that intimacy requires effort.

The idea of commitment in marriage is another crucial, misunderstood concept. Couples in healthy marriages are committed to fostering each other's growth and enhancing the "aliveness" of the relationship. When "till death do us part" means that you're now stuck with each other, it loses its intended value. Marriage becomes a life sentence without the possibility of parole. It connotes a type of "stuckness" rather than a dedication to being and growing together. Commitment is a genuine effort to engage emotionally with the intent of fostering growth through openness and caring. Conflict is inherent in this intimate relationship. Problems are grist for the mill; they are not ignored. The relationship evolves to a peership through sharing decisions while establishing a future.

Healthy marriages are not necessarily smooth, tranquil relationships. There is a certain amount of upset and struggle involved. Over time, growing relationships encounter and even create tension. The vitality of two people remaining dedicated to themselves while also loyal to each other doesn't come without friction. The marital contract is not permission to keep score. In fact, healthy marriages experience dozens of emotional divorces. Whether they last 5-minutes, 5-hours, or 5-days, such experiences can be intense, the sense of loss overwhelming. As difficult as these times can be, the committed couple knows there will be a tomorrow. While this doesn't guarantee they'll never divorce, they know that it won't happen on impulse. They have the courage to face each other, address their differences, and at least try to make the relationship work. Their level of investment ensures that neither will cut and run at the first sign of disillusion.

Growing relationships revere the ''we'' and value the ''I's.'' The ''we'' is what soothes our aloneness, calms our isolation, and relieves our angst. Through marriage, we discover more and more about who we are individually. One of the joys of an intimate relationship lies in the discovery of unknown aspects of oneself. The marriage offers the opportunity to discover and develop new interpersonal strength. Healthy marriages focus on sharing and communication. Affective expression, in a relationship that values the ''we'' as well as the ''I,'' is powerful.

Marriage has a developmental life cycle with predictable crises and issues that require attention. Warkentin and Valerius (1976) spoke of the seasons of marriage, foreseen stages of falling in and out of love and times of distance and recommitment. They saw marriage as a struggle for ownership and separation, an attempt to develop an independent identity while remaining intimate with another valued person.

PARENTING

Carl often talked of the sailing metaphor when describing family life. Despite a clear destination, life zigs and zags depending on shifts in the wind. It is easy to be blown off course, feel scared, and hope for rescue. The key is to find a safe harbor, rechart the course, and continue the journey.

The job of guiding children from infancy through childhood, adolescence, and beyond is invigorating and at times overwhelming. The startling realization of dependence and responsibility interrupts the joy of bringing a new baby home from the hospital. The new parent faces the awesome task of deciphering the baby's needs as the dyad becomes a triad and attempts a leap to normalcy through establishing new routines and patterns of interaction. The mother-infant dyad is a blissful unit that can leave the father on the outside. Mother learns to respond to the child's cries in a soothing manner. The family choreographs the rhythm of their interactions.

Parenting is at times a difficult and puzzling process. The issues are infinite, the struggles endless, and the impasses intense. Parenting has its ups and downs. The highs are exhilarating and the lows devastating. Yet, this is all part of the normal process of development. In order to fully enjoy this most profound experience, it's helpful to keep the following thoughts in mind.

Parenting, by its very nature, is an inherently complicated process dominated by polarities. At one moment parent and child are close, cuddly, and connected, at the next they're distant and disengaged. These shifts from friend to foe and back again occur in a heartbeat, often without the parent realizing what has happened. The infant can shift from cooing to raging precipitated by a sudden hunger pang or gas bubble. Children come to us for security when afraid, then just as abruptly push us away. One day our teenager may confide in us, sharing a trauma or joy. Twenty-four hours later it's as if we've contracted leprosy. These shifts, often triggered by the normal developmental needs of the child, require an empathic parent. A 6-year-old was angry with his mother one afternoon when she was too busy to play with him. He stated dramatically, "You used to be a nice mommy before you got a job." Despite her devastation, she recognized the truth in his words. Children have a way of getting to the heart of the matter.

Typical developmental issues become even more confounded when we factor in parents' human limitations and foibles. Parents, all parents, project onto their kids. It's not anything we try to do; it just happens. It's part of the experience of being a parent. We look at our children and see ourselves, or, worse yet, we see behaviors that remind us of some dreaded relative. As they grow, the primitive identification increases. Little Sally reminds her mom of how she loved to dance. Young Sammy throws a football just like his dad. As we relive our childhood through our children, we want the best for them. We're so invested in their turning out well that we go into trance. We know what they should do, how they should act, what will be best for them. Our certainty makes it all the more disturbing when things don't go according to the plan. Disappointment sets in, and power struggles begin.

By imposing our ideas and beliefs onto our children rather than responding to their needs, we lock into an adversarial set. It devastates us when 5-year-old Johnny screams "I hate you" for not stopping at the candy aisle in the local grocery store. In a flash we think to ourselves, "I never said anything so horrible to my parents," "I don't deserve this," or "I've given to him all day and this is the thanks I get." It's normal to test the limits at age 5. Hearing the words "I hate you" coming from the mouth of a child you love is difficult to handle. It's hard to know what to do next. When we break into tears, sharply scold him with "You're a bad boy," or thoughtlessly whine "You don't really mean that, do you Johnny?" we're missing the point. The child's developmental needs must take precedence over the parent's emotional reactivity. This is where Carl's notion that the secret to being a good parent is in the enjoyment of being hated fits in. It suggests that we relax, take a step back, gather our thoughts, and respond based on our convictions rather than hurt feelings.

The next "truth" of parenting is that, despite our efforts and caring, there's no way to do it perfectly. The abundance of parenting literature speaks to our insecurity with the role. We're bound to make mistakes, to overreact at times and underreact at others. It's important to accept the fact that you'll make mistakes, without giving up on your ideals. The feedback we receive from our children can push us to reconsider our tactics. Five-year-old Chris had just received a spanking for hitting his younger brother. As he was sitting on the steps pouting, he jumped up indignantly: "I don't get it. How come big people can hit little people, but when little people hit little people, they get in trouble?" One can learn valuable lessons through children's naïve honesty. The process is invigorating despite complicated issues.

The final point to keep in mind regarding parenting is to recognize the difference between public and private relations. The rules of social behavior don't necessarily apply when dealing with the parent-child relationship. Parenting isn't about political correctness or fairness. It's a relationship, not a set of rules. A parent attending an open house was amazed at the positive descriptions of her 10-year-old son. Finally, she couldn't contain herself any longer and asked, "Are you sure you're talking about Bobby?" She had many more struggles with her son at home than the teachers were experiencing. Maybe her parenting was better than she thought. At least her son behaved well in public.

THE PARENTAL UNIT

The importance of the husband-wife bond is nowhere more apparent than in the process of raising children. The parental team emerges directly from the depth and lovingness of the spousal relationship. The couple's connection is the primary source of rejuvenation and energy when either partner feels depleted. It is joyous when this system is working and the husband and wife can openly relate and share the excitement of the child's arrival, despite the added stress. This deepens their emotional contact. When the spousal relationship is on the rocks, the addition of a child merely adds stress to an already debilitating situation. Both partners become more exhausted, more drained. While they may temporarily pull together, the impact of the added stress eventually pushes them further apart. The addition of children tends to topple relationships that are already in trouble. It amplifies the preexisting relationship. Good relationships are enhanced; bad ones are stretched further.

The quality of the connection between Mom and Dad is crucial for the children. While the mother-child and father-child relationships are vital, it's the strength and adaptability of the parental relationship that leads to the development of happy, secure children. It's as if the children are directly plugged into the emotional tone of the parental relationship. When the parents are in sync and feeling close, the children can relax. When the parental connection is tense, the children are anxious. If you ask kids how their mother and father get along, they can tell you without hesitation. They don't have to ponder a question they haven't considered. They're cognizant of the atmosphere that exists between their mom and dad. Their vigilance is automatic and profound, even when not readily apparent. Studies of divorced parents have shown that children's adjustment directly relates to the amount of conflict between their mother and father. If parents are civil to each other, children do better. When there is chronic discord, children suffer.

The process of moving from being a couple to being a family involves a number of predictable shifts. As the pregnancy progresses, the natural mother-infant symbiosis develops. As the mother invests more of herself into her baby, that relationship becomes the center of affect in the family. Dad, no matter how happy he might be about the pregnancy, typically feels left out. If he's mature enough to accept and even enjoy the mother-infant bliss, the family has a chance to move ahead. The tension increases when he becomes jealous and resentful or when he sulks and has tantrums because his sexual needs are blocked. Mom is in the impossible position of attending to the needs of the infant or the neediness of her husband.

The process of raising young children has the potential to increase or diminish the commitment the husband and wife have in each other. The relationship is damaged when the parents are unable to collaborate. They polarize, and a cross-generational alliance solidifies with the mother and child united as the father bails out emotionally. The gap widens when the father turns to golf, his work, or another woman for attention. This establishes the pattern of the family turning away from each other. This pattern of emotional infidelity further distances the couple. Each time they feel lonely or overwhelmed by the stress of living, they revisit the issue of "What do we do now? Pull together or turn away from each other?"

A less obvious but subtly disruptive parenting problem occurs when the couple exists to serve the children. The children's wants and needs are the primary focus of the family. The couple relates through and about their children. The couple bond is secondary, with minimal energy directed toward the adult side of the family. The children's needs shape all family decisions. Over the lifetime of the family, this interactional pattern creates distance between the couple that may not become apparent until the children leave home. At this point, it becomes painfully evident that the children are the glue for the relationship. Without them, there is not much common ground.

The capacity to pull together and operate as a cohesive unit is essential to effective parenting. It's good for parents to have the experience of being on the same team. They feel connected rather than alone, and their power is amplified. The idea of a united front comes easily with issues the parents agree on. When they see eye to eye on the value of education, the importance of manners, or the evils of alcohol, the teaming is effortless. Rest assured Johnny is watching when Mom and Dad disagree over the importance of his cleaning his room or playing outside. It's important for kids to see their parents arrive at a consensus when differences arise. Their willingness to work together and come to a mutual solution sends a clear message to Johnny. He learns that Mom and Dad respect each other, that they value the opinions of each other enough to do what it takes to reach a solution. This stance, while reducing the child's ability to manipulate, also provides security and stability. Children learn to respect the parents as a team. Parents don't have to be clones. They don't have to begin from the same position. They do need the capacity to suspend their own certainties long enough to actually hear each other and find common ground. A similar issue for parents is to stay out of sibling struggles. Parents do children a disservice when they step in too quickly to settle things. Working out problems provides skills for future relationships.

Another essential ingredient to successful parenting is for both parents to develop their capacity to parent autonomously. Each parent must find his or her own way of connecting with, relating to, and struggling productively with the children. While the parents have the "we" to lean on, they also need to be able to comfortably stand alone. Prematurely calling your partner in to mediate an impasse with one of the kids will do little to build a workable relationship. The old strategy of threatening your child with "Wait until your father gets home" or bailing out with "Your mom is better with those kinds of issues" does little to earn respect. Our children need to have the experience of connecting and struggling with us as individuals. It's the avenue to a more personal, more intimate relationship.

In developing this capacity, it's important that you find your own path, follow your own beliefs, and use your own style. Trying to emulate your partner in the name of consistency is a mistake. You need to find and take responsibility for your own approach. Common errors for parents include giving up, being too lenient, and being too strict. Parenting is a juggling act, learning to balance the emotions of tenderness and toughness. Parents' decisions are not always popular.

SUMMARY

The healthy family is in a process of perpetual evolution. It continues to grow in spite of whatever obstacles it faces. The rules and regulations are not etched in stone but develop implicitly out of the operation of the family. Family members express their identity through their daily living.

Carl was fond of saying "A healthy family holds its past in perspective, is optimistic of the future, but lives in the here and now." Health is signified through the choices we make today, not those of the past or future. The healthy family has a sense of an integrated whole, lives with the facts of its inconsistencies, acknowledges the passing of time, and always seeks to expand its experience.

The family life cycle is a prominent model for understanding the evolutionary change in a family system. Predictable markers in the family life cycle are birth, death, and marriage. Other markers include changes in income, illness, and family mobility. The family therapist must take note of these important events, because they contribute to cumulative stress within the system.

Life cycle stress is resolved through repression, avoidance, or open struggle. Healthy families solve problems by asserting customs, myths, and family rules. Self-doubt and frustration can provide the impetus for change.

Family life is both painful and deeply moving. The power of the family, like that of an infant, is both seductive and threatening. Openness and vulnerability lead to growth and a reparative experience. Much attention has been paid to the problems of families and how some families are failing to meet the needs of their members. The characteristics that make strong, healthy families successful receive too little attention. Understanding the inner workings of these types of families is beneficial to therapists committed to helping problem families grow.

Chapter 5

Generating an Interpersonal Context

I don't believe in individuals; we're all fragments of our families.—Carl Whitaker

When Carl first started seeing families, he had to strategize about ways to get them to come to therapy together. The culture supported individual analysis. Everyone who was socially "in the know" had a private analyst. Today, with the proliferation of family therapy and the cultural emphasis on family values, it is not so difficult to persuade a family to come to an initial appointment. It is our experience that if you believe it is important to see a family together, they will show up.

Still, when a family enters your office for the first time, they instinctively tighten up a bit and brace themselves for the unknown. We all experience a twinge of anxiety when trying something new. This is a natural process, one that's to be expected. The family typically begins an initial visit by offering to tell the story that led them to treatment. They want to be clear about why they came and are eager to present their view of the problem, believing that if they relate the problem in enough detail it will be easier for you to solve. Within minutes, the family scapegoat emerges. This introduction gives the therapist a sense, almost palpable at times, of who's scripted to talk first, how the situation will be presented, and, certainly, who will be implicated in the problem. Unconsciously, the family members collude in an initial presentation that keeps their anxiety in check and their role structure intact.

The family's story often portrays the destructive influence of one member, the identified patient, and the united efforts of the family to help this individual. The family isn't intentionally trying to mislead the therapist. Usually they have experienced a specific problem with a family member. Typically, an outside agency, such as a school, the police, social services, or an employer, has become involved. The family feels stuck and believes that the way to fix the problem is to "cure" the identified patient. The therapist's initial goal is to disrupt the family's belief that they are in therapy to "cure" someone and replace the family's description of the problem with a broader perspective. The therapist needs to expand the symptom by shifting the focus from the identified patient to the entire family system. This generates an interpersonal context.

The therapist's primary effort in therapy is to disrupt the deadening hopelessness of the initial presentation. The family needs to come alive, to move beyond their hopeless recollections from the past and experience their collective power in the present. The key to disrupting this "identified patient/healthy family" framework is to help family members see that their lives are interconnected. The idea is to redefine the problem as embedded in an interactive process rather than within the "patient." The therapist's persistence in moving from a singular scapegoat to a "we're-all-in-this-together" perspective creates the entire context for therapy.

When the family views itself as an entity and takes a "we" perspective, the accumulated anxiety within the system is redistributed and becomes a powerful catalyst for change. Rather than being singlehandedly shouldered by the identified patient, each family member is required to carry his or her own share of the distress. For example, a family recently came to an initial session because the 17-year-old son had been arrested for underage drinking. His mother had confided during the initial phone call that she thought the real problem was that her son was depressed and needed medication. The family mandate to the therapist was to cure the son. They, of course, would help in any way they could. The session was flat until the therapist persisted in getting the family to talk about itself. At this point, the boy's sister spilled the beans about her parents' constant pot smoking and her own suicidal fantasies. The collective anxiety about how family members felt about themselves brought the therapy encounter to life.

Carl often stated, "I am not interested in curing the identified patient or fixing the family's car, so rather than focusing on the kid, I head for the accumulated anxiety in the family" (Simon, 1985, p. 30). While dealing with our own anxiety is difficult, it's also the only way to be alive. Life is not about avoiding pain and discomfort but is about embracing it and living a full life in spite of it—and, perhaps at times, because of it.

Carl's belief that "there is no such thing as an individual, only fragments of families" runs counter to our culture's belief that an individual is a selfcontained entity. We are all part of a larger system that includes family members. The family legacy reverberates within us and always will. We can act as if we don't care and pretend it doesn't influence us. We can even cut ourselves off emotionally but only at tremendous personal cost. To be truly alive, we must discover ways to belong to the group while developing our own individual identities. Therapy must acknowledge and facilitate the difficult process of helping the family develop a sense of curiosity about itself without destroying the integrity of individual members. Generating an interpersonal context provides an opportunity for the family to broaden their perspective by viewing their situation from a variety of positions.

This stage in therapy of establishing an interpersonal context is organized around uncovering and expanding the family's diagnostic set. This phase of therapy is facilitated by the following types of interventions: (a) expanding the symptom, (b) highlighting cross-generational and intergenerational influences, and (c) redefining pathology.

EXPANDING THE SYMPTOM

Expanding the symptom is similar to the process of shifting from a view that captures only the intrapsychic world of an individual to a view that brings the rest of the family into focus. It redefines the patient as "a set of relationships," not an individual psyche. Each of us face difficult problems throughout life. People experience losses and must struggle to find meaning in their experiences. We believe that it's easier to face life problems within the context of a family. Our efforts, therefore, are focused on what is occurring within a family that has resulted in a loss of the family's confidence in facing problems collectively.

In the following example, Carl consults with a couple in their 40th year of marriage. The last 25 years of their relationship has been organized around Mary's diagnosis of schizophrenia and Steve's focus on "helping" her. When a chronic illness becomes the centrally organizing principle in the relationship, the couple is in trouble. While the husband's effort was obviously well intended and a real sacrifice, a certain deadness had descended on the relationship. The couple's interactions had become stiff and automatic. Together they seemed to be living out a tightly scripted, dark drama. Illness consumed their lives and drained their vitality.

Mary had been hospitalized 4 days before the consultation. In this segment Carl interviews Steve, hoping to free him from his dedication to his wife's "craziness" by introducing him to his own.

Carl: I assume since your wife's crazy, you are crazy too. Tell me about your craziness.

Steve: Oh, I'm not crazy.

Carl: I know, but tell me about it.

Steve: You know, that's funny. I was in the Air Force during World War I and on my first solo flight I turned the plane over before I took off. The mission was ruined, and I was really embarrassed.

Carl: Sounds pretty crazy, but it was actually pretty smart. You could have been killed if you went on that mission. Tell me some more.

Steve: Later, when it was my turn to be mission leader, I forgot to calibrate the bombsight. We dropped our full load of bombs 2,000 yards short of the target.

Carl: Well, that was crazy, but it kept you from killing a lot of people. Tell me another one.

Steve: Man, you're crazy.

Carl: Yeah, but go ahead.

Steve: When I finished my 50 missions, the commanding officer asked me to take over as the lead flight instructor. I was so mad. I reamed him out. I got up in his face and cussed him out. You can't do that in the Air Force; I thought I was going to be court martialed.

Carl: Well, I want another.

Steve: When I was a little boy, I got in a fight with my brother. I was banging his head on the concrete. Not just banging it, but really pounding it. Thump! Thump! Thump! If Dad didn't stop me, I probably would have killed him. . . . Wow, is that a weird memory!

Carl: That sounds like enough. I'll forgive you for all the rest.

As Steve recalled his own childhood craziness, he became quite emotional, making contact with himself again. This exchange gave Mary something as well. For the first time in years, Mary experienced her husband actually sounding like a human being. His ''aliveness'' was in stark contrast to the deadness he typically manifested. She sensed a glimmer of hope. He was back from the dead. Carl asked the husband about his craziness to broaden the framework or expand the symptom. His intent was for the couple to experience the ''we'' of their craziness rather than the wife continuing to suffer alone.

For Carl, expanding the symptom often involved an invitation to be crazy or just relax and enjoy the process. Carl believed that one-person craziness is lonely, but two-person craziness can be intimate and family craziness fun. As the husband continued to talk of his own craziness, he became more relaxed, and the tone of the preceding encounter softened. Expanding the symptom allows all participants in the encounter to lower their defenses.

The following example illustrates Carl's work with a couple and their two daughters during a consultation interview. Carl expands the symptom initially described as the husband's loyalty to his business by covertly communicating to the wife that her overinvolvement with the children may equally contribute to the distance in their marital relationship. He encourages her to see herself as a participant in the relationship rather than feeling victimized by it.

Carl: [to wife] Mom, can you say where you see the family pattern and how it operates?

Wife: At this time?

Carl: Well, I was thinking over the years really. It's easier to take a look at the past than it is to look at today.

Wife: I think we were close when we got married; then we had the children, and we were close to them. I think that's when we started drifting. I was pretty stationary; Paul went in another direction. He went into business. I think that was the beginning of the separation and distance.

Carl: Did you have any sense of the children belonging to you, and he being married to the business?

Wife: Exactly! I feel like I raised the children and he raised the business.

Carl: Did you ever figure out what trick you used to make him do that?

Wife: You mean, did I turn him into an workaholic?

Carl: No, not that. Do you think he was threatened by all the fun you had with the kids? Did you keep them all to yourself when they were young and cuddly?

Wife: Well, I guess I did. I could have used some help at times, but even when he was home he always seemed to get in the way. I guess at times it was easier when he was gone.

Carl implied that the process is bilateral and encouraged everyone to think about how he or she contributed to the presenting problems. No one is to blame, yet all participate in maintaining the process. Symptoms can be reframed within the context of the relationship. In this case, infidelity in the marriage is defined as a bilateral process. The husband becomes obsessed with his career, while the wife falls in love with the kids. Unfortunately, this is often a difficult process to resolve in our culture. Couples avoid the agony of struggling to develop more intimacy by seeking meaning outside their personal relationship.

A final example of expanding the symptom is illustrated in an initial therapy session with a 16-year-old girl and her parents. The daughter had just been released from a 10-day psychiatric admission for "delinquent" behavior.

Therapist: Dad, can you get us started?

Dad: Sure. We're here because our daughter Mary is depressed. Her grades have dropped from A's and B's to D's and F's. She's sneaking out of the house at night and recently took our credit card and charged $900 on it.

Therapist: Wow, it sounds like she's having a great time to me! Why do you think of it as depression?

Dad: Because it's such a change. It's so out of character for her. She's gone from being a really good kid to being a juvenile delinquent. She's not at all pleasant to be around anymore!

Therapist: Do you have any sense of how you fit into the picture?

Dad: Well, no, I'm just trying to help her grow up.

Daughter: [yelling] Oh right, you're sure helping me grow up by treating me like a 2-year-old! Just get off my case and leave me alone. Stop bugging me for every little thing I do! Get a life!

Dad: [yelling] Well, you act like a 2-year-old! I teach a lot of young people every day. They're only a couple of years older than you chronologically, but they're miles ahead emotionally—they get to class on time; they handle their assignments. You're not anywhere near ready for the real world. You'll end up being a nobody if you don't change.

Therapist: [Mom is quietly sobbing as she fights to hold back her tears] So, Mom, can you put some words to your tears? Let us in on what they're saying?

Mom: He's always so tough on her. He never really takes an interest and just listens. He just gets loud and yells. Then he storms out of the room and pouts.

Therapist: And I assume your tears are saying that's how he treats you, too?

Mom: Yes, if I choose to deal with him. Usually it's not worth it, so I just fade out and keep to myself.

Therapist: Do you have any sense of being depressed, too?

Mom: No. I'm not doing too badly.

Daughter: Not doing too badly? Are you out of your mind? You're doing horribly. You cry almost every day. All you do is sit around and stare at the television. You used to spend all your spare time painting. I haven't seen you pick up a brush for a year! Don't tell me you're not doing too badly!

Therapist: So you've diagnosed her as being depressed, too. Do you think she just doesn't know it?

Daughter: I guess she doesn't know it. I don't know. . .but she is depressed!

Therapist: So let's see. . .you're depressed and having fun, Mom's depressed and isn't enjoying it much. . . . What about Dad? What's he doing?

Daughter: He's just mad! He's always mad and in a bad mood. All he does is crab and complain!

Mom: He's depressed, too. He just takes it out on us.

Therapist: So, you guys are the depressed family. [to daughter] If I had to choose, it sounds like yours is the most fun.

Five minutes into the therapy, the frame has shifted. Rather than focusing on a depressed, acting-out teenager, the attention is directed to the three forms of depression this family manifests. The anxiety is now communal. We believe that when anxiety about a problem is shared by the family rather than residing in an individual, it is easier to manage.

By expanding the symptom, we teach the family to think systems. We begin by acknowledging the presenting problem and convey a sense of caring in response to the family's pain and suffering. We then work quickly to take the focus off the identified patient and implicate the entire system. In the previous examples, discussion shifted from a wife's schizophrenia to the couple's "craziness." Marital distance was reframed as a bilateral process whereby the husband and wife were held equally accountable, and a 16-year-old's delinquency was reframed as "family depression," all within the first session.

Many family therapists adhering to a variety of family therapy models profess an interest in the family system. They view individual problems within the context of a larger interconnected web of relationships. However, they are often willing to meet only with individuals. The client is then sent back for "home visits" to work out areas of conflict. In contrast, we prefer to challenge the identified patient myth with the entire family present in the first stage of therapy.

In this stage, we want to get the family members to talk to each other directly about their life together. The therapist intensifies the encounter, highlighting affectively loaded issues underlying the family's initial stale description of the problem. It's usually possible to expose the family's life cycle stress, patterns, and despair in the first stage. Of course, once therapy is under way, individual problems can be dealt with, but preferably out of the individual's initiative, not as an attack by the family on a single scapegoat.

HIGHLIGHTING CROSS-GENERATIONAL AND INTERGENERATIONAL INFLUENCES

Another way to broaden the therapist's and family's view of the problem is to widen the lens even further, this time taking a look not only at the nuclear family but at the extended family as well. The therapist may inquire about Mom and Dad's parents and grandparents to see how the family's pattern of living has unfolded. This increases the family's awareness of symptoms and interactional patterns that have occurred for generations. When viewed as responses to life stresses, family symptoms become more understandable within a historical context. It's easier on a family to talk about previous generations than to talk about themselves. Defenses are lowered as the family shares stories of the past and repetitive family patterns begin to emerge.

We assume that symptoms have continuity through generations. Rather than focusing solely on present problems, it is important to ask questions about previous generations so that individuals emerge as products of their history. Family patterns repeat themselves over time. A daughter may engage in rebellious behavior as an extension of her father's delinquent adolescence and her mother's unexpressed resentment of her own oppression. Awareness of this repetitive process allows the daughter and the family to take responsibility for deciding, today, how they will contribute to their evolving story. The daughter may continue her rebelliousness, but now she can accept ownership of it within the context of her family history. The family must consciously decide on the current direction their legacy will take.

The therapist highlights cross-generational and intergenerational influences by encouraging parents to tell stories about their own childhood, parents, and grandparents. Sharing stories in this way leads to a funny combination of being taken off the hook and being held accountable. Family members feel partially absolved as they realize, to some degree, that they have been programmed to act the way they're acting. At the same time, however, they are painfully aware of the responsibility they now shoulder. The way they handle today's dilemma is etched into their family history. Each of us is adding to the legacy as well as being affected by it. Once grasped, it is impossible to forget the elegant beauty of this simple reality.

The following example is an excerpt from an initial session with a couple and their 15-year-old son Matthew. The family is struggling to learn how to deal with conflict. Ten-year-old Jake was not in attendance because the parents didn't want to expose him to the family's problems. Dad's father, who moved in with the family a year ago, also refused to come to the session, saying he didn't believe in wasting good money when there weren't any problems to deal with. While the session began with a focus on Matt's individual issues, it quickly expanded to include the three-generation unit.

Therapist: So you're worried that Matt is too shy and socially withdrawn.

Mom: Yes. It was so painful for him during the last few years. He did so poorly in school because of his social upset I decided to home school both of the boys this year, and they're doing just wonderfully. Matt's grades are up, and he's beginning to enjoy learning again.

Therapist: And how's he doing socially?

Mom: Well, okay. He's getting along with his younger brother now. He still doesn't get out with the neighborhood kids very much. He's much more open and talkative with me now that he's home.

Therapist: And with the other family members?

Mom: Well, Grandpa picks on him. He's old and crabby. He has a hard time walking, so he asks us to do a lot of things for him.

Therapist: How about it, Dad? Do you see this in your dad too?

Dad: Well, sometimes, but he is old and getting confused. He really doesn't ask for too much.

Matt: Not too much! Just every time he sees me! I don't even go downstairs anymore. I try to avoid him as much as possible. I can't even go downstairs anymore to play pool.

Therapist: You're willing to give up pool so you don't have to deal with him? Why don't you just tell him, "Sorry, Gramps, I'm here to play pool. I need to have a little fun."?

Matt: He'd go crazy on me. He'd yell and curse and get all worked up. I can't do that. He might have another heart attack. Besides, I'd feel bad.

Therapist: You can't even be honest with your own grandpa? You can't be yourself? How about it, Dad? Can you talk to your dad and straighten things out?

Dad: Oh no, not with my dad! He can't handle conflict. He's not much of a talker. Life works out better if you do what he says. Besides, he's really not that much to handle.

Mom: Not for you! You're at work all day . . . all week! I'm at home with him every morning. I feel like a cook at a restaurant. He gets out of bed in the morning and announces what he'll have for breakfast. He doesn't care what I've made for everyone else. He treats me like a waitress. It makes me mad! I can't stand it! I told my husband last night that he's going to have to side with me and deal with his father. His dad is going to have to eat what we all eat. I don't have time to prepare special meals for him.

Dad: Well, okay, but it's really not that hard to cook up an omelet and make some bacon! I mean, he's 82 years old.

Mom: I'm not going to become your mother. She catered to him for more than 50 years! I've never even seen him pour a cup of coffee, let alone do something nice for her! She died a worn and exasperated woman who was still saying "Yes, dear" to his ridiculous demands. He'll always be welcome at our house. I do feel it's our duty to have him live with us now that he's alone, but he's got to learn to adjust. We're not all going to change to suit him.

Therapist: So this must seem familiar, maybe even comfortable for you, Dad. Your wife is complaining to you about your dad just like your mom used to. It's kind of cozy.

Dad: Well, it's not really cozy. I just want everyone to get along and be happy. I don't like to upset anyone.

Therapist: Well, I can certainly understand that, but tell me, is that how it worked out for you as a kid? Did you go through your childhood without being upset?

Dad: No, it was tough at times. I avoided my dad whenever I could. Mom and I would talk about how crabby he was.

Therapist: So now you've got to decide if your chapter in the family history book will read the same as the chapter from your childhood.

Dad: What?

Therapist: So far, it sounds like you're allowing the same damned thing that drove you crazy as a kid to drive your own kids crazy. Matt is upset with Grandpa and tries to avoid him and complains to your wife. You keep busy and act like there's nothing to deal with. You don't like it when your wife complains and says to do something about it. She's tired of feeling like a short order cook. Are you ready to pick up a pen? How will your chapter read?

As this vignette evolved, Grandpa's influence and the multigenerational pattern of withdrawing from conflict became apparent. During the past year, the level of unspoken tension in the family had slowly risen, but the process remained unchanged. Suppressed affect was beginning to spill over, and the voltage was at an intolerable level. When Matt and Mom began directly addressing the issues, the game was over. Dad was then in the position of needing to consciously decide what action to take. He had to either endorse the painful replication of his own childhood experience as it ensnared his son or face his own fear and apprehensions related to confronting his father. It was definitely his time at bat!

While anxiety evoking and deeply unsettling, the option of facing his father represented an opportunity to develop a real person-to-person relationship in the present. Through a confronting of the rigid roles that had been depleting the family for generations, the possibility of intimacy appeared on the horizon. If the family had the courage to remove their masks and face their fears, a sense of hope could begin to build.

Carl often described marriage partners as "two scapegoats setting out to reproduce their own families of origin." In the vignette to follow, Carl challenges a couple to think of themselves as a multigenerational unit. Here he amplifies the theme of secretiveness in the family. He encourages the couple to think about how patterns have repeated from one generation to the next.

Wife: He's always been so secretive about everything. You have to drag things out of him. Sometimes I wake up in the morning and look over at him and think I've lived with this person for 22 years and I don't even know him.

Carl: Can you see the pattern repeating from your family or his family? I don't think you do it to him or he does it to you. I think you all do it because it came down from a previous generation. Does that make any sense to you?

Wife: I guess I badger him at times, just like my mother badgered my father. She was always trying to reach him. At first she wanted real closeness. Later she just wanted him to react to something. My sisters and I gave up on him. We figured, he just wasn't interested in people. It was so much easier to get attention from my mother. She was always interested in us. While she could be smothering, she was always available.

Carl: [to husband] How about your family? Were they secretive too?

Husband: Um . . . I think we were typical '50s people. We weren't people who were looking at our feelings, we were looking at TV.

Carl: Were your mother and father under stress?

Husband: Undoubtedly, at times.

Carl: Did you know about it, or was it kept secret from you?

Husband: Well, I was born in 1940, and my parents were divorced in 1949. There was a war in between, and my father was overseas for 4 years. I don't know anything about his personal struggles. My mom was divorced twice. I know she cried a lot, but she never talked about it

Carl: Do you have any sense of repeating that pattern?

Husband: I don't know. I'd have to think about that.

Carl: Do you have any sense of who you pattern yourself after?

Husband: I wasn't close to my biological or my first stepfather. By the time my mother remarried for the third time, I was 18-years-old and in the army. I guess the big influence was my mom. I'm probably more like her.

Carl typically invited the extended family into the therapy, believing that this was crucial, especially when clients were stuck and therapy deadlocked. As a consultant in the next example, Carl breaks through the family's tough exterior and identifies affectively loaded issues by asking the extended family to share their life stories. Carl asks Dad about the relationship between his daughter and wife. While Carl and Dad converse, the mother and daughter listen to what is being said about them. Carl had a habit of talking indirectly to a person through someone else, as a way of sending covert messages. Through cross-generational storytelling, the therapist can draw parallels between the nuclear and extended family. The therapist looks for issues in stories that may reflect current blind spots. In this case, Carl pushes the sensitive issue of Mom's miscarriages to increase anxiety and mobilize the system.

Carl: [to therapist] Do you want to catch me up and give me some idea of where you've been and what you're looking for?

Therapist: I've been working with Nicole and Allen for 4 months. We've been stuck around the issue of Nicole rethinking her decision to have children. Allen has two teenaged children from a previous marriage and says his days of parenting are over. When Nicole and Allen married, they agreed not to have children. He's upset she's breaking the contract.

Carl: There are people missing. Allen's children and his previous wife. I was wondering how they happen not to be here today. They certainly are part of the scene.

Therapist: Allen couldn't imagine asking his ex-wife. He didn't think she'd be willing to come. His children are spending the weekend with their mother. Nicole invited her parents.

Carl: I'd like to start with you, Dad [Nicole's father], if I may. Can you say something about what you think is "cooking" in the family scene and how I can be useful?

Dad: Well, I think my wife is concerned about Nicole being depressed. She gets down, and we worry about her.

Carl: I'd like to stay with the group scene rather than the individual, if that makes any sense to you.

Dad: Well, we came to talk about Nicole's condition. My wife and I are doing fine. We've been married 34 years and we're still together. [As Carl attempts to focus the session on an intergenerational set, the dad objects]

Carl: Well, that's perfectly all right, and I want to be clear that I don't expect you and your wife to be patients here. The patients are the people who ask for help. And I think of you and your wife as consultants who try to help me be more useful to them.

Dad: My wife does everything for everybody. She's such a worrier. We have two children, Nicole and her older brother Rob. My wife does fuss over Nicole a bit more. She gets down when Nicole's down. Rob lives in Nebraska, so he's a little harder to track down. [After Carl defines the grandparents as "nonpatients," Granddad plunges in]

Carl: Do you think your wife's a supermom? Does she go so far that she beats herself up with it? How do you protect her from that?

Dad: Well, there's not much I can do about it. She's always been this way. The kids are her life. She'd do anything for them. We would have liked to have more. We had two and six miscarriages in between, but we're thankful for the two we have!

Carl: How did you take it when it turned out Nicole was going to marry somebody who was divorced and had a couple of kids?

Dad: Well, whatever makes her happy. We want her to be happy.

Carl: You don't worry she might try to be a supermom like your wife and take on these other two kids that don't belong to her?

Dad: Well, she is a lot like her mother that way. I don't know how she feels about taking care of teenagers. She seems to have a good relationship with them. She's always running here or there. They've got busy lives.

Carl: What do you think, Mom, about the situation? Is it scary for your daughter to be a stepmother instead of a mother? Did that business raise all your pain and suffering of the six pregnancies that didn't make it?

Mother: Well, I really don't think of it anymore. [pauses, becomes tearful] I would have loved to have had more children. We really tried. It just wasn't meant to be. One child that I lost, I carried almost full term. That was painful.

They tell you not to blame yourself, but I always wondered if I could have taken better care of myself, not pushed myself so much, relaxed more. [Once the grandmother had so easily revealed her continuing pain, Carl instinctively moved to highlight the role of the spousal relationship in the grieving process]

Carl: Were you and your husband able to share the sadness, or did you have to be tough?

Mother: Oh, he's been good to me. It was upsetting for him, too. We didn't talk about it much. You just have to move on.

Carl: Were you ever able to find anybody that you could really cry with about that?

Mother: Well, I was all right. Everyone gets dealt something in life. People have worse things to deal with. It was painful at the time, but I was all right.

Carl: Do you think that has anything to do with Nicole having married into a situation where she has two grown children? This way she can't lose them. [Here Carl underscores the obvious but unnoticed parallels between them]

Mother: Oh, I don't think she planned that. It's just how it turned out.

Carl: Nicole, where are you with all this? Besides having changed your mind.

Nicole: Pretty stressed out. When we married, I was 26. The idea of not having children didn't bother me. Now that I'm 30, I sort of started panicking, worrying that maybe I was missing out on something—doing it wrong. I'm pretty committed to my career. I do a lot of traveling and didn't really have a desire to have children. I'm not sure why I'm so confused now.

Carl: I had the craziest feeling that maybe you were thinking or dreaming of having kids for your mother. All those that she lost.

Nicole: I know she's always wanted more children; that was a disappointment for both of my parents. They both came from large families. Mom says she's gotten over it, but she cries whenever someone brings it up.

Carl: Well, so you suffer then. That's their problem. You can make it yours if you want to.

Nicole: I guess so. My mom's just been wonderful to me. There isn't anything she wouldn't do for me if I asked her.

Carl: Well, after all, she lost six, you know. Look at all these babies you represent. Now if all six had been born alive, you probably wouldn't even be noticed. Do you think if you and your husband and your mother and father got into therapy that she could get the courage to wail out her guilt about all those missing children?

Nicole: I don't think they'd do it. She truly believes she's over it.

Carl: Well, boy, is she crazy. Those missing children are right in front of you and me and her and Dad and your husband. Every one of them and maybe a couple more she doesn't know about. I think it's inevitable. She may not know it, but someplace in her head all these pregnancies are a terrible haunting sadness. She's held together for you and your brother and her husband and if she gets the courage to fall apart, you know, it's going to be a mess. I think it's maybe worthwhile, though.

Carl: [to Nicole's husband] Can you say where you are with all of this?

While Carl highlights and intensifies the issue of the mother's miscarriages, he is careful not to turn her into the patient. He draws a parallel between Nicole's confusion regarding the decision to have children and her mother's unresolved grief. After intensifying the encounter, he suddenly changes the subject, asking Allen to talk about his experience of family life. By overattending to the mother's losses, he plants a seed implying that, perhaps, she is projecting her unfulfilled dreams onto her daughter. He does not try to convince the family of this or make elaborate interpretations. He merely shares his "crazy thoughts" and moves on, leaving them to do what they want with it.

By the end of the first stage of therapy, we want the family to have a significant awareness of their patterning and a better sense of their hopes, fears, and dreams. We want to highlight how patterns of dealing with stress repeat themselves over generations and identify themes or affectively loaded issues that continue to drive the family's affect and behavior. Some families go to extremes to avoid conflict. Other families somaticize when stressed. Some families are secretive, others explosive. Some families expect perfection, while others sabotage members' attempts to grow and individuate from the family.

Families unconsciously replicate patterns of interaction that keep the family's legacy alive. "The Marshalls never buckle under pressure," "The Smiths always give 110%," and "The Johnsons never get sick" are slogans that result in generation after generation organizing family life and behavior in a similar way. We want to identify the powerful themes underlying the family's life. Is the family struggling to carry out some type of family legacy? Are they projecting unfulfilled dreams and desires on the next generation? When the family becomes more aware of family themes and cross-generational patterns, we believe it is in a better position to do something about them. We want to facilitate experiences that challenge family myths and patterns and create new themes of family life.

REDEFINING PATHOLOGY

The concept of "craziness" occupies a strange and distorted position in our culture. While we revere the craziness or freedom of youth, we are terrified by people or things that are different and difficult to explain. They make us uncomfortable. We use the term *craziness* with a sense of admiration toward someone willing to go against the grain. We can also use the term to compartmentalize and devalue people. It's a way of washing our hands of the frightful or bizarre.

We derive our conception of craziness from the medical model, which pathologizes behaviors that stray too far from the norm. Society defines what is normal. The problem is that cultures vary in their definition of *crazy*. What is crazy in one culture may be considered the norm in another. For example, body piercing, dreadlocks, and cross dressing are considered bizarre and unusual in most small, conservative rural communities. However, in more cosmopolitan areas, a variety of diverse and sometimes deviant or outlandish behaviors are the norm. It only takes one ride in the subway of New York City to discover that crazy is "in."

We have all internalized the image of the frazzled, frayed, and bedraggled insane individual being ostracized, spit at, and carried away to seclusion in order to protect society from his or her contagious disease. It's this unconscious, internalized image of "crazy" that we hold onto—fearing that craziness results in falling off the edge with little hope for return—that's so destructive.

As therapists, we continue to be faced with the arduous task of dispelling the myth of going crazy. Those who experience a sudden onset of depression often don't get help for fear they're "losing it." Family members often turn their head the other way and tell loved ones to "get it together" and "snap out of it." One of the authors made the following statement to a tearful, depressed woman who feared that her life would be over if she relied on medication: "If I told you that you had diabetes or a thyroid problem, you wouldn't hesitate to get help. This isn't any different!" Momentarily, there was a gleam of hope in her eye. Maybe she wasn't going nuts after all.

One of Carl's most significant contributions was to challenge the cultural belief that we don't have any control over our "craziness." Psychopathology pigeonholes people and bypasses their personhood. Craziness becomes dangerous when it is isolated. The image that craziness involves "out-of-control" affect can be countered by adding a cognitive, more rational ingredient to the mix. Carl often told his clients "It's okay to be crazy as long as you're smart about it. If you're stupid you'll end up eating frozen peas in a mental institution." Being smart means being selective about how and where you choose to express your craziness. Carl admitted that he, too, was crazy. He said the trick is to learn how to make a living at it.

Carl reframed family pathology as an effort to grow. He redefined "crazy" as the ability to be unique, spontaneous, and playful. He encouraged the family to accept its craziness and taught members how to channel it creatively as a way to enhance and add spice to their living.

When the family points to one member as "crazy," it's important for the therapist to redefine or normalize the process. We all have crazy experiences. By defining pathology as normal idiosyncratic experiences, the therapist removes the stigma and creates room for creativity.

The following case illustrates Carl's work with a schizophrenic client and his family. Carl shares his belief that "craziness" is really just "stupidity," and there is hope for that problem. You can't do much about being crazy, but you can do something about being stupid. There is an odd tongue-in-cheek quality to this message that creates hope where before there was none. It also develops a language in which to talk about the belief that just because someone is crazy, it doesn't mean he or she can be totally irresponsible or unaccountable. If you see the symptoms as the forefront, the patient becomes the background. Carl wanted to keep the person in focus in hopes that things could be different.

Son: I've been defeated by my craziness?

Carl: Well, that's because you're stupid, you know, and you can get over that.

Son: I can't get over stupidity.

Carl: Sure you can. If you are stupid, it just means you're doing dumb things you don't need to do. It isn't a question of being feeble-minded; hell, if you weren't smart, you wouldn't be able to go crazy. [Here Carl counters the father's effort to define craziness as being beyond stupidity]

Dad: Unless you are really psychotic; I suppose that's something different?

Carl: I think psychotic is merely a hardened variety of craziness. It's like a black hole. It's difficult to escape. Everybody thinks you're crazy, so you act more and more crazy.

Dad: Compacting the black hole. [mimics making a snowball]

Mom: And there's no way out.

Carl: I think you can get out, but, God, it is really hard work.

Mom: I'm thinking about people that are psychotic. They just stay that way.

Carl: But that is because they're disregarded.

Dad: Or the family gets smarter or more objective about things . . . stops trying so hard.

Carl: And kicks them out further. I think there are different ways to go crazy, different kinds of craziness. I think you can be "driven crazy." That to me is really being kicked outside the family so you're sort of malignantly isolated. There's "going crazy," which is what you do with a good friend. It's when you're really high as a kite and you're out of your cotton-pickin' head. Then there's "acting crazy." If you've really been crazy once and the tension gets too high, you can sort of imitate yourself.

This dialogue suggests that, to some extent, craziness is a social function. Being devalued or extruded from the family creates an experience of isolation and alienation that erodes personhood. Once you are defined as a clinical syndrome, your sense of humanness fades, and you become a figment of the family fantasy. The binding dance of a self-fulfilling prophecy is under way.

As this session continues, Carl shares the belief that craziness is an elected office. Within the context of the family psyche, subterranean elections are held, typically by secret ballot. Votes are tallied determining who will play what role. Terms are open ended. Another election is the only way to change the outcome. Carl continues:

> I think one of the big factors that makes a difference is the family's voting rights. Just like Mark Twain said about the town drunk, "It's an elected office." Somebody runs for it and everybody votes. I think you were there first and they thought you were crucial. Parents get awfully anxious about the first kid. I had one story that's always been fascinating to me. This guy was very crazy, and I asked his parents when it started. The mother said, "I know exactly when it started. I got up at 3 o'clock one morning to go to the bathroom and there was a light under his door. I knocked on the door, went in, and said, 'What's the matter? What are you doing up at 3 o'clock in the morning?' He said, 'I've been sitting here for 5 hours trying to think of an English thesis for tomorrow and I can't think.' So I ran quickly and got daddy and told him to come in. 'He's been sitting here for 5 hours and he can't think.' And, you know, he's never been the same since. We stayed up for the rest of the night." That's election. Mother and father were so terrified that they really believed he couldn't think and that this was the end of the world, and he went right on. He stayed crazy for a long time. In a strange kind of way, the person who is crazy gets all the investment, all of the caring that both parents have about each other and about themselves. So they're really tremendously endowed.

Initially, Carl implies that the parents may have created their son's craziness. Then he reframes this joint effort in positive terms, stating that they didn't know what they were doing. Their investment in their son was understandably an act of caring.

As therapists, we need to dispel the myth of craziness. Our goal is not to fix the family or cure their craziness but to normalize and redirect it in a healthier way. We encourage the family to think about how and why the member in question was elected to be crazy in the first place. Labeling and devaluing individuals robs them of their personhood and drives them further outside the family. The intent is for the family to take collective responsibility and invite the alienated and extruded member back into the family.

We redefine family pathology as an effort to grow. Crazy is revered. We believe that people have the right to their own unique craziness, that they are entitled to their own paradigms for living. This is not to say that we aren't responsible for our actions; rather, craziness is controllable. We differentiate craziness from stupidity and stress that how one chooses to live out one's craziness is a conscious decision.

SUMMARY

The primary goal of the first phase of therapy is for the family to discover its capacity for self-repair. If we are successful in generating an interpersonal set, the spotlight dims on the identified patient. Each member shares his or her own experience of family life, and the family begins to talk to each other about their inner struggles. During the first stage of therapy, the goal is to empower the family as a team, to develop a sense of hope and the belief that together they can gain the momentum to continue their journey.

As each generation recounts their experience of family life, we get a picture of how the family has dealt with stress and anxiety. Parents and grandparents share anecdotes that elicit family themes of depression, denial, perfectionism, secretiveness, and so forth. As the story unfolds, the entire family system becomes aware of its patterns. We highlight significant repetitive processes to broaden the family's perspective. Once they have a better sense of where they've been, they can decide where they're going.

When the family can see past the identified patient, it's easier to reframe pathology as a creative effort at growth. Carl's story about the boy who sat up until 3:00 in the morning implies that he didn't become schizophrenic overnight. The family unconsciously colluded in electing him for the role. His parents were not completely to blame. They really didn't know what they were doing. Their overinvestment, which perpetuated their son's behavior, was the only way they knew to convey their caring. We all get crazy; the trick is not to be stupid. By the end of the first phase of therapy, we want the family to have a more collective view of themselves, a better sense of their origin, and a desire to tackle their craziness.

Chapter 6

Creating a Therapeutic Alliance

Tseking asked, "Is there one single word that can serve as a principle of conduct for life?" Confucius replied, "Perhaps the word reciprocity will do.—The Wisdom of Confucius

The task of creating a therapeutic alliance is paramount once an interpersonal context is firm in the family's mind. Now that the problem has been expanded to include more than the identified patient, the goal of the second stage of therapy is for the family to experience the therapist as an ally who is strong enough to tolerate their emotional voltage without defeat. At this point, the therapist begins to share more of himself or herself, encouraging the family to be more of who they are. If the therapist is successful in creating a therapeutic alliance, the family loosens up a bit and begins to let down its guard. This facilitates a more spontaneous process. While the therapist aligns with the family, he or she maintains control of the therapy hour by setting explicit conditions to maximize the probability of success, such as reminding the family that they are ultimately responsible for their growth. The therapist must be effective in blocking character assassination or glorification.

It is up to the family members to commit themselves to the therapy process. The therapist merely offers the opportunity for therapy, under his or her conditions. This is conveyed from the earliest contact. Sessions do not take place if the family breaks rank and some members do not attend. Carl often said, "It's better to fail at the start than to start and fail later on."

Creating a therapeutic alliance is a challenging task for the therapist. It's also not an easy or natural process for the family. Relating to a stranger about emotionally charged issues can be awkward. If the therapy is to be successful, the family needs to risk exposing its underbelly. Behavior reserved for private is difficult to exhibit publicly. Families are reluctant to open themselves up until a sense of trust and connectedness with the therapist has developed. This process is an active, anxiety-driven one that occurs with every family. Family members are not sure how to define themselves in relation to the therapist. They want some ground rules for behavior.

Perhaps the idea of a blind date best captures the spirit and atmosphere of this stage of therapy. A meeting of strangers is no sure thing. Neither party knows in advance what will occur, whether it will work out, or if they will decide to continue seeing each other. While a blind date can lead to a connection that is ultimately intimate and deeply personal, it may not begin that way. The first step in any new relationship is to establish one's capacity to connect with another while being true to oneself. This process is the platform from which the therapeutic system evolves.

When working with a family, Carl often engaged in a repetitive process of joining and disengaging. He viewed himself as a catalyst for change but did not become part of the actual reorganization process. He moved in to experience the family, stimulated interaction, and then pulled out. He engaged the family in a personal, intimate encounter and then disconnected, often leaving them perplexed about the experience. By means of joining, Carl was adept at getting to the heart of the family, revealing their inner complexities. Carl was a master at initiating confusion. He felt it was the therapist's responsibility to disrupt the status quo, especially in the early stages of therapy. He did not apologize for his methods; even skilled surgeons cause pain. Out of this pain, the family has the opportunity to regroup in a more productive way. Initially, some families found Carl abrasive, but few had no reaction to him. One client described Carl as being like sand in your bathing suit. Carl provoked controversy, both in therapy and in his professional life. He wanted people to think for themselves, to react as honestly as he did. He didn't much care what the response was, as long as it was real.

Carl believed that family therapy was not for the timid. The therapist has to be capable of tolerating tremendous levels of anxiety. This anxiety may be internal or stimulated by the family. Therapists must be able to engage the anxiety present in the room without panicking or overreacting. It is crucial not to neutralize the family's fear out of our own apprehension.

Early in the therapy process, Carl engaged the family by (a) joining with them, (b) adopting their language, and (c) participating in parallel play. These were his "connecting maneuvers." They were complemented by "distancing or disengaging maneuvers" in which he would pull back and insist that the family both initiate the discussion and provide the energy to carry the session. Perhaps one of our clearest convictions is that the family has to bear the full responsibility for their own living. The ultimate goal of therapy is to encourage the family to follow their own beliefs and assume the opportunity or burden of calling their own shots.

JOINING AND DISTANCING

The idea of joining is one of the most misunderstood concepts in the psychother-apy literature. While widely recognized as essential to the therapy process, it is commonly viewed in a distorted, oversimplified form. Joining is typically thought to emanate from a foundation of unconditional caring the therapist instinctively holds for each family he encounters. When viewed from this per-spective, joining is relegated to an automatic superficial function similar to flash-ing a social smile when meeting a stranger. At best, it means nothing; at worst, it's a lie. Carl openly admitted that, early in the therapy process, he didn't yet ''care'' about the people in the room. They were still fumbling on the blind date. Caring about virtual strangers is improbable. Despite the obviousness of this observation, the family and the therapist often have unrealistic expectations for the first encounter. Genuine caring can evolve only through the reciprocal process of getting to know one another.

Joining doesn't have to be difficult. We each have an intuitive sense of how to connect with different types of families. One family with young children arrived at the therapist's office early in the morning. The therapist was running late because he had stopped to buy a muffin for himself. When the family entered the room and sat down, the therapist asked the kids if they'd like to share a muffin with him. At first they were reluctant, and then they sat on the floor to join in. The therapist told the children it had been a while since he had the pleasure of sharing his breakfast with any kids. On another occasion, the children in the family asked the therapist whether he had any pictures of his children. This turned into a lively conversation about similarities among the kids. The youngest asked what the therapist did to his kids when they were bad. The issue of joining will vary from family to family.

In the following example, a family, new to therapy, is midway through the initial interview when the session goes flat. The family members finish their opening presentation, saying something about needing better communication, and nothing happens. A pause in the conversation extends for a full 2 minutes. The room is suddenly getting warm, eye contact is being avoided, and the kids are squirming. Dad tightens his jaw to suppress a yawn. Seven-year-old Johnny responds with an unashamed, mouth-wide-open yawn. Carl chuckles and play-fully joins with Johnny.

Carl: You know, that looks like a good idea. Let me try one too. [stretches and lets out a broad yawn] Ah...that's better.

Mom: [Mom's eyes are blazing as she glances at her husband and then turns to Carl] Well, I'm sorry we're boring you. We've told you about our problem and that we really need help. Do you think you could do something other than yawn? Aren't you interested in us?

Carl: Oh, I suppose I'm interested enough. Actually, it's probably more accurate to say I'm interested in getting interested in you, but so far it's kind of boring.

Johnny at least has the guts to let out a real yawn. Dad tried to hide his. I guess I like Johnny's style better and decided to be more honest myself. It's a tough job waiting for you guys to get serious.

Dad: What do you mean, ''get'' serious? We're already serious. We're here, aren't we? It takes a lot to do something like this.

Carl: Sure it does, and I respect that. But now that we're all here at the ballpark, I need to let you in on something. I'm only a coach for this baseball team, I'm not playing on it. You guys will need to be the ones on the field making the plays. So far it feels like you're not sure about leaving the dugout.

Mom: Okay, well, then coach us! Tell us what to do.

Carl: I'm sorry...I said I'd be the coach, not the mother. I don't know what you should do. I suppose you guys need to take the field and show me your stuff. Maybe then we can get started.

Dad: But that's why we're here! We don't know how to play the communication game very well.

Carl: Okay, then...I'll do some coaching. Dad, why don't you take the mound and throw the first pitch? You know, look around the room and take off on something.

This vignette illustrates Carl's belief that people can't really care about someone they don't know. He resonated to Johnny's authenticity through his involvement. He maintained his distance when the parents complained about his yawning, questioning whether or not he was really interested in them. He shared his own personal reaction to the process, revealing that it was hard on him to wait for them to begin. Carl also conveyed the message that he was not willing to be their mother. He would only be a coach.

Most therapists are worried about the image they portray. Creating a loving illusion is a dangerous precedent. Even more dangerous is for the therapist to act as if he or she really cares about a family in a ''pseudocaring'' manner. This runs the risk of colluding with the family to ''let sleeping dogs lie'' and guarantees that the encounter will be superficial. It calls to mind the sociopath's motto: ''Always be sincere, even when you don't mean it.''.

Most family therapists tend to be delusional ''supermom'' characters. We tend to be victims. With this stance, it doesn't take long to burn out. As family therapists, we must fight against the cultural conviction that if society damages people, we ''magicians'' will give our own life to whoever doesn't make a good life for themselves. Family therapists often agree to straighten out three generations of culturally induced poverty, degradation, and dysfunctional living. If it takes years to correct, no problem, society is glad to let us try. They won't pay much, but we don't mind! Before you do family therapy, you need to be clear about the pathology of uncontrollable caring and the destructiveness of not fighting for your own priorities in living.

One of the authors' young supervisees called one evening, upset about a family he had seen. "You know, I've seen this family for three sessions already. They haven't done anything I've asked them to do and they aren't any better!" The supervisor chuckled. "I've seen some families for years and they aren't any better. Relax and get to know them. Don't try to be supermom!" The point is that you can't assume responsibility for the family's living or you will become overburdened and give up. Therapy is not about influencing families to live as we do; rather, it is about guiding them in efforts to live their life. This can be a complicated lesson for therapists to learn. It is usually learned through failure rather than success.

To counter these potential pitfalls, a better foundation for therapy is to begin from the belief that the family is paying you to be honest even if, at times, your honesty is off-putting. This is your contract with them. While families are often surprised or shocked at this beginning, on a deeper level they know therapy must transcend social pleasantries. Honesty reflects a profound level of caring.

Intimate relationships are developed through the complementary processes of joining and distancing. While being distinctly different psychological experiences, they fit together to form a more complete, transcendent gestalt. These divergent processes collaborate in a synergistic fashion. The more connected you are, the more capacity you have to separate and explore life as an individual. The more confident you are as an individual, the more free you are to belong to a system without losing yourself. Rather than being adversarial, these processes feed and energize each other. Distancing may involve withdrawing from family interaction, or it may involve breaking social etiquette in a playful manner to convey to the family that therapy is going to operate differently than is socially acceptable. For example, it may mean saying to a child, "That's my computer, you can't touch it" or "Stay out of my drawers." This interaction clarifies your role in relation to the family. The interaction is personal, not a function of the social establishment. It is necessary to take this kind of responsibility and ownership in creating a therapeutic alliance. It provides a vacuum between the family and therapist whereby the family must decide how to fill the space created by the therapist's distance. This facilitates an honest therapeutic encounter.

Relationships require the capacity to hold on and to let go, to give and to take. It is essential to learn to tolerate the anxiety of being abandoned, as well as the terror of being engulfed. The situation is similar to learning to swim as a child. Children are confident in their abilities as long as their hands touch bottom or someone is buoying them up. The sheer terror of realizing the first time they are moving under their own power is exhilarating! All of the rules change instantly.

During the initial phase of therapy, Carl joined with families by highlighting similarities. He believed that we're all more similar than different, that the commonalities of the human condition far overshadow the differences of our idiosyncratic life experiences. Referring back to his OB-GYN days, he would say, "You know, a body is a body. They're 90% the same on the outside, and we're all the same on the inside.'' Carl would frequently tease grandparents who made reference to their age by discussing his own age-related concerns. When men expressed feeling outside of the family, he shared his experience of living on a dairy farm where his mother attended to the family's emotional living, while his father worried about the farm. When mothers complained of being unappreciated, he spoke of their "deadly maternal instincts." Connecting with families frequently took the form of sharing beliefs that reflect universal experiences.

Carl joined with families by sharing part of his own past because he believed the concept of empathy was not effective. Being empathic requires the therapist to focus on the "other" rather than on him- or herself. Carl was not interested in becoming a "Peeping Tom." He discovered ways to join with families by becoming actively involved while being careful not to invade their system. He began the relationship by being honest and fully present with the family in therapy. Carl was fond of saying that "in therapy, a family pays for your ear but must capture your heart."

In the following example, Carl joins with a three-generation family of women by teasing them about age and gender issues. The grandmother has been talking about "giving up on men." She describes her boyfriend as unreliable and considers breaking up with him. Carl flirtatiously makes the encounter more personal and humorous.

Grandmother: I don't want any more to do with him. He drinks too much and never calls.

Carl: You mean you're going to give up on men?

Grandmother: Oh yeah, definitely.

Carl: [looking around] Do you think she's going to give up on men? She's not that old; is she?

Mother: [laughing] No.

Grandmother: Oh, I am too! I'm 61.

Carl: Oh, let's not brag. I've got 5 years on you. [laughing] See, you were wrong again. You shouldn't marry anyone this old. It's hopeless.

Joining with the family is an integral process of the therapy. The therapist, although a participant in the process, does not assume responsibility for the direction of the therapy, only the structure. Communication with the family establishes the therapist as coach rather than leader. The initiative for the process must come from them. Therapy must move beyond the boundaries of social interaction into the experiential realm.

ADOPTING THE FAMILY'S LANGUAGE

Carl was intrigued with the language families use to portray their lives. He was not as concerned with what was said as he was with how the family said it. He listened for the subtleties, the inferred meanings, the descriptors, the mood painted by the speaker. He observed other family members while someone was speaking, looking for unexpressed reactions. He was aware of who listened, who ignored, who distracted, and who furthered the discussion. He focused on peculiar expressions, nonverbal gestures and manners. He had an uncanny way of mirroring the family's tone. He communicated to the family in their language, using fragments of their dialogue. This was not a deliberate action or a conscious process but one that evolved through the belief that the family will tell you all you need to know about them if you are receptive. Carl was sensitive and responsive to families' unique customs.

Family experience is the data the therapist draws from. The family's stories are key. The therapist will not understand the real reason the family came to therapy without spending time listening. We want to avoid systematic replacement of the family experience with our language. Symbolic-experiential therapy differs from other therapies by broadening the family's symbolic descriptions of issues rather than narrowing them. It involves an effort to understand issues from the patient's perspective and life context. Too often therapists fit the family's description of the problem into their treatment modality. Seemingly crazy behavior makes perfect sense when viewed from the context of the family's life. At times we're amazed at how well the family is actually doing.

This is a good point to discuss the issue of culture and diversity. A therapist cannot know all there is to know about culture and diversity. Nuances are both numerous and subtle. We feel it is important to address cultural issues and know how culture affects families. We try to take what we know about culture and view it from the family's perspective. We rely on them to tell us what we need to know through the description of their family history, reasons for living in this country, and experiences they have had assimilating into the environment. Often these experiences are very different for parents and children. Children tend to acculturate at a quicker pace, often challenging the family norms. Parents can feel one-down to children who understand the language and customs better then they do.

For example, in one Hispanic family the 10-year-old daughter kept complaining of "being boring." The therapist was confused about the message and asked the girl what made her so boring. She got mad when her brother laughed. He said, "She means bored, but really she's boring; that's why the kids don't like to play with her." This led to a discussion about the problems family members had expressing themselves when they were not quite sure of the meaning. The therapist assured them that his Spanish would be much worse, so he appreciated their willingness to struggle with the language difference.

In another instance, the father said, "Well, I'm not really sure why I need to be here, but if you want me here, I'd like to talk about my mother-in-law."

The therapist was then able to carefully augment the therapeutic alliance by stating, ''Well, I had trouble with my mother-in-law early in my marriage and I never did resolve it! I hope you guys can help me figure out some things about it.'' Thus, the therapeutic alliance evolves from the family's initiative and the therapist's sharing of his or her own past experiences.

In the following example, the session begins in a superficial and polite manner. The family's focus is on where they have come from rather than where they need to go. Carl confronts the family on their lack of motivation to change. The father continually comments that his ''vision'' and ''hearing'' have changed. Carl then uses the words *vision* and *hearing* throughout the encounter to communicate with the father in his own language.

Carl: You guys just don't seem desperate enough to be working on anything today. Do you think that's true for you?

Father: No, there was a time I was real desperate. That's before my vision and my hearing improved. Now I see things differently. My desperation became a catalyst and I tried harder with my family.

Carl: Did your desperation change your life any or just your vision?

Father: I think it changed my life.

Carl: Oh, that's nice. Did it change for the better or worse?

Father: Definitely for the better.

Carl: So what are you doing here?

Father: I just came down to watch you.

Carl: Well, then, all that's really changed is your vision.

Father: My hearing has also improved. I can hear Lorraine. Years ago I became tone deaf to her voice and I couldn't see my children even though they were all in the house.

Carl: And after you saw them, was it any easier to make contact with them, or was it just easier to stay away?

Father: It was almost impossible to make contact with them.

Carl: If it was impossible to make contact with them, clearing up your vision didn't help much, did it?

Father: It gave me the opportunity that I have now.

Carl: You just haven't taken advantage of it.

Father: I have taken advantage of it!

Carl: Oh, I thought you said it wasn't working. You said you were using your vision and hearing, but nothing was happening.

Father: After working hard for 15 years, 12 hours a day, and coming home night after night to dinner with these people, I finally woke up and said, ''Who are these people?'' And my daughter said, ''Who are you?'' And I said, ''I'm your father.'' They didn't know who I was.

Carl: Did you find out who you were?

Father: To some degree.

Carl: Did you show them?

Father: That's what we're doing now.

Carl: So you are adjusted enough to do that?

Father: Oh, yes.

Carl: Do you think there will be a time when you get desperate enough to make contact rather than just sharing your vision and hearing?

Father: I think as they get older we'll connect. Right now it's, ah, just not happening.

Carl: That's one of my delusions—that they'll get older but I won't. [laughter] I wish I could make that happen. It's a crazy fantasy. If I ever get to be God, I'll give you some time to wait for them to grow up without your aging. I don't think you should plan on it, but you never can tell.

Adopting a family's language involves more than paying attention to the family's words. It requires a sensitivity to the emotional tone of individual members and the family collectively. It means paying attention to the way the family describes their life experience and their relationships with other family members. It also involves the therapist being aware of and using his or her own internal reactions to the family process.

PARALLEL PLAY

Parallel play is a critical process in symbolic-experiential therapy. It is a method of establishing a therapeutic alliance where the family and therapist work side by side to forge a connection, a joint project in which the family assumes the initiative. Instead of taking the lead, the therapist parallels the family by running along beside them. This process is similar to the play of 3-year-olds. You can play alongside them, but if you attempt a joint project before they are developmentally ready, they will retreat. If you build your block tower beside the child's block tower, then the two of you can co-exist, although you are not yet a real team.

The same process exists with families. Early on in therapy they are not ready for a joint project, despite the explicit contract to the contrary. When the family brings something up that they want to change, the therapist can begin very carefully to augment the ongoing process by sharing thoughts or experiences similar to those of the family. The therapist does not take the initiative but responds only to the family's offerings. The therapist elaborates on an experience and begins to present a fantasy of what might be different based on his or her perspective. Parallel play moves the therapist out of a one-up position and into a more collaborative exchange that helps the family break out of their insular viewpoint.

Whenever the therapist goes one-down and shares slivers of his or her own pain and impotence, the family has an opportunity to reassert its power. Parallel play involves taking a component of the therapist's life that is analogous to what the patient is discussing and presenting it from another perspective. It is a way to expand the family's experience indirectly by sharing an experience of your own. For example, when a client talked about suicide, Carl talked about his suicide attempt and how lucky he was he didn't make it. In talking about his own life, he was careful not to invade the client's world. This encouraged the family to deal with their own symbolic world. Carl hoped that families would infer something about themselves and their world from what he said about his own world. It is important that you don't take their life into your hands but keep pushing them, through your inferences, to augment their choices and power. Conversely, experiences offered by the therapist are not open for problem solving.

Parallel play requires that the therapist be responsive to the therapy process, not responsible for it. Therapy is an endless series of sharing similarities and differences in experiences. The therapist can never know what is best for the family; he or she responds to the process, and the family does what they want with it.

Carl responded to families in a free associative manner. He believed this opened the door for more honesty in the therapeutic relationship. When describing this process, he referred to an experiment conducted with children who were given two exams. Prior to the first exam, children were instructed to answer questions with the first response that came to mind. When given the second exam, they were told to think about each answer carefully. The off-the-cuff answers, which aligned with Carl's way of thinking, were 80% correct, and the thoughtful answers were 50% correct. Carl believed that therapists were more effective when they responded from experience rather than from logic or reason. The family's defenses were lowered when Carl modeled the process of being human by engaging in parallel play. When you have the courage to expose your vulnerabilities, the family gains the courage to become more of who they are. Vulnerabilities become less deadly. There is greater opportunity for creativity in exploration.

In a classic example of parallel play, Carl was consulting with a family consisting of Mom, Dad, 6-year-old Ashley, and 18-month-old Mike. Midway through the session, Carl found himself squatting and making grunting noises in concert with the baby, who decided to squat in the corner and fill his diaper.

The impact was unmistakable as this previously constricted family began to loosen up.

In the following example, the father of a schizophrenic son recounts an experience that was socially and personally mortifying. He felt foolish when approaching a woman he thought he knew. He got a glimpse of his capacity to distort life to make it fit with his internal needs. Carl normalizes the experience by sharing a social anxiety story of his own.

Father: When I was younger, there was this girl that I liked. One time I was skiing with a group of guys and I said to myself, "That's her." I wanted to see this girl so badly that I made her into the girl I liked. I went over to her and she wasn't anything like her. She was blonde; that was as close as it came. As I got closer to her, I started bursting out in a sweat. It was terrible because I realized it was all in my head. It had nothing to do with that girl whatsoever.

Carl: Yeah, that's great. I think everybody has those experiences, and most people can never recall them. They're scared to death of them. Of course we all have them in the middle of the night.

Mother: You don't feel so bad about the ones you have in the middle of the night. You can say, "Oh well, it was dark and in the middle of the night." But if you have some sort of experience like that in the daytime it makes you blush to think about it. You're more apt to think.... Well that reminds me of when I was in high school and would say something really dumb. It was usually when I wanted something to happen so much that I'd trip over myself. Then of course I'd think to myself, "Oh, I'm just nutty!"

Carl: Boy, you're talking about high school. I remember walking down the street once. I was so shy, I was a junior in high school. There was a guy in one of my classes coming towards me, so I practiced a smile so that when he got along I could turn it on.

Father: Were you able to pull it off when the time came?

Carl: Yeah, but it was still awful "fakey."

Parallel play is a form of associative communication that emerges from the therapist's awareness of self and from her or his capacity to be truly present in the moment as the session unfolds. It is not something you preplan. It is a spontaneous act of sharing that is best captured by the spirit of play. It's handled in such a casual manner that the family is not left with the sense that the therapist is fragile or needs caring. In fact, the family doesn't have to respond to it at all. They just hear it and experience it. It offers a model for simply sharing experiences without intellectual censoring.

Parallel play differs from joining in that it is more personal, more revealing. When a therapist talks about "practicing a smile" or his or her social anxiety and family members share similar awkward moments, a feeling of connectedness ensues. The level of intimacy increases. Parallel play takes the therapist out of the role of expert. The therapist and family relate more as peers. The therapist steps down from the pedestal and becomes more human.

In a final example, Carl responds to a family member's revelation of feeling insecure with his own experience.

Patient: I feel really insecure.

Carl: You know, it's amazing. I've been in this racket for 55 years and I know I'm competent, but inside myself I feel like a stupid farm boy to you city slickers. I feel you're going to get me. It's still there. It's been there since 13, and I don't think it's changed much. It's like the character structure never changes. Your personality, your adaptation, and your functional relationships can develop, but, underneath, the "who you are" never changes.

SUMMARY

Developing a collaborative relationship is necessary for therapy to progress. There are many ways to create a therapeutic alliance with a family. Much of the joining process occurs naturally and spontaneously as you get to know one another. The family may share a private joke with the therapist or in some other way let him or her see their vulnerability. Similarly, the therapist may look around the room at the family and be reminded of an extended family member or a good friend and share that recognition with the family. Both the family and the therapist must find ways to connect without compromising their underlying belief systems. The therapy system must be able to engender a bilateral respect between the therapist and family, with each accepting responsibility for their positions in living.

During this stage, a type of generation gap must be established between the family and the therapist. The family must accept your control of the therapy hour so that the family does not dominate the process. The therapist needs to believe in the professional style and approach he or she is using and must have a determination to be effective. A family therapist needs to take charge out of caring, not out of a need to dominate. When a therapeutic alliance is created, the family and therapist become attached in a way that is acceptable to both parties. There is a joint belief that their experience together will create opportunities for the family to discover its capacity for self-repair. Through methods such as parallel play, the family members begin to experience their vulnerabilities in a less deadly manner. Their creative energy is tapped as the therapeutic alliance is solidified.

Chapter 7

Stimulating a Symbolic Context

It seems to me we've got to have the guts to let our Alice-in-Wonderland trip take us where it will and dare to come back to tell the story.—Carl Whitaker

Perhaps the tale of Alice-in-Wonderland best captures this stage of therapy. The story begins with Alice perched in a tree cuddling her cat, Dinah, while her sister sits below and staunchly reads from a text. The sister's patience wears thin when Alice dangles her leg one too many times in her direction, interrupting the flow of her reading. The exchange between Alice and her sister goes something like this:

Sister: Alice, will you kindly pay attention to your history lesson?

Alice: I'm sorry, but how can one possibly pay attention to a book with no pictures in it?

Sister: My dear child, there are a great many good books in this world without pictures.

Alice: In this world, perhaps, but not in my world. In my world, the books will be nothing but pictures.

Sister: Your world, what nonsense!

Alice: Nonsense? [caresses her cat] That's it, Dinah. If I had a world of my own everything would be nonsense. Nothing would be what it is, because everything would be what it isn't and contrariwise, what it is, it wouldn't be and what it wouldn't be it would. You see? (Sharpsteen, 1951)

As Alice slips further into a daydream, she chases a rabbit who is running late and falls into a deep ravine that leads to the magical world of Wonderland.

After careening down the river in a bottle, she first discovers herself in a house where everything is upside down, including Alice. Here, her adventure begins. There are no rules in Wonderland; the nonsensical and illogical replace logic. Fantasies come alive, and anything is possible.

In a similar way, this stage of therapy involves creating a context in which the family invites us into their fantasy or symbolic world. We want to gain access to the family's primary process, their inner world of fantasies, impulses, and dreams. We want to get at the infrastructure of the family, to go underground and engage the family in uncensored spontaneity. The world of reality is not abandoned by this shift to the symbolic. It's an integrative effort that brings together the worlds of fact and fantasy. It can be likened to the family learning to reach into fantasy with one hand while holding onto the shoulder of the therapist with the other. The therapist's task is to maintain a dual role, simultaneously being real and symbolic to the family (Whitaker, 1952).

This contextual shift creates an atmosphere of play that gives the therapy a dreamlike quality. The family experiences a shift in its defensive perimeter. The boundaries change to include the therapist in rather exclude him or her from the family circle. As the therapist and family engage in a more personal process, the relationship shifts to a deeper level. The family shares more of their inner life that has been reserved for private. They interact more spontaneously without censoring responses. The therapist is trusted with their inner secrets and emotions.

In this stage, it becomes clear that the therapy has moved beyond the realm of fact and is more deliberately non-rational. The world of impulse, intuition, and primary process has become central. Stepping through the looking glass and participating in the symbolic world of the family intensifies the therapeutic relationship. By engaging in joint fantasies, the therapist and the family might ''spin a fairy tale'' that reorganizes their experience of living (Whitaker & Warkentin, 1965). One family had a great time exploring how life would be different if they won the lottery. Each person listed all the things she or he would do. They enjoyed suspending their problems to laugh and construct an outrageous tale of wealth. The rebellious adolescent even joined in. In another family, the children talked about the similarities they saw between their family and the fairy tale Cinderella. The 10-year-old felt picked on by her older stepsisters and unsupported by her stepmother. The family was able to talk more honestly about the issues of being a blended family and how each person felt burdened at times.

Once inside the system, the process between the therapist and family is reminiscent of what occurs during play therapy. Children communicate symbolically through play. As one puppet lashes out at another, the therapist invites the enraged child to experience anger. The therapist might pick up another puppet and mimic or mirror the child's play to intensify the experience. In this way, the therapist becomes a participant in the child's symbolic play. Once accepted in the drama, the therapist can intervene by offering the child's puppet a tissue or providing a compassionate hug. The therapist could also pretend to be injured or send the child's puppet to time out depending on the feel of the moment. The play is the thing. The experience is the therapy. Talking about it may be anticlimactic.

Similarly, the family uses metaphors or slips of the tongue to communicate symbolically. The wife says her husband "lives in a cave," or the daughter says she feels like "a pickle in the middle" of her parents' arguments. The therapist incorporates these words into the process, asking the family to elaborate as a way of shifting from literal to metaphoric language.

Stimulating a symbolic context is pivotal to developing a primary process relationship. The therapist facilitates access to the family's primary process—their inner world of fantasies, impulses, fears, and dreams—by joking, telling stories, and sharing free associations. For example, when a 29-year-old daughter complained about not knowing much about relationships, Carl turned to her mother and asked, "Did you ever tell her about the birds and bees?" The mother fumbled around, mumbling something about having a book about sex that she kept on top of the kitchen cabinet. Carl, with tongue in cheek, remarked, "So, if she ever gets really desperate, she could crawl up on the kitchen shelf to get it." Sharing his association to the imagery, the mother introduced the long-repressed theme of sexuality. The therapist's capacity to respond to underlying anxiety in a casual but pointed manner can open new territories for discussion. By responding from the pool of her or his own internal associations, the therapist hopes to encourage the family to access their inner world. Carl believed that the unconscious responses of the therapist belonged to the family.

An awareness of self and a trusting relationship with another person predicate interacting at the primary process level. The therapist shares fantasies or metaphors that further primary process relating. Depicting family problems leaves the family with powerful images to relate to. Carl believed that the therapist must assume a parental role in order to "get in" and have an impact.

> If the client comes as a child saying, "Daddy you're strong. Help me lift life's burden," we must learn how to encourage his strength. If he comes with an identity crisis like a late teenager trying to find himself or a college student stumbling in his confusion over life, we must find the guts to sit with him while he works through the defects he got from his parents, his transference to us, and his effort to thrust on into more vital living. Maybe a few will come as integrated adults who want to speed their growth, a poet who wants to gain a greater sense of beauty, the man who has bound himself and wants to have increased courage in finding a relationship to a significant other. Maybe they'll grow beyond us. (Whitaker, 1973, p. 51)

Carl's work with schizophrenics taught him the importance of symbolic communication. In order to make significant contact, he discovered it was necessary to attend to more than the spoken word (Whitaker, 1952). Bodily reactions, proprioceptive sensations, and muscle tension contribute to the overall communication. Nonverbal aspects such as voice quality, tone, timbre, breaks in timing, and posture modify and define the actual words. Words alone are of limited use in therapy. The therapist must go beyond words to create a symbolic context. The affective investment of the therapist is also crucial. For example, Carl often used silence to push the process. "You know how powerful it can be to have a patient stare at you and the patient will tell you how powerful it is when you stare at him" (Whitaker, 1952, p. 3). Nonverbal communication confirms or disconfirms what the family said. During this stage, the therapist might also question a mom's comment that she no longer holds a grudge against her mother-in-law, when she seems tense and upset during the discussion. It is important for the therapist to attend to his or her physical reactions to the family's story. If a father describes himself as a bully, saying that he just doesn't give a damn about anybody, but the therapist senses a tenderness in his tone, he or she might share a story about being sensitive. The therapist might also pat the father on the back, making nonverbal contact, at the end of the session. The therapist watches for the discrepancy between the overt and the covert. When they are not congruent, it is important to focus the therapeutic lens.

During this stage, the process of therapy is more spontaneous. When therapists, without explanation, share thoughts that pop into their head, or comment on a bodily sensation, they leave the family to make sense of the disclosure. They're free to discuss it, wonder about it, or simply ignore it. Often a more open, spontaneous interaction emerges. For example, as a family was discussing the disruptiveness of their adolescent son, the therapist told them of a sudden pain in his chest. The tone of the session immediately shifted. They began discussing their own physical symptoms. Each family member actively participated, with no scapegoat in sight. When the therapist is free to engage in non-rational communication, the family is more free to leave their script. The sharing of free associations does not represent a conscious effort to influence; rather, it represents an openness to inner experience.

The therapeutic relationship is a person-to-person relationship. The family risks exposing their weaknesses and struggles with their anxiety. The therapist strives to connect with and genuinely respond to them. This process does not involve the therapist sharing unresolved personal issues, although such interactions can be free associative.

The therapist's posture allows freedom for the relationship to develop. There is maximum responsiveness to authenticity and growth. Carl stated, "I assume that everything that comes to me belongs to them. I don't try to make an examination before or after I talk. I just tell it. I'm not trying to get them anywhere. I'm just trying to offer what I have" (Barrows & Zeig, 1981, p. 9).

Engaging the family at the symbolic rather than the literal level of living is a way to have a more powerful impact. The therapist directs effort toward expanding the family's view of the problem, broadening their belief system, and developing alternate solutions. Through symbolic communication, a shared language evolves that makes the therapy personal and more intimate. The follow-ing are three classic interventions used to stimulate a symbolic context: (a) exploration of symbolic bits and fragments, (b) expansion of fantasies, and (c) use of play, humor, and absurdity.

EXPLORING SYMBOLIC BITS AND FRAGMENTS

For the experienced clinician, this process can be great fun. As the family tells their story, the therapist pays particular attention to the family's affect, becomes aware of emotional undertones, and attaches symbolic meaning to the family's words and actions.

The therapist typically begins by responding to a word or phrase that catches his or her attention. As the family focuses on the content of events in their lives, the therapist listens "through" what is being said rather than "to" it in order to stimulate primary process relating (Whitaker, 1966).

The therapist moves beyond the reality events of the family's daily living and into the family's symbolic understructure. For example, one therapist, when working with a couple who had become increasingly more distant since their children had left home, quickly went underground. The wife, rambling on about specific arguments she had had with her husband during the past week and making numerous attempts to defend herself, complained, "It's like I have this house and he can't get in." The therapist shifted the focus away from the content of the arguments to the image of the house and the obstacles that prevented the husband from getting in.

The therapist initiated the shift to the symbolic context by asking the wife to describe the house. The wife described it as having many different rooms without doors. The wife's description of the house represented a shift to a metaphorical language. She talked of having no control over which room she was in at any particular time. She described one room as being "like a dark, suicidal room" that was scary but somehow safe. She felt her husband could not get in because he did not understand this house. The husband said he wanted to "get in" and felt he was capable of overcoming any obstacles in his way. He then began to describe his own house. Metaphorically, the couple engaged in an intimate discussion of their differences and the marriage. The symbolic understructure of a family is similar to the infrastructure of a city. While city leaders may want residents to attend to the beautiful skyscrapers and fine restau-rants, the electrical wiring and plumbing underneath are what actually keep the city running. It is the family substructure, its plumbing and wiring, that must be stimulated during this stage. Staying on the surface feeds the illusion of a quick fix.

This technique occurs spontaneously as the flow of the session unfolds. It's not preplanned. A family member might begin to use a more introspective lan-guage while talking about her or his problems and painful family dynamics. Rather than complaining about his lack of a social life, the isolated father calls himself a hermit. The therapist, picking up on this image, goes a step further and free associates about the cave in which the hermit lives. Through the therapist picking up on words that seem to have special meaning, the session becomes more lively. The whole family becomes engaged in a playful fantasy regarding Dad as a hermit, Mom as Mrs. Hermit, and the chronically whiny kids as hermit crabs. These spontaneous side trips touch on hidden aspects of the family's relationships that were central to their struggles for intimate involvement with one another. This random element can give the process an unexpected twist and help the family transcend the presenting problem.

The following example involves a wife blaming her husband for treating her like his slave. She takes care of the children, cooks, cleans, and has no time for herself. Her husband is demanding, uncaring, and indifferent. He accuses his wife of being a perfectionist. He offers to help on numerous occasions but can never do anything to please her. He feels she is constantly criticizing the way he deals with the children. He feels like a child in his own home and is angry that all she does is mother him. "Slave" and "mother"—words that carry symbolic meaning—are embedded within the family's account of their life together. By attending to symbolic meaning, Carl shifts from reality to the symbolic, getting a glimpse of the inner world of the family.

Husband: I'm sick and tired of it. I'm in charge of nine men at work. I'm under a lot of stress. Things get crazy, you know, but they respect me. I come home, walk through the door, and immediately get orders. She complains about the kids. She tells me to do this and that. She mothers me.

Carl: [to wife] How did he trick you into being his mother? Doesn't his own mother want the job anymore? How did she relinquish her duties? Maybe you could learn to bail out like she did. I don't know, you look like a softy to me. Of course some mothers are pretty rough under the exterior.

Wife: I don't mother him. He doesn't do a thing I ask. He takes me for granted. I'm his slave. He doesn't want me to work. He walks through the door and expects me to wait on him. I feel secluded or locked up.

Carl: Well, maybe you could get your own mother or the kids to help you find the key. I don't know, the slaves were emancipated years ago. There may be hope for you yet.

Another example involves Carl quickly shifting to the symbolic when working with a 30-year-old woman who had never lived with anyone other than her parents. She was the youngest of five children and had no identity other than that of caretaker. She reported no social life. Her world consisted of working during the day and tending to her ill parents at night. Her father had Alzheimer's, and her mother, a serious heart condition. Family members occasionally offered to help, but she refused their services. She adamantly defended against her siblings' suggestion that perhaps she was hiding behind her parents for fear of growing up. As the woman described her daily duties, she commented, "At times I feel like I'm only half here." Carl picked up on this symbolic fragment and, using her language, inquired as to where the other half of her was.

Carl: Where is the other half?

Client: The other half of me, I guess, is back on the farm with Mother and Daddy.

Carl: Can you see this half of you?

Client: Oh yes, I am dressed in a Buster Brown suit and am playing in the back yard.

Through attending to picture images that open a window into the family's world of unreality, therapy shifts to a metaphorical language. In the preceding example, the woman went on to talk about the part of her she had left behind on the farm. Recapturing those aspects of her personality was vital to her life as an adult. Lowering the family's defenses allows family members to begin to depict their problems in picture images. These images portray unconscious family dynamics and give the therapist a better sense of the family's infrastructure. They also alert the therapist to forgotten or minimized aspects of the family that are overwhelmed by current problems.

As therapy progresses, nonverbal cues and patterns of interaction between the therapist and family may also become symbolic. These encounters between the therapist and family may produce a lasting effect. During the later stages of treatment, they are often symbolic of earlier experiences within the therapy sessions. For example, a male therapist worked with a family concerned about their teenage son, who had a history of stealing, lying, and acting out. During the first four sessions, the son refused to talk and was quite bitter. At the end of sessions the therapist had, on occasion, walked behind the boy to the door, patted him on the back, and, in a comforting tone of voice, said, "Take care." Upon termination, the boy seemed reluctant to leave the room. He waited until the therapist, engaged in conversation with other family members, headed for the door. The boy walked behind him, patted him on the back, and, in a voice that conveyed a similar sense of caring, encouraged the therapist to "Take care." The phrase "Take care" and the emotional response of caring, communicated through both tone of voice and touch, were a symbol shared by the boy and the therapist. The symbol represented a mutually experienced connectedness, a special bond, that had evolved over the course of treatment. Using symbols throughout therapy is a means of increasing the level of intimacy, thus providing a context in which change is most likely to occur. Every intimate relationship has a private language. This is the stage during which that private language evolves.

EXPANDING FANTASIES

A natural extension of the technique of picking up on symbolic bits and fragments is to focus on expanding family fantasies. Carl engaged in symbolic communication by participating in joint fantasies with clients. This process involves first picking up on symbolic words and phrases embedded in what the client has said and then asking the client to expand on them. The therapist then adds to the fantasy symbolically, communicating with the client about his or her inner world.

Carl believed that unconscious communication between the therapist and client was an essential element of therapy. In the 1960s, Carl wrote an article, "Training for the Unreality Experience" (Whitaker, 1966), that provided a detailed description of how to shift to the symbolic or move into unreality. The therapist begins by attending to an affectively loaded word, embedded in what the client says, that infers visual imagery. According to Carl, "The word may be a unique one, a word that has special significance for the client, or the word may be an ordinary one used unusually or repetitiously" (Whitaker, 1966, p. 43). For example, the client may say, "I just feel like I have this wall up." The therapist asks questions about the wall to expand the fantasy. After establishing a visual construct, the therapist "gradually pushes the client into seeing him or herself in this visual picture" (p. 44). The therapist asks questions such as "Can you see yourself there?" and "What are you doing?" and then pushes the fantasy further by asking "Can you see me there?" and "What are we doing?" The therapist encourages the client to describe some type of movement or action and asks "What happens next?"

In the following example, Carl metaphorically discusses a husband's relationship with his wife. The husband, like his own father, had isolated himself from the family. He was preoccupied with work on the farm, his tractor, and "things," according to his wife. She had given up on their relationship, believing he had lost interest in her. Midway through the second session, the husband said, "I just feel like I have this wall up." Carl pushes the fantasy, which eventually seems to spark some emotion.

Client: I just feel like I have this wall up.

Carl: Try to picture the wall.

Client: Well, it isn't a brick wall. I had not thought of such a wall.

Carl: Will you think about it now?

Client: Well, I think of a wall of trees.

Carl: How far apart are the trees?

Client: They are touching now, and my wife's name is across the front. The letters are 4-feet-high, and the sign is 20-feet-long.

Carl: Can you see over the wall of trees?

Client: No.

Carl: Can you see yourself there?

Client: Yes.

Carl: How are you dressed?

Client: In a field uniform.

Carl: Can you see me there?

Client: No...yes.

Carl: Is your wife on the other side of the trees?

Client: Yes.

Carl: We need to get us to the other side. Will one of us go first, or will we have to go together?

Client: We can both go together.

Carl: Are we going?

Client: Yes, we are going.

Carl: Are we on the other side now?

Client: Yes.

Carl: I guess I'd better duck back through the trees.

Client: I suddenly remember a song. "I'll meet my darling when the sun rises." (Whitaker, 1966, p. 44)

Carl encouraged the husband to visualize the wall. It was not easy for him to engage in fantasy. It took some coaching. After creating the image, Carl encouraged the husband to include him in the fantasy because he believed that the therapeutic relationship was the crucial component in the encounter. Carl felt it was important to structure the dream or the unreality experience in such a way that a relationship was established in it (Whitaker, 1966). Once the visual construct was established, Carl pushed for some type of movement or action. He encouraged the client to take the initiative, to decide what action would occur. In instances in which the client did not respond, Carl proposed some kind of action. The client was then free to participate, add to, or change the picture in a way that was meaningful.

In the following example, a therapist works with a couple that wants to save their marriage and avoid divorce. While both members were bright and seemingly dedicated, nothing was happening. Whenever they made progress, it quickly unraveled, leaving them at another impasse. The couple could describe the type of relationship they had in mind, yet the rut deepened. During the session, the therapist flipped out of the impasse by moving to the symbolic. The therapist encouraged the wife to expand on her fantasy of life without her husband.

Wife: I'm determined to make this relationship work. We've been through so much together. I'm not interested in a life without him. I can't even imagine a life without him. The story of my life has been and will always be "Life with Dan."

Therapist: What's happened to your imagination? I've always thought of you as being quite creative.

Wife: Well, I didn't mean it literally. Of course I could imagine life without him.

Therapist: Well, that sounds better. Do you trust him enough, I suppose yourself, too, to talk about your creative fantasy? To put words to your imagination?

[Husband leans forward and is all ears, with a quizzical look on his face]

Wife: Well, sure, I guess so. [giggles] Don't take this personal, Dan, but I picture a small white house. A white house in a lush green alley. No one, nothing else is in sight.

Therapist: Where's Dan?

Wife: I don't know. He's not in this fantasy. [laughs] This is about simplicity, about being free to be me. It's about not needing to compromise or negotiate with anyone else.

Therapist: So this place off in the woods is your place, not the couple's place?

Wife: Right! It's mine and I'm calling all the shots.

Therapist: You're not willing to visualize it as a duplex, or to imagine another home right next door?

Wife: Bingo! You've got it. Maybe he could build his own place the next valley over. Then I'd need a fence.

Therapist: Tell me about the house.

Wife: It's bright and sunny. There are windows everywhere, but it's still private. And there are lovely hardwood floors. It's quiet and peaceful.

Therapist: And what about the kids?

Wife: That's why it's so quiet and peaceful. [pauses] Well, maybe I'd dedicate a room to Dan and the kids. You know, like a portrait room. They'd all be there, right there on the wall. Dan would be dashing and the kids angelic.

Thus, for the first time, the couple broke their pattern. The sense of a life-and-death struggle to convince one other to accept and live the other's fantasy was gone. Through the house metaphor, the wife was able to describe her desire to be a person, not just a feature of her husband's fantasy. When she stepped out of the reality realm, her image easily evolved. No longer constrained by the feeling that she was making a reality decision, she was able to put words to a long-unexpressed feeling.

The therapist can also shift from the reality to the symbolic by highlighting symbolic meaning underlying family interactions. For example, a family sought treatment for an out-of-control 8-year-old boy. As the session progressed, it became clear that Johnny was loud and aggressive when his father was critical of his mom. When Dad's blood pressure began to rise, Johnny would spring into action, typically targeting his 6-year-old sister Mary. Halfway through the session, Dad's face turned crimson as he excitedly corrected his wife. At this same instant, Johnny hurled a wooden block in his sister's direction. As it zipped past her ear and crashed into the wall, the adults-only conversation stopped. All eyes turned to Johnny.

Therapist: Wow! That was a great throw. You may have a future in baseball, maybe football if you get a little meaner. Of course you'll need to work on your accuracy.

Mom: Get a little meaner? What are you talking about? We've got too much meanness in our home as it is. He could have really hurt his sister. He's dangerous.

Dad: Get off his back, will you? He's just being a boy. Your little darling Mary isn't so innocent. She asks for it half the time.

Therapist: You could pat him on the back for such a good effort. Maybe a little practice in the yard would improve his accuracy.

Dad: I'm not saying I approve of him throwing things at his sister. It's just that Susan makes such a big deal out of everything. She just can't let people be themselves. He didn't hurt Mary, and when he does he feels terrible. He apologizes and means it.

Therapist: Have you and Susan figured out what he's up to?

Dad: I don't know what you're talking about. He's just being a brat.

Therapist: Well, I think you're wrong about that. The block he hurled past Mary reminded me of the insults you were hurling at Susan. It's just that your aim is better. You scored a direct hit. He just hit the wall.

While the therapist could have made other interpretations, in this case he responded to the symbolic implications of Johnny's actions as a reflection of his father's behavior. This reaction planted the idea that there was a relationship between the concrete behaviors of one of the family members and the impulses or actions of another. It complicated and expanded the possible meaning they could give to their real-life interactions. Another perspective could have identified Johnny as a hero for trying to distract his parents from their fighting. Perhaps he was a mentor trying to teach his mother to get mad and fight fire with fire when assaulted by Dad.

THE USE OF PLAY, HUMOR, AND ABSURDITY

Upon greeting the family, the therapist is in a double bind. The family desperately asks for help, hoping the therapist will do something to fix the situation. At the same time, the family works together to sabotage any efforts made by the therapist to change them. They simultaneously seek and defy assistance. While they are miserable with how things are, their dysfunctional patterning offers them security. It's all they've known. The therapist can playfully sidestep the family's defensive process through humor and absurdity.

Play, humor, and absurdity are ways to move the family into the non-rational realm of being. When the family is engaged through teasing, telling jokes, or reversing statements, they are thrown off balance. The family often comes in with one way of viewing the problem and tries to maintain a tight grip on what they perceive as the only solution. Through play, humor, and absurdity, we attempt to break through their rigidity.

The goal is to produce transcendent experiences, to help the family move above their pain and stress and view their situation from a completely different frame (Whitaker & Keith, 1981). We connect with the family through telling a joke or offering an anecdote that tickles their fancy, gets them laughing so hard they expand their viewpoint. We want them to enjoy the bumps in the road. We give them a license to make mistakes and not take themselves so seriously. When the car comes to an abrupt halt in the middle of the road, they look at us perplexed, as if asking "Now what do we do?" We glance back, shrugging our shoulders as if to say "I don't know. It's up to you. I'm just along for the ride. I trust you to lead the adventure."

Society's passion for art, music, and literature reflects a deep-seated desire to escape the world of law and order, social niceties, restrictions, and rigid daily routines. We hurry off to the theater or symphony or lose ourselves in a Pulitzer-winning novel to get at the non-rational core of life. The non-rational is where we find relief from the pressure and stress of everyday living, in much the same way Alice did when she escaped to Wonderland. Just as drama, music, and literature have developed their own non-rational core, the accumulated and organized residue of experience makes up the non-rational core of each individual. Through play, humor, and absurdity, we access the collective unconscious and primary process of the individual or family.

At the beginning of his career, Carl was criticized for his non-rational therapy. His opponents referred to his techniques as "irrational." Carl and colleagues (Malone et al., 1961) addressed such criticisms by writing a rebuttal that differentiated irrational from non-rational therapy. Carl concluded by stressing the importance of moving clients into a non-rational experiential realm of relating. It is possible for an outsider to talk about problems in a logical rational fashion as a way of getting at underlying family dynamics. As the family listens to this conversation, they have an opportunity to see their issues from the perspective of someone else. Conversely, the family system opens up when nudged slowly into the non-rational realm. The therapist then has the opportunity to view the family drama from behind the curtain, to work with the characters and props before show time. Perhaps Carl best expressed his rationale for the non-rational in the following statement:

> The freedom to be non-rational is an important part of human experience. For deeper satisfaction, we want the capacity to be silly, to be humorous, and to laugh at jokes. We want to experience those aspects of our self not ordinarily experienced when we are responsibly doing our everyday jobs. Our dreams, intuitions, unique momentary sensations, temper outbursts, mediation, fantasy, and prayer connote a freedom to move beyond the experience of everyday life into a recognition of the creative interior of each person. For this deeper satisfaction in living, we need a rich feeling life as a foundation for a rich idea life. (personal communication, 1988)

Play

Play is universal. It promotes health and facilitates growth. In a recent therapy session, a mother of a 10-year-old child made it clear that she considered play a frivolity, a waste of time. She preferred her daughter use her extra time to get ahead in her homework or practice her piano. She could not believe that her daughter was socially maladjusted and never invited to parties. Other kids did not like to play with her. No wonder, she was a stick in the mud. She was no fun because she was never allowed to play. Her parents had not thought it worthwhile enough to encourage this activity. Therapy consisted of assignments to help the family learn ways to play, to experiment with new activities and to be silly together. The example to follow illustrates the process of encouraging the family to be creative with their play by offering outlandish activities.

Therapist: Let's see how many wild play activities we can come up with, you first Dad.

Dad: Gee, let me see, it's been so long. Maybe we could play a game.

Therapist: Come on, you can do better than that. What did you like to do as a kid?

Dad: I guess we didn't play much. I remember playing at the beach and hide and seek in the woods.

Therapist: Good. How about you, Mom?

Mom: We used to make cookies, paint with watercolors, sometimes we'd play tag. My brother really liked playing with water balloons.

Therapist: That reminds me of a time when my kids and I started to have a water balloon fight. Next thing I knew, the kids had glasses of water, chasing me around. Well, you know I had to top that, so I got a bucket of water. A few minutes later I looked up and my youngest son had the hose in the living room. Oh boy, did we get carried away. They still laugh about it. That's what I'm talking about, playing where you just have a great time!

If the family does not know how to play, our first task is to play with them. Play encourages the family to let down their guard, lower defenses, and diffuse their anxiety. It is a way of connecting that says it's okay to relax. Children are particularly good at this activity in that they are uninhibited, and spontaneous. All of us have picked our children up from school and asked them what they have done during the day only to hear "All we did was play." To the alert adult, this is good news, as play is the key to our development and curiosity as adults.

It is essential for therapists to have activities in their office for children: paper, pencils, crayons, puppets, puzzles, blocks, and books. Children gravitate to hands-on materials. It is absurd to think young children can sit through an hour-long therapy session without becoming bored. Play materials serve several functions. They allow the child to be entertained but also permit an opportunity for the therapist to observe the interaction within the family as the children attempt to engage the parents in their activity. It is important for adults to play as well. A reserved adult noticed the Play-Doh on the therapist's shelf. She asked, "Can I play with that? I loved Play-Doh when I was a kid and haven't seen any for years." Another therapist keeps a puzzle in his office that kids can put together quickly. Interestingly, adults have been known to struggle for several sessions to figure it out.

In a recent interview, a family was discussing their reasons for coming to therapy while their 5-year-old son was quietly drawing. Midway through the session, the child presented his artwork to the therapist for inspection. "That's an interesting picture," the therapist said. "Can you tell me anything about it?" The child answered, "It's a picture of Daddy hitting Mommy, you know he does that sometimes." This interchange altered the tone of the therapy and precipitated a discussion on the physical aggression of the husband. This issue may have surfaced eventually, but it was dealt with much sooner because of the child's unexpected disclosure.

Humor and Absurdity

Humor induces regression by way of confusion. With tongue in cheek, we often use humor to shatter the family's gestalt. The process is similar to a good joke that makes us laugh by creating a sudden shift in our thinking. The punch line typically catches us off guard, abruptly changing our train of thought.

For example, a couple had been coming to therapy for a while to work on the conflict in their marriage. Partway through the session, the couple was in their usual stalemate. The therapist said, "You two remind me of a greeting card I read yesterday. It was a card with a couple in bed separated by a barbed wire fence. The wife was looking particularly sour and the husband was saying 'Apparently I have done something to upset you.' It put me in mind of the two of you!" The husband went on to say that's how he feels most of the time. His wife gets upset, maybe sarcastic, stops talking but never discusses issues in a civilized manner.

Another example is that of an elderly woman attending therapy with her husband. She usually begins a session with a joke or anecdote. It is amazing how often these jokes get to the heart of whatever the couple needs to discuss that week. It has become a ritual for this woman to begin sessions in this manner. A recent encounter went like this:

Mrs. S.: What is a neurotic?

[Therapist, thinking this is a serious question, struggles to answer]

Mrs. S.: What is a psychotic?

Therapist: [catching on to the fact that this isn't a serious discussion] I'm not sure how to define it for you.

Mrs. S.: Well, you must know what a therapist is!

Therapist: I don't have a clue.

Mrs. S.: [laughs and slaps her leg] A neurotic is someone who builds castles in the sky; a psychotic lives in them; and a therapist is someone who collects the rent! I thought you would have heard that before!

Mr. S.: You know how she loves to kid you. On a serious note, we've been talking about memory loss. You know she's worried about that.

The couple and therapist went on to have a serious discussion about fear of Alzheimer's disease and early senility. The couple had realistic fears because of their family histories. Humor enables a therapist to communicate on multiple levels with the family. Humor expands the family's narrow focus or reality. Humor makes it possible to say something indirectly without actually saying it. Through the use of humor, the therapist provides covert messages to the family. When it became obvious that a parentified child was running the show, Carl would tease the child, saying "If you're your mother's mother, that must make you your own grandmother. What a crazy thought!"

When absurd comments are added to the interaction, the situation seems not so dreadful. It's impossible to be ridiculous and serious at the same time. "Flipping the therapy situation into absurdity provides a way to escape the gravitational pull of reason and places both patient and therapist in the realm of the unknown" (Keith & Whitaker, 1978, p. 70).

The following example illustrates an absurd interaction between a therapist and a mother who had been having difficulty with a young child. The mother was not willing to try anything that had been suggested to her.

Therapist: When you talk about your son, it reminds me of the problem I'm having training my dog. Nothing seems to work. You know, I found a place where you can drop your dog off and pick it up when it is trained. Sounded great to me.

Mother: That's ridiculous; can't you do it yourself?

Therapist: Why stress myself when someone else is willing to do it for me! You know, maybe the trainer would be willing to take your son on too. I think he will learn much quicker than my dog.

At this point, the mother was getting annoyed but was more aware of the dilemma she was causing herself. In order to parent her son, she needed to be less passive. She was skilled at defeating any feedback or suggestions the therapist made.

In another session, a couple was in a stalemate trying to figure out ways to disrupt their arguments. The therapist related an incident from his own experience.

Therapist: When my wife and I were first married, she would get furious with me when I would go to bed rather than stay up and argue. One night, she waited until I went to sleep, snuck into the room, threw back the covers, and doused me with ice-cold water. Not that I'm suggesting that for you, but I can tell you, it sure put a different spin on our arguments. Tell me the craziest thing either of you have ever done to get the other's attention.

Wife: I'm embarrassed to say. One time we were fighting, my husband was at work. I waited for him to come home, then jumped out from behind the door with only an apron on! I got his attention.

Therapist: I wonder why you two have given up on your creativity.

SUMMARY

In this stage of therapy, the therapist stimulates a symbolic context to induce primary process or uncensored spontaneity. By sharing free associative slivers and attending to the family's metaphorical language, the therapist pushes the process to a deeper level. When defenses are lowered, the family invites the therapist into their symbolic or fantasy world, exposing their infrastructure. It is here that unconscious family dynamics are revealed.

We emphasize a non-rational experiential approach to therapy. Play, humor, and absurdity are relied on to move families momentarily out of their rigid role structure and into a dreamlike "as if" world where anything is possible. The family simply needs to trust their own unconscious creative process and needs the patience to discover where their adventure will take them. At this point, the family becomes more interested in being themselves than in pretending. We believe it is at this stage that the family is most susceptible to taking in new experiences that facilitate change.

Carl provided detailed descriptions of interventions used to access a family's symbolic world. However, he cautioned against their preplanned use, emphasizing that the person of the therapist and his or her affective involvement is the primary catalyst for change. Carl believed that, if he was successful in shifting from reality to the symbolic, the client could ''move on to more experience in the world of unreality'' (Whitaker, 1966, p. 45). In this stage, Carl created a symbolic context in which further symbolic experiences could occur.

Chapter 8

Activating Stress Within the System

Don't just do something. Sit there.—Carl Whitaker

Anxiety is the central catalyzing ingredient in activating stress within the therapy system. It is essential for growth and critical to any lasting change. During this phase of therapy, the therapist is active in terms of pushing the family beyond the constraints of their comfort zone. Both the therapist and the family must tolerate the stress of venturing into new territory. The therapeutic system is powerful enough and the relationship intimate enough to permit this activity.

Following the experience of moving from concrete to symbolic processes, families feel a bit disoriented. There is a natural, reflexive tendency to reestablish the familiarity of dealing with specific problems. This is a pivotal time in the therapy. The family attempts to calm their anxiety by reverting to the status quo. When families regress to this earlier stage of relating or when they are overly complacent, their desperation isn't high enough to facilitate growth. It is essential for the therapist to amplify the anxiety level to fuel change. The intent is to shake things up so that the family can't continue in the comfort of their familiar misery. Now that the therapeutic alliance has been established and the therapist is more deeply connected with the family, the therapist is free to challenge the status quo. The therapist's caring is the anesthesia that allows the family to tolerate the pain of the surgery. If the operation is successful, the family is free to resume growing and to reorganize itself in a more productive fashion.

Carl differentiated between positive and negative anxiety (Whitaker & Malone, 1953). Anxiety that promotes growth is positive anxiety. Feelings of expectancy and tense hopefulness predominate when anxiety is positive. Hopelessness and a cautiousness to share thoughts and feelings contribute to negative anxiety.

The habituated response to affect creates feelings of panic and apprehension that become overwhelming.

Confronting anxiety is a bilateral undertaking. Not only do families come face to face with issues, but similarly therapists must tolerate their own anxiety when families move toward solutions they would not choose for them. It is not our task to push families in directions we feel would be good for them in order to decrease our stress. For example, one family had been dealing with a rebellious adolescent for several months. The couple reached a decision to let the child drop out of high school and move into an apartment. The therapist was saddened by this choice because he felt the couple had acquiesced too easily. During such times, therapists must be able to manage their own sense of failure. It is a profound experience to sense a family's desperation as they grapple with each other. A natural reactivity is triggered in the therapist. Whether therapists are intimidated, angered, envious, or bored, one thing is certain: They are not neutral. The experience of participating with families in distress does not leave us untouched.

The affect that emerges from the shared experience of this stage belongs to the therapy process. It is not private. When working with a family in distress, the therapist's hidden fears, anxieties, and worries are central to the process. The therapist's ability to use this anxiety is central to the therapy flow. Sharing pieces of themselves that are stimulated by the family's presence is a way of encouraging family members to grow. It pushes them to drop their facade and risk higher levels of vulnerability. When the therapist's internal reactions are accessed and shared, they contribute to openness within the session. When denied and hidden, they contribute to stuckness. The therapist must be careful to not become too absorbed by or isolated from the family. To be effective, "the therapist's affect must be attached to the family, yet he may not belong to it. The therapist must be 'in' yet not 'of' the family and its subgroups. He must be available to each person, yet belong to none. He must belong to himself" (Whitaker, 1962, p. 335).

Clinical impasses frequently occur as a result of a therapist's inability to tolerate the anxiety present in the therapy room: his or her own or that of the family. Whitaker, Warkentin, and Johnson (1950) defined *impasse* as "a stalemate in the therapy process which consists of a deterioration in the therapeutic relationship. The therapeutic experience loses its emotional voltage" (p. 641). Impasses often result from the therapist's unresolved countertransference issues. For example, a couple in therapy may need to have a fight in order to deal more directly with conflict. If the therapist comes from a family that never raised their voices, facilitating any direct confrontation may be difficult. A therapist's inability to tolerate increasing levels of anxiety may result in an impasse, draining the therapy of the affect needed for progress.

When therapy is at an impasse, one way to challenge the standstill is for therapists to take responsibility by admitting that they have failed to move the process forward. The therapist's openness provides a model for the family, who may then dare to take more risks in therapy.

During this phase of the therapy, the therapist's openness moves beyond the level of sharing characteristic of the previous stages. By virtue of the growing relationship with the family, the therapist can access deeper levels of personal associations and is more free to step beyond the constraints of politeness or social etiquette. In parallel play, the therapist responded to the family's actual words and actions. The therapist now moves beyond mirroring, or responding to underlying affect, and focuses on pushing the family to actually grapple with the issues they steadfastly avoid. The full range of affect is now fair game. It's the therapist's job to push the family into new territory.

ACTING IN AND ACTING OUT

Carl also differentiated between "acting in" and "acting out." "Acting in" refers to the therapist intensifying her or his participation by increasing anxiety. "Acting out" involves the therapist functioning in a way that decreases her or his anxiety. For example, when a child refused to listen to Carl's repeated requests to stop playing with his phone, he shouted in a louder tone of voice, demanding that the child sit down. This example of "acting in" resulted in the parents being more firm with the child when giving directives in future sessions. In this case, Carl used his anger to facilitate movement within the system.

In a series of articles published in the 1960s, Carl identified ways in which the family and therapist "act out" (Whitaker, 1962, 1965a; Whitaker & Malone, 1963). Carl defined acting out as a method of diminishing affect (Whitaker, 1965a) or avoiding emotional closeness (Whitaker & Malone, 1963). For example, the family could act out by fighting with the therapist, fighting among themselves, scapegoating a family member, or discussing the sessions with a grandmother or someone who functioned as a social therapist outside of therapy. Acting out behaviors promote distance between therapy participants and drain the system of the affect necessary to move forward. Acting out behaviors by the therapist include intellectualization, withdrawal, being late for sessions, and affective spill, which involves dreaming and/or talking about the family between sessions. Carl described acting out as a "joint project carried out by the patient and the therapist" (Whitaker & Malone, 1963, p. 418).

Acting out serves different functions depending on the stage of therapy (Whitaker, 1965). Acting out in the initial phase can be a way to avoid development of an intimate relationship. During the middle phase, acting out decreases the level of anxiety needed to facilitate change. Acting out in a later phase may be a way to prolong termination. Acting out can be prevented if the therapist and family learn to express anxiety more openly during the interview.

Techniques commonly used to access the undercurrent anxiety of the therapy experience are (a) active waiting or silence, (b) challenging roles, (c) deviation amplification, and (d) establishing differences.

ACTIVE WAITING

Use of active waiting or silence is one way to increase anxiety within the system. It is a technique that provides experience rather than insight. While an intellectual understanding or awareness may follow, the essence is experiential. It offers the family the opportunity to look inward, to attend to their inner rumblings without the distraction of the therapist's perception. The therapist's posture of active waiting is not to be confused with passivity, ineptitude, or disinterest. In an odd sort of way, it's the therapist saying "I take you seriously." By waiting for the family to take charge, the therapist conveys confidence in them. The therapist shows respect for the family's capacity to make decisions about their living and their right and responsibility to live life according to their beliefs. When the therapist jumps in and is directive, the message is implicitly demeaning.

This technique also describes those situations in which the therapist underscores the fact that nothing is happening by literally sitting back and waiting for the family to step forward. When the session has gone flat, comments about the process can activate the family's anxiety. When the therapist says "Had enough for today, or are you just catching your breath?" "Maybe it's too dangerous to continue on," or "Do you think it's possible to nap with your eyes open?" the family is reminded that they're the players, the game belongs to them.

For example, as the family sits in silence, a typical exchange might go like this:

Therapist: You know, sitting here and watching you all fidget around reminds me of our first couple of sessions. You all sat there looking at me, expecting that I would know what to say. Have any of you slipped back into that delusion? I thought we were past that, but I suppose it's okay to keep hoping.

Dad: Well, we don't seem to know where to go. You know us a lot better now. Maybe a little direction would help.

Therapist: You know, I don't think I've gotten much smarter. Maybe a bit more cagey though. The temptation to jump in and try to convince you to be like me isn't very compelling.

Dad: We're not looking to become you, just to get some guidance.

Therapist: That's what I mean. The important thing is that you learn to follow your own instincts. My nose won't do you any good. You need to learn to use your own sniffers. Anyone up to being the family bloodhound? Can you pick up a scent worth following?

The level of tension increases as the therapy hour unfolds and the therapist sits back, refusing to lead. Time comes to a standstill as the distortion of the "60-second eternity" emerges. Each family member nervously scans the room and then retreats into the sanctuary of his or her inner world. As they realize the therapist is not going to take over, they become more focused, more serious. Operating from the premise that nothing worth knowing can be taught, the therapist allows the family to have the experience of being on the field while the coach remains safely tucked away in the dugout. The next move is theirs; they have to take the initiative.

One elderly couple had attended sessions to discuss how to handle their wills. This was a second marriage for both. Midway into the session, following a period of silence, the husband said to the therapist, "Well, aren't you going to say something?" The therapist stated, "I was waiting to see where you were going to take this point." The husband said, "I don't much like the quiet." The therapist chuckled. "I knew a therapist who waited the whole hour for a family to get started and didn't say a thing." The husband laughed. "What an easy way to make a living." The therapist said, "Actually, it's quite difficult to wait until someone has enough initiative to talk about what is on their mind. It is much easier to tell them what to do." Following a bit more silence, the husband began to share his concerns in earnest.

The following excerpt is taken from *The Family Crucible*, a book Carl coauthored with Dr. Augustus Napier. The authors began by describing how they refused to meet with a family who sought therapy because of their teenage daughter's rebellious behavior until all members were present. From their first contact with the family, they shifted the focus from the identified patient to the entire family. The example to follow illustrates how, as the therapy proceeded, Carl used silence to facilitate the family's effort to carry the therapy process.

After a long period of silence, the father commented, "I guess we're waiting for you guys to start us off." Carl tilted back in his chair casually and took a puff of his pipe. "We were waiting for you to start with each other. Bet we can wait longer!" His tone, though pleasant and teasing, had a serious feel. The silence returned. Finally, the father began to discuss his concerns about the family (Napier & Whitaker, 1978, p. 61).

The authors provided a rationale for encouraging the family to decide what to talk about in sessions: "If we had continued to question, probe, and interpret, we would have set a dangerous precedent by implying we were assuming the responsibility for pushing change. That would have been unfair to the family. If therapy was to succeed, they had to know that their initiative, their will to fight, struggle, push, and try was essential to a successful outcome"(Napier & Whitaker, 1978, p. 61). Silence was used to increase the level of anxiety and encourage the family to take the lead. The father eventually responded to the challenge.

A final suggestion about using active waiting to increase anxiety is that, following each session, the family should wait 24-hours before discussing anything related to the therapy session. This "24-hour rule" affords each family member the opportunity to more fully digest whatever happened in the session. The family's experience of the hour is left intact. They receive the benefit of stewing in their own juices before discussions begin to alter or reshape the experience. This "crock pot effect" leaves each family member in touch with him- or herself and ultimately more able to engage in a discussion without losing perspective. Premature discussions typically serve to realign the troops and establish a consensus. Any emerging anxiety is deflated. Intellectual discussions have a way of diminishing emotional impact.

CHALLENGING ROLES

One of Carl's favorite sayings came from Mark Twain: "Even the town drunk is an elected office." Role assignments are powerful. Social groups instinctively strive to define and assign role functions to their members. It's a way of establishing a framework to create order from chaos. On the positive side, roles permit a group to function more smoothly and effectively. Everyone knows what to do, what not to do, how to relate to and interact with each other. The negative side, however, reflects a situation in which roles not only guide and clarify but limit, restrict, and even contort the group members into positions that are painful and unnatural.

While role assignments are obviously an integral part of familial as well as societal functioning, they can also be damaging. It really comes down to the issue of the amount of flexibility or rigidity the roles carry. The technique of challenging family roles most commonly attends to themes of flexibility/rigidity and balance/imbalance. This entails identifying roles played by various family members (e.g., victim, bully, white knight, pushover, peacekeeper) and challenging the family to alter these roles. Suggesting that there is a reciprocal relationship connecting seemingly adversarial role pairings makes it even more appealing. For example, the bullying 14-year-old brother might be questioned as to how he's so easily controlled by his 8-year-old sister, who can get him grounded for a week by simply provoking him until he hits her. The counterculture, drug-using 17-year-old daughter might be complimented for bringing her parents together, while the 13-year-old "white knight" brother might be diagnosed as self-absorbed and as an "isolate in the making."

The process might also include tinkering with the family's interpretation of gender roles and their differing expectations of male and female members. A common therapeutic pattern is to recommend a role reversal for couples who are at an impasse. The following excerpt shows how a therapist might use this approach with a couple stuck in the distancing effect of rigid gender roles.

Therapist: Do you think you could help her get out of the supermom role with you? It might do wonders for your sex life. It's hard for women to feel sexy with men they feel they're mothering.

Husband: That would be great. I keep telling her to take better care of herself.

Therapist: How about it, Mom? Does becoming a wife hold any appeal for you?

Wife: It sure does. I'd love to be an equal rather than feel that I'm taking care of him. But by the time he gets home and I get dinner together while he watches the news, I'm already getting upset. He relaxes with TV and a couple of beers while I prepare dinner and struggle to keep the kids quiet so they won't disturb him.

Therapist: That gives me a great idea. Why don't the two of you just flip roles? One could do Monday, Wednesday, and Friday and the other could cover Tuesday, Thursday, and Saturday.

Husband: What do you mean, flip?

Therapist: You know. When you get home you could take over and prepare the dinner while Julie takes a break and has a cocktail. You could keep the troops calm while she finds a way to relax. How does that sound?

Husband: I'm not sure you understand how we run our life.

Wife: It would be wonderful! I don't even need the help three nights a week. A night or two a week would do it. I'd be thrilled with that. Let's not overdo it.

Challenging roles can also take the form of changing multigenerational role assignments. When 9-year-old Nancy is allowed to occupy her father's chair, take command of the television remote control, and order Mom and Dad to get snacks for her, the pattern begins to shift. When Mom and Dad play along and take on Nancy's role of whining, complaining, and tormenting the family dog, the impact is even more profound. It creates a sense of openness and playfulness that contributes to the family's overall ability to deal with life adaptively.

One of the classic role confusion patterns is to refer to a child who is actually in the role of mothering her own parent as being her own grandmother. This automatically conjures up associations from the parents' past and indirectly raises the question "Is this the way I want to parent my child?"

Therapist: So, whenever Daddy gets mad like this, do you try to calm him down?

Daughter: Sure. He can't help it sometimes. He works so hard that he deserves a rest.

Therapist: Do you know if his mommy gave him neck rubs like that when he was a little boy?

Daughter: I don't know, but I think so.

Therapist: Wow! I just had the craziest idea. Do you know that when you do such a great job of taking care of Daddy it makes you your own grandmother?

In the example to follow, Carl challenges a mother's role as "supermom." The mother has been unhappy with her role within the family but is unwilling to give up any of her functions to other family members. Carl increases the anxiety by implying that she is a nonperson, in hopes that she'll find the courage to take herself more seriously. He challenges the mother to think about whether the supermom role is really desirable and increases her awareness of this unidimensional role in order to expand it.

Mother: I don't know that my husband would understand.

Carl: I think that's true. Most men don't understand much. I get worried for fear if women get independent, they won't keep on babying us and we'll never grow up. It would be terrible, you know, if women turn out to be nonmothers to their husbands. It's going to be a gruesome world to all us little boys wandering around lost.

Mother: Well, I was very surprised. I can always tell when my daughter is depressed the minute I talk to her, whether it's on the phone or in person.

Carl: Of course. That's one of the things it's very hard to get over, being a supermom. What do you do now? With the kids grown and gone, who do you supermom now?

Mother: No one. I belong to clubs, things like that.

Carl: Well, that's just complaining with other mothers about their world.

Mother: No, I very seldom tell anybody any of my family problems.

Carl: You don't let them know about you? Well, have you thought of working for hospice? Some of you supermoms are just wonderful taking care of people who are dying of cancer.

Mother: No, I haven't. I worked at a rest home for a couple of years, but it got to me. I couldn't take it. Later I worked in the parish kitchen where they serve underprivileged people.

Carl: Did it work? Does it help? Do you feel good afterwards?

Mother: Well, it helps for awhile, and then all of a sudden it gets to you that you feel so sorry for the people.

Carl: You suffer too much. Have you been able to learn anything about how to be tough? You seem like a super softy, you know. Like I could crawl up in your lap and you'd cuddle me.

Carl was really challenging the rigid sex roles of both men and women. He described men as "little boys" who require a great deal of nurturing and women as eager to take on this role. Carl believed that both men and women were hopeless, men for being unable to connect and women for believing that men could change. Although the women's movement changed many of our ways of thinking about the roles of men and women, our daily activities haven't been dramatically altered.

By challenging the mother, Carl was also communicating to the mother's daughter (who was present) that this is how she could end up if she carried out her mother's legacy. As Carl talked to the mother, the daughter had the opportunity to think not only about her mother but about herself.

A final method for altering roles is to challenge the idea that people are one way or the other. Rather than seeing people as good or bad, smart or stupid, the effort is to see them as good and bad, smart and stupid. Through a more inclusive point of view, constricting role structures can be shattered. We're all both weak and strong, courageous and cowardly, giving and selfish. By simply attending to qualities that are being overlooked by a family member, a therapist can greatly facilitate relationships. This is particularly true when working with families in which the presenting problem is child focused. Parents can become so centered on negative or problematic behavior that they overlook the times the child is behaving well. Asking about times the child is well behaved or doing things the parents enjoy helps them focus on positive qualities. They begin to notice that there are times when their child is pleasurable.

For instance, a young couple came to therapy with their 16-month-old son. They were referred to therapy because the son had violent temper tantrums. During the session, the child was pleasant and well behaved and engaged in age-appropriate behavior. Both parents commented a dozen times that he had never acted so good. When asked what was different about this situation, the couple replied that maybe his behavior was better because they were concentrating only on him. They had a $2\frac{1}{2}$-year-old and a 6-month-old at home. They did not accompany the parents because they both had colds. The therapist and couple went on to have a discussion on the difficulty of managing three active children and the importance of spending special time with each child as well as each other. As the couple was leaving the clinic, the therapist overheard the husband saying "Maybe he's not such a bad kid after all."

DEVIATION AMPLIFICATION

A third way of helping the family generate enough anxiety to fuel the growth process is to begin with their perspective, join with them, and then jump two or three steps ahead to an outlandish conclusion. When the limits of their conscious logic are extended, the family is pushed into new territory. This technique is based on the idea that each family follows the path of its own belief system as far as it will take them. A dead end or impasse occurs when, after following their logic to its natural conclusion, they're unwilling to live with the results. From this "back against the wall" position, each family member attempts to force other members to submit to her or his preferences. Once an entrenched stance is in effect, the impasse is complete. Family members remain locked in place with nowhere to go. Although drained and depleted, they're unable to even consider alternatives. They prefer to hold their position rather than face the possibilities that are available but unacceptable.

The therapist's task in this situation is clear. The family must be moved from the territory that is familiar but killing them into the realm that is terrifying but offers hope. It's really another way of inviting them to take themselves more seriously. For example, when a couple seems stuck on the simple issue of not spending enough time together—especially when the argument has gone flat but remains compelling—the therapist's simple question of "How much time do you think he should dedicate?" can get the process flowing again. It moves them into the territory of how they "choose" to spend their time. It clarifies the issue as one of priorities, not of a lack of time.

The following vignette is an excerpt taken from a case in which Carl identified a couple's lack of investment as the primary factor contributing to the impasse in therapy. Carl increased the anxiety within the system by amplifying the situation. He suggested that the couple was not desperate enough to change. Rather than exploring ways to resolve marital issues, Carl pushed the couple to think about what it would be like when they separated. Could they help each other find better spouses? Who would the children live with? Through being pushed further in the direction they were already leaning, the couple had the opportunity to directly face the reality they had been avoiding. It broke the fantasy that somehow the therapist would save them from themselves.

Later in the interview, Carl expressed his own frustration regarding the couple's reluctance to discuss divorce: "I have a feeling you're laughing at this. I don't understand why. The separation is clear. I was trying to make believe you're going ahead the way it's already going and see if I could help you plan for 2 years or 6 months from now."

Carl: Do you think it's probably going to go on like this for the rest of your life?

Wife: Yeah, it could unless we do something.

Carl: So, I don't understand why you're going for therapy. Why don't you just let it happen the way it's happening?

Wife: I'm crazy, I can't go on. And he's crazy, and our poor children are going to get crazy. I mean...I don't know how he feels, but I'm at the point where I'm almost ready. This is, like, our last-ditch effort and that will be it. I feel like I've been unhappy for a lot of years now. It's both of our faults. It's just, you know...

Carl: Do you think he may do better with his third wife?

Wife: His third wife? I don't know. That's an interesting concept. They say you pick the same mates over and over, so I don't know.

Carl: Had you thought of trying to help him find the right kind?

Wife: Find his third wife? I don't think so, but I know a lot of people who really like him, so I don't think he'll have a problem.

Carl: Have you tried to get any help from him in choosing somebody that would be compatible with you?

Wife: No, I don't think he'd go for that.

Carl: Well, he might, and knowing you he might know of somebody that would be compatible with you.

Wife: He'd probably get Jack the Ripper.

Carl: I wasn't being facetious; I was serious.

Carl suggested the couple quit working on the marriage and help each other find someone new in an attempt to move them beyond the disabling impasse that had become their life. The couple presented as emotionally dead. Carl's intent was to move them into an area they were not comfortable with but needed to face. If he pushed the symptom out far enough, they might do something different. By increasing the anxiety, he might make them angry, make them laugh, or do something that would change their view of the situation. By talking about quitting, he challenged them to either consider divorce or decide to actually be married.

Deviation amplification is not a paradoxical maneuver. The couple in the preceding example felt hopeless and uninvested. Carl gave voice to a process that was obvious but unspoken. Unlike paradox, the purpose was not to induce a specific reaction. The intent was simply to disrupt the family's habituated process (Whitaker & Keith, 1981). Carl believed that if he could create enough confusion to disrupt a couple's normal way of operating, the couple might restructure itself. How they reorganized, by divorcing or reinvesting energy in the relationship, was up to them.

In the next vignette, a mother and daughter discuss their frustration with men. The mother describes her relationship with an alcoholic husband. Both the mother and the daughter express hopelessness about the situation and reveal that they have given up on men. The vignette demonstrates how Carl challenged roles and used deviation amplification to disrupt rigid patterns of thinking. Carl implied that the mother had taken on the role of a nonperson by participating in a relationship in which she neglected her own needs. While the situation was clearly painful, it had become too familiar. Their misery was leading to lethargy rather than change. Carl responded to the absurd living situation by offering absurd answers. The hope was that by pushing them beyond the realm of their typical logic, they would recognize the ridiculous quality of their dilemma and be moved to become more creative in facing it.

Carl: Did you and your husband drink together?

Mother: No.

Carl: That's a mysterious thing to me. I've often thought that's the best way for women. You could cure your husband that way. If you got to be a drunk, I bet he'd stop.

Mother: I've often thought of that, but I can't take it—a couple of drinks and I'm through.

Carl: Well, that's just practice. You just have to work on it.

Mother: I wouldn't be home to cook his meals.

Carl: Then he would rapidly learn how important it is to stay home and cook meals. He'll have a meal ready for you when you come home. [laughs]

Mother: Oh sure. That would be something, wouldn't it. [laughs] No, I don't mind anybody having a sociable drink.

Carl: I agree with you. You'd have to go at it full time, and a sociable drink doesn't count. If you get to be a real drunk, then I bet you he'd stop.

Mother: He watches the time go. He doesn't drink until noon. [laughs]

Carl: You should get him one of those watches that says ''5'' all the way around and then he wouldn't have to worry about it. It would always be time to drink.

Mother: For sure. He'd put on the television or something.

Carl: That raises another problem. [to daughter] If you got to be a drinking woman, you might very well marry a sane, nondrinking man. If you stay non-drinking, you may follow your mom's path.

Daughter: No, I drink now. [laughs]

Carl: Oh, you drink now? Oh well, that's not too bad then.

Daughter: If you can't lick 'em, join 'em.

Carl: Sure, and they may have to take on the job of the nondrinking one in the family.

Mother: That's not the way it works. If I went to a party and had a few drinks, he'd be hollering that I'm drunk. I never take my car when I'm drinking, and he doesn't drive. He wouldn't tolerate my drinking.

Carl: Oh, don't listen to him. You can't really be an alcoholic if you listen to somebody else.

Mother: I guess not.

Carl: You just listen to your own needs.

When working with rigidly stuck families, Carl contributed confusion by exaggerating the process. He stated, ''I live in a world of confusion. I can instigate confusion for anything. You set it up, I can confuse it. I revel in nonorganization. I think that's part of what my therapy has to do with. It has to do with disorganizing whatever the family brings in and enjoying my disorganization as well'' (Barrows & Zeig, 1981, p. 9). Carl often told families that he was confusing them on purpose: ''I'm not trying to get them anyplace, I'm trying to confuse them so they won't go on the way they have been going. If you can screw it up so they can't enjoy the way it's going anymore, they'll work out ways of making a more adequate living'' (Whitaker, 1973, p. 3).

The next vignette is an example of how Carl induced confusion by amplifying the situation. In the therapy session, the daughter became upset with Carl's approach and confronted him about it.

Daughter: Can I ask you one? How come I've got the really strong feeling that this is like a comedy you'd watch on TV?

Carl: Oh, I'll tell you. One of the ways I try to be useful is to cut across the usual way we think. The problem with me and everyone else is that we think in a rut. We run in the same circles, and I think many times the most important thing I can do is to think different than they do, and I'm not sure it makes any difference how I think different. It's just that it helps to switch around some of their routine thinking. It breaks the old rut and offers a new path. I'm not really laughing at you. I'm trying to be useful. I'm not being derisive or sarcastic. I've been doing this for a long, long time and I think it works. It's a funny kind of business. I had a couple, both psychiatrists who I worked with for some time, who were having terrible fights. They just beat each other up. I finally broke through this and in the middle of their fights they'd start laughing at themselves. The fighting stopped. That's what I'm trying to get to. I really take your life seriously. I think the guy you find shouldn't be embarrassing to you. He's a human being who appeals to you. I think having him in here and our trying to help you guys see what that is may be useful to you in your living. Does that make any sense?

Daughter: Yeah. [wipes eye] I'm just trying, you...

Carl: Let me say another thing that may be part of the answer to the same thing. I think confusion is very valuable. I think as long as you aren't confused you probably don't change anything.

Daughter: That's true. You completely confused me today, I'll tell you that much.

Carl: Good. Let me see if I can go a step further. It may not make any sense to you, but part of the way I do that is to be confused myself. I'm not trying to be reasonable or rational. I'm trying to share with you my confusion about what's going on with your lives in the hope that that will be useful to you.

Carl talked about the therapist's need to be both caring and tough. He described caring as the ''anesthesia for confrontation.'' Carl developed a tremendous caring for the families he saw. His caring could be both supportive and challenging. In this case, his caring took on a provocative tone. Simple support or empathic listening would not have led to change.

In a classic example of deviation amplification, Carl once consulted with a family that was organized around the psychotic symptoms of a young adult male who believed he was Christ. As the session unfolded, the isolating rigidity of the identified patient's "pathology" and the family's "health" remained intact. Carl was feeling useless when he suddenly responded by pushing the family to participate in the identified patient's world. By assigning various family members the roles of the Blessed Virgin, Mary Magdalene, the apostles, and so forth, he moved them beyond the security of an identified patient and supportive family. The session came alive. The paralyzing rigidity was broken. The identified patient, uncomfortable with this shift beyond his preestablished realm, eventually leaned over and said to Carl, "Come on, Doc. What are you doing? I'm not really Christ."

Another way to increase productive anxiety is to guide the family into taboo topics that are unacknowledged or ignored. While the content may seem inappropriate from a social point of view, it's essential from a therapeutic perspective. Exploring such split-off topics often triggers growth. As a somewhat reserved man was listening to his wife rail on about his emotional inadequacies, Carl responded.

Carl: Do you ever get crazy inside while Sally is sharing her feelings with you?

Husband: What do you mean, crazy?

Carl: You know...just lose it. Find your mind wandering all over the place from one fantasy to the next.

Husband: I don't know. [hesitates] Maybe once in a while.

Carl: Any you care to share with us now?

Husband: Well, nothing too exciting. Sometimes I begin to feel a little annoyed, so I just shut down. It helps me relax. [laughs] Otherwise I might pop.

Carl: You know, I just had a crazy idea. If someday you really flipped and just went crazy, what would it look like? Would you get a rifle and head for the nearest tower? Or maybe just wander off into the woods and build a hut and eat berries? Maybe drive to San Francisco and jump off the Golden Gate Bridge?

Husband: I don't know. I've never thought about it.

Carl: Well, you're just not trying. I have the fantasy I'd head for the woods. I might come out again someday, but I think it would take a long time.

Husband: Well, I guess I'd take off for San Francisco. Not to jump off the bridge but to live a freer life. Not be so bottled up.

Carl: How about becoming a sex addict out there? People tell me it's the thing to do. A great way to experience highs and lows. Sometimes euphoric, sometimes absolutely self-loathing. Exciting and dangerous.

Asking this sort of "inappropriate" question can sometimes help families consciously delve into areas that are typically too loaded to face. If they can tolerate the expression of uncensored dialogue, they have the opportunity to integrate these previously unexperienced interactions into their social living.

ESTABLISHING DIFFERENCES

We live in a culture that sends mixed messages. While we overtly talk of valuing individualism, at the covert level it's not tolerated. Conformity and political correctness dominate the social landscape. We are programmed to seek consensus. When someone disagrees with us, we feel nervous. We can't fully relax until we "resolve" the fact of an overt difference of opinion. This can take the form of trying to convince the other person to see it our way, discrediting the person by getting others to agree with us, or changing our point of view to agree with the person. These moves close the gap and restore consensus. When this isn't possible, we often seek to smooth things over to create an illusion of agreement. Overt, ongoing disagreement is uncomfortable. The commonly held philosophy that couples should never go to bed angry reflects this position.

Psychotherapy as a corrective process must resist this unquestioned pursuit of comfort. A powerful method for increasing the amount of productive anxiety in the therapy room is for the therapist to take a position that stands in opposition to one of the family's central beliefs about themselves. Through identifying an area of differences, a feeling of angst begins to emerge. The level of stress is further amplified when the therapist then stands by his or her belief, resisting the family's effort to change his or her mind or minimize differences. The therapist's separateness is established. Over time, this can lead to clearer boundaries and a basic sense of respect for others.

During a therapy session with a suicidal adolescent, an optimistic father, an angry mother, and a "perfect" 8-year-old daughter, the therapist opted to take on the father's nearly giddy degree of optimism. While it served him well in his highly successful sales career, it seemed almost delusional in the context of the family's overall level of pain.

Therapist: So, Dad, how do you handle your son's pain and your wife's anger when you come home from a business trip? It looks pretty heavy. Are you secretly depressed?

Dad: Depressed? Me? Not at all.

Therapist: You look depressed to me.

Dad: Well, it's not true.

Therapist: Well, I'm not really debating whether it's true or not. I'm just telling you I think you're depressed. Your son nearly killed himself and your wife is furious at you. At least Susie is still smiling. [Dad begins to slightly tear up] You don't have to buy it, though. I'm not really trying to sell you on the idea. I just want you to know that I see you as depressed and that I'm worried about you. I worry about fathers.

Dad: Thanks, but I'm really not depressed. [Dad is smiling through his tears]

Therapist: Maybe you are and you don't know it.

The idea was not to force a diagnosis on the father but, rather, to establish the fact that at least one person in the room doesn't believe he's as unaffected as he acts. The father and the family are left with an overt opinion about Dad that they can't easily ignore. The comfort of their surface-level denial is contaminated.

SUMMARY

Anxiety is a catalyzing ingredient of the therapy process. If change is to occur, it is essential that the family experience enough anxiety to push them beyond the constraints of the status quo. Families have a tendency to reestablish a sense of comfort, to calm their anxiety after feeling challenged to push beyond their normal mode of interaction. This is a natural process, but at this phase of therapy, it is important for the therapist to amplify the family's level of anxiety to continue to generate change. The therapist's willingness to use anxiety is central to this stage of the therapy.

During this stage of therapy, the therapist and the family must learn to express anxiety more openly during the session. Differences are recognized and acknowledged. The therapist punctuates the fact that he or she is not part of the family and is not coopting them. Techniques commonly used to activate the underlying anxiety of the therapy experience include waiting, challenging roles, amplifying family deviations, and highlighting differences. If therapy is to succeed during this stage, the family must experience their will to fight, push, and disagree as essential to a successful therapeutic outcome. The family must take charge, and the therapist must convey confidence in them.

Chapter 9

Creating Symbolic Experience
Through Associative
Communication

There is perhaps no challenge more threatening to the family therapist than the opportunity, indeed the necessity, to be involved, to be fully a person in the therapy hour.—Carl Whitaker

Alice's excursion to Wonderland wasn't all fun and games. As her fantasy world came to life, her experience in this nonsensical world became a stressful adventure. Her persistence in following a white rabbit that constantly scurried about exclaiming "I'm late! I'm late! For a very important date" became a frantic chase as Alice experienced being lost in a world that made no sense. Much to her chagrin, the rabbit had a knack for remaining slightly out of sight. Unable to catch up with him, Alice became discouraged and panicked that she'd never find her way home.

Her curiosity about the white rabbit waned as she became preoccupied with seeking direction on how to get out of the world she had longed to enter. Once in Wonderland, the theme of how to escape and return to reality predominated. However, no one was particularly helpful. If anything, the world with no rules made things all the more confusing. In fact, most of the creatures in the forest seemed to relish in their refusal to help.

The singing flowers shoo Alice from the garden when she requests help. They insist she is a weed after inspecting her scrawny legs. Offended Alice continues on midway through the forest until she notices a series of signs posted on tree branches. Abruptly she stops, hoping to get some sense of direction. To her dismay, the signs are contradictory in nature, reading "This Way," "That Way," and "Up." Befuddled, she stops a moment to think. From nowhere, the Cheshire cat appears.

Alice: Don't go, please. I just wanted to ask you which way I ought to go.

Cat: Well, that depends on where you want to get to.

Alice: Oh, it really doesn't matter as long as I can...

Cat: Well then, it really doesn't matter which way you go. Oh, by the way, if you'd really like to know, he went that way.

Alice: Who did?

Cat: The white rabbit.

Alice: He did?

Cat: He did what?

Alice: Went that way?

Cat: Who did?

Alice: The white rabbit.

Cat: What rabbit?

Alice: But didn't you just say? I mean, oh dear!

Cat: Can you stand on your head? However, if I were looking for a white rabbit, I'd ask the Mad Hatter. [Alice peruses the sign—MAD HATTER]

Alice: No, no. I don't.

Cat: Or there's the March Hare in that direction.

Alice: Thank you. I think I shall visit him.

Cat: Of course, he's mad too!

Alice: But I don't want to go among mad people.

Cat: Oh, you can't help that. Most everyone's mad here. You may have noticed that I'm not all there myself. [laughs and disappears] (Sharpsteen, 1951)

After this encounter, Alice wearily continues on. As a last resort, she approaches singing teapots. The teapots appear interested in her quest and are kind in nature, but they have a habit of changing the subject, often losing track of the conversation. They express their interest and then quickly lose the point altogether.

The fairy tale culminates when Alice, at her wit's end, sits in the middle of the darkened forest crying profusely, worried she has exhausted all options. She sobs, realizing she must rely on her own advice. "That's just the trouble with me. I give myself very good advice but I very seldom follow it and that explains the trouble I'm always in."

For Alice, it was the struggle that resulted in her transformation. If it had been easy, if she could have snapped her fingers and returned home, she would have missed the experience necessary for growth. This is the experience of the middle stage of therapy, which symbolizes the journey, the push and pull of the family and the therapist. There is an intimacy, a sense of knowing, of communicating in a more meaningful way. The family has tested the therapist on more than one occasion. By now they have made a decision to invest themselves in the therapy process.

Once the family becomes invested in the therapeutic process, they may experience a sudden sense of panic, a desire to turn around. If the relationship is solid, this panic is short lived. Once the ball gets rolling, therapy takes on a life of its own. While the therapist is there to lend a hand, it is important to maintain a role similar to that of the white rabbit, always remaining slightly out of sight, often out of reach. The therapist's task is to get things moving, stimulate interaction, and shake things up, to upset the order or unbalance the system and then quickly extricate from the process as the family reorganizes itself. For example, a couple was in marital therapy as a result of the husband's affair. The wife was describing how hard she was trying to work at the marriage. According to her, the husband was aloof and uncooperative. His periods of absence fueled her suspiciousness. She was smiling and pleasant but was adept at subtly zinging her husband. The therapist smiled and said, "Wow, I barely saw the scalpel, you stuck him so quickly!" The husband nodded. "I thought I was bleeding." Exposing her covert behavior challenged the illusion of her goodness. The system was unbalanced.

By sharing fantasies and metaphors, the therapist shifts the process from content to symbolic. As the family begins to be more real, the therapist has a window into their symbolic world. Listening to their dreams and free associations allows the therapist to hear what is significant to them. The therapy encounter encourages the family to follow their heart and let their intuition guide them.

Family dysfunction, rigid patterning, and anxieties manifested in repetition and compulsion bind the family in its own defensive processes. They perseverate in their attempts to repeat unsuccessful solutions to their problem. They are stuck. This nonadaptive behavior appears beyond their control. It's as if they have blinders on. Human behavior is both absurd and ridiculous, and cognitive knowledge is impotent to alter the absurdity. What is not ridiculous or absurd is the depression, anxiety, and terror that accompany repeated behaviors. For example, a couple came to recognize that their conflict escalated whenever they became too intimate or too distant. Conflict was the release valve that either pulled them together or pushed them apart. The dance remained the same. It is reminiscent of someone talking louder to a person who doesn't understand English. The volume doesn't translate into better understanding.

In order to access the family's creative processes, the therapist must be skilled in stimulating a symbolic context for therapy. The therapist relies on facilitating primary process relating and associative communication (the language of inference and the language of options) to communicate symbolically with the family (Connell, Mitten, & Whitaker, 1993). We want to move into the nonrational realm of relating as a way of bypassing defenses and getting at their understructure. Therapists accomplish this hurdle by helping families understand the complexity of their culture. The problems expressed at the surface level are more complicated at the interpersonal level. It is a challenge to help the family endure their not knowing. This ambivalence is stressful for both the family and the therapist. The therapist serves as an example by tolerating uncertainty and anxiety. The goal of this stage of therapy is for the family to discover that their story contains the solution, if only we can be jointly patient so as to fully understand it.

This is the most crucial stage of therapy. The dynamic interplay between the family and therapist is complex. Interaction is based on a myriad of factors, many of which are beyond the scope of the therapist's and family's conscious awareness. The therapy experience consists of moments that are "beyond technique." The essence eludes definition. We hope to illuminate those processes that intensify the therapy experience and become symbolic for the family.

A recent experience comes to mind. A therapist was seeing a family with a profoundly depressed mother. During the session, the discussion had focused on whether hospitalization was an option at this point in her depression. Based on a past experience with hospitalization, the family was against it. As they prepared to leave the office, the therapist hugged the woman. This spontaneous gesture was out of character for him. As he hugged her, as much for his own security as hers, she whispered, "This reminds me of being a kid and I don't know if I can cope with that uncertainty." Later sessions focused on the fact that no one in her family provided comfort for her growing up. This simple gesture had been significant for the woman and got her in touch with an alienated part of herself that was desperate for solace.

This phase constitutes a joining of kindred spirits (Connell & Russell, 1986). Through mutual sharing of fantasies and storytelling, the encounter between the therapist and family increases the level of intimacy in the system. This stage involves accelerated movement. As the therapist intensifies the experience or turns up the thermostat, the system reaches its maximum heat. Although this chapter highlights several techniques, success depends on the therapist's finesse in shifting from one to another, in a manner similar to the cat in the tale of Alice. Here we focus on using associative communication to bypass defenses and access the symbolic infrastructure of the family.

TYPOLOGY OF LANGUAGES

During this stage of therapy, the therapist communicates with the family through a series of languages. As usual, the family begins by expressing their distress via the language of pain and impotence. They describe their struggles and explain the problems they want the therapist to solve. Rather than responding to their pain on a literal level and offering concrete "solutions," the therapist moves to expand their experience of the problem. New possibilities open as the therapist sidesteps the family's usual way of viewing the dilemma. Using the language of inference accomplishes this task. The family expects "advice," but the therapist offers stories or fantasies triggered by their story. The key is to listen to what the family says and then infer beyond their presentation. This enhances the possibility of change (Connell, Mitten, & Whitaker, 1995).

By enlarging the family's narrow view of the problem, the therapist moves to expand awareness of the multitude of untried modes of resolving their dilemma. This is the language of options. While the options "suggested" can be reasonable or ridiculous, the underlying message is clear: There are more options to consider, more solutions to try. This typology of languages has the therapeutic effect of establishing a sense of hope, of creating possibilities where once there were none.

During an impassioned but stuck family session, a mother tearfully pointed to her youngest daughter, saying "My baby is leaving me." The therapist responded to the mother's pain by commenting, "That's why they cut the umbilical cord. You know that's a fascinating thing, when they cut the cord the mother often flinches as if she's experiencing actual physical pain even though there's no physical sensation. It's all psychological. I suppose it never really stops hurting, though. They're never grateful enough. Do you think your husband could tie the cord?" By inference, he was saying that the daughter's leaving home was part of the natural cycle of life. He also validated the legitimacy of the mother's pain while implying that it was unavoidable. Bringing Dad in as the nursemaid suggested the possibility of a way to survive the loneliness. This associative, metaphoric, storytelling style of communicating often circumvents the family's repetitive defenses. While they are busy guarding the front door, the therapist sneaks through the side.

Carl communicated symbolically through a language of options. By presenting a string of ridiculous solutions in response to family pain, he communicated that there were many options in life (Neill & Kniskern, 1982). At times his associations seemed absurd, even outlandish. The family often says, "We've tried everything. There's nothing else we can do." Options convey that there are many other ways for them to try. To a mom who was complaining about her inability to control her son's temper tantrums, the therapist might say, "Have you considered getting a squirt gun to soak him while he's throwing himself around? Perhaps you could throw yourself on the floor and have a bigger tantrum! The whole family could get involved and roll around kicking and screaming!"

The intent is to create experiences for a family that go beyond understanding. These shared experiences generate the most intimacy and have the greatest potential to keep the system alive and growing. Creating real and even absurd experiences that touch on areas the family has not yet integrated or resolved furthers the relationship. For example, if a family needs to experience Dad as more caring in order for their perception and symbolic meaning of "father" to change, the therapist encourages the father's vulnerability in sessions. Therapists rely on their own creative unconscious processes to produce a context in which new experiences can occur in therapy. Symbolic experiences facilitate change in the interpersonal world of the family. The sections to follow provide examples of (a) sharing free associations, fantasies, visual images, and metaphors; (b) telling stories; (c) communicating through the language of inference; (d) communicating through the language of options; (e) creating symbolic experiences; and (f) using roles.

SHARING FREE ASSOCIATIONS, FANTASIES, VISUAL IMAGES, AND METAPHORS

By sharing personal beliefs and free associations, the therapist facilitates primary process relating. This type of relating involves uncensored spontaneity, or being on automatic pilot. The therapist's fantasies create "picture images" that may become powerful metaphors for the family. For example, when a family was describing the level of conflict between adolescent siblings, the therapist said, "I just had an image of a free-for-all at a hockey game. God, I hope you guys aren't that brutal to each other!" This fantasy conveyed concern that the home environment might be abusive. On a symbolic level, the therapist acknowledges the seriousness of the situation. However, by owning the fantasy, she or he leaves nothing for the family to fight against. The family is free to use or discard these associations. This process relies on the therapist's creative ability to think beyond the concrete experience the family is describing and make a connection to a more abstract or metaphorical experience from her or his private or professional life. These images are clearly the therapist's rendering of the family's experience.

Carl described communication between the doctor and family as one of the central problems in the field of psychotherapy (Whitaker, 1961, 1964). This problem resulted from psychiatry's early emphasis on understanding the patient's background story and, later, the patient's behavior. This resulted in one-way communication, with the therapist functioning as a blank screen. One of Carl's major contributions was focusing on the role of the therapist in relation to the family as an active partner in their growth process.

Carl challenged the traditional methods of psychotherapy by emphasizing a need for increased communication from the therapist to the patient. He believed that free associations, fantasies, and visual images that the family triggered within him during the session belonged to the family. He did not need to understand them. He was only responsible for sharing them. He often said to families, "I have a conversation with you and I don't even know what I'm talking about sometimes, but I believe in it because it's what has occurred to me." Therapists must have a basic trust in their own intuitive life.

In a consultation Carl conducted with an extended multigenerational family, an adult son was rambling on about how his life was, what he had learned from therapy, changes he wanted to make, and so forth. Carl looked quizzically at him and said, "You know, I haven't heard a damn thing you've said for the past 5 minutes. I was thinking about the infrastructure of the city. It's a wonderful thing that goes on down there. There is a maze of stuff that supports life up here and no one has a clue about it. It goes on all the time!" After Carl had shared his fantasy, there was a moment of silence. The son looked at Carl like he was nuts. Interestingly enough, he began to more openly disclose his disappointments, fears, and loneliness. The tone of the interaction changed dramatically.

Carl referred to his free associations as similar to what Zen masters call koans. The idea was for Zen masters to provide students with a challenge in which logic was useless. This required students to attend to their inner selves in order to make sense of the experience. Carl offered his free associations to families in a similar way. The free association, or koan, stands only as a bare statement (Whitaker & Warkentin, 1965). It is always up to the family to make their own sense of the statement.

Carl described his reliance on the nonrational components of therapy as similar to the Zen master's effort to deprogram rational or logical thinking. Therapists need courage and wisdom to deal with seemingly impossible problems. Carl's methodologies were based on Eastern thought, which focuses on enhancing growth, rather than Western psychotherapy methods, which correct pathology (Whitaker, 1976).

Carl offered his free associations and fantasies to activate the therapeutic relationship. By sharing his inner thoughts, he encouraged the family to share more of themselves. This often facilitated a more genuine interpersonal relationship. In the following example, a husband talks of his wife's illness. After the wife's diagnosis with bone cancer, the husband busied himself with household tasks. He was proud of how he managed to maintain the house, do yard work, prepare meals, and care for his wife. Despite the extended family's suggestion that he rely on outside assistance, he tackled even the strenuous job of lifting his wife in and out of bed for meals and baths. When asked how he was doing emotionally, he remarked, "It's a little tough, but I can manage. I've always been independent. I'm a survivor."

Carl believed that the husband was as dependent on caring for his wife as his wife was dependent on him. His preoccupation with the caretaker role made it possible for him to suppress underlying fear related to losing his wife. Carl responded to the husband's denial of dependency on his wife by sharing a fantasy.

Husband: I really am doing fine. The kids can't believe how well I'm managing. You just do what you have to do.

Carl: I have this fantasy about myself if my wife died. I think I'd disappear into the woods. I don't know how long it would take before I would be able to come back. I don't believe I'd really kill myself, but I'd be in bad shape.

The fantasy infers that the husband may be more dependent on his wife than he thinks. Carl did not say this directly. By sharing a fantasy about his own wife, Carl was able to bypass the husband's defenses. Carl suggested that by owning the inferences you make from a family's pain and impotence, you don't invade their field. Speaking from the "I" position is irrefutable and nonintrusive.

Carl offered families metaphors to "help them visualize various struggles within family life" (Whitaker & Keith, 1981). For example, he referred to a parentified child as "grandmother" or described Dad as a fictional character such as Archie Bunker. Metaphorical language must communicate to the family indirectly about its own process of relating. When working with military families, Carl informed parents that they had equal rank. He suggested they were both five-star generals and neither could boss the other around (Keith & Whitaker, 1982). In this way, it is possible to rearrange family symbols to facilitate change.

Carl did not intentionally construct metaphors that fit for the family. Instead, he used his own primary process by listening to his inner-self. He described this process through his work with a couple who had recently launched two teenagers. He initially joined with them, saying "You know this looks like the typical empty nest syndrome and that's very painful. I realize how painful it is." Midway through the session, an image occurred to him that he shared with the couple. He said, "You know, that's the funniest thing. I just saw the emptiness of a bird's nest and the problem was that it was full of shit. You know, that's exactly the problem. It's not the emptiness. It's the fact that it's full of shit that's destroying you." The picture of an empty nest inferred that it was really the marriage that needed work.

Carl described his use of metaphor as similar to that of a cartoonist. He moved from metaphor to metaphor to dramatize character. In the following example, Carl responds to a wife's description of increasing distance in the marital relationship (Whitaker & Bumberry, 1988). She had talked of her husband's preoccupation with work on the farm, his tractor, and so forth.

Wife: I try to talk to him. He never seems interested. I feel so lonely. He can't wait to get on his tractor or tend to the animals.

Carl: How long after you were married was it before you realized he loved the cows more than you?

Wife: Well, I don't know. I can't remember. I had one kid after the other. It's hard. I don't know.

Carl: What did he substitute when you started loving the kids instead of him?

As the wife dejectedly spoke of the loneliness in her marriage, an image of the husband tenderly caressing his cows came to Carl. He left the family with an absurd but eerily accurate picture of the distance in the marriage by sharing this image. If an image is bizarre enough to penetrate a family's programmed thinking, it may become a symbol capable of leading them to reorganize their way of experiencing each other. It may disrupt their comfort with the interpersonal distance by creating a few sparks. In the preceding example, Carl, by identifying the mother's parallel love affair with her children, established a picture of mutuality. Both partners were implicated in the marital distance. This, of course, suggested that with enough desperation, they were both also capable of triggering change. Neither was helpless.

In the next example, an adult daughter of the previous couple expresses frustration related to difficulty maintaining intimate relationships with men. Shortly after she becomes involved with a man, he tends to break up with her (Whitaker & Bumberry, 1988). Carl responds with a visual fantasy.

Vanessa: I don't choose the right men for relationships. One was withholding and not affectionate. One went off with another woman. Now Mark [her most recent boyfriend] has a new girlfriend.

Carl: Is he afraid you're going to eat him up?

Vanessa: I think a lot of men are afraid of my intensity.

Carl: Do you think you eat them up to fill a hole inside of you?

Vanessa: Yes.

Carl: You can't fill a hole inside of you with someone else.

Vanessa: I know! I have to do something with myself. I don't know how to fill it, though. I've been eating a lot the past few days, trying to fill myself up.

Carl shared an association that occurred to him while Vanessa was talking. The image that she might eat men up to fill a hole inside of her inferred that her intensity and neediness might scare men away. He conveyed the importance of being able to meet some of her own emotional needs.

In another example, Carl engages in dialogue with a mother about her daughter and son-in-law's marriage. The couple had a history of not being committed to therapy. However, the mother refused to give up hope, saying "They've got to sit down together and work it out."

Mother: I think they're just stubborn. They've got to sit down together and work it out.

Carl: No, they don't. It would be nice if they did, but...

Mother: They should work together to save their marriage. Even if it's just for the kids' sake.

Carl: Maybe they don't want to.

Mother: Well, that's up to them. There's nothing I can say or do. It's their lives, not mine.

Carl: There may not be anything they want to say or do about it either. It may be that their backturning is more satisfying than turning around.

The image of the couple back-to-back provides a vivid picture of the marriage inferring that both husband and wife are stubborn and equally responsible for their unhappiness. Carl always accepted a system's decision to maintain the status quo. He resisted any residual anxiety that compelled him to lead.

In the next example, Carl confronts a father about his alcoholism. In response to the father's ongoing minimization and denial, Carl paints an unsettling picture of a cirrhotic liver by comparing it with "Italian bread that's so hard you can't get a high-quality knife through it." Using words to discuss the father's drinking didn't seem to help. Carl's intent was to convey a message about how the alcoholic was destroying himself through metaphor or inference rather that direct confrontation.

Carl: How long did they tell you to quit?

Father: They told me to quit forever.

Carl: Oh well, that's not very fair. How long did you quit?

Father: Oh, I don't know, how long was it, 3 months, 4 months?

Carl: And they said your liver was all right after that?

Father: I haven't really talked to them since. They said the liver was failing, but I was able to use an herb to cleanse my system out. Cleaned it right up.

Carl: Have you ever seen a liver with cirrhosis? It's wonderful.

Father: Well, they didn't mention cirrhosis. What did they say it was?

Sister: They said you're doing it. Your body can't take it anymore. That's the problem.

Carl: It's a fascinating thing when you do an autopsy and you see a cirrhotic liver. It feels like Italian bread, you know, the bread that's so hard you can't cut it. It's like that. You can hardly get a good, high-quality knife through it, it's so solid. It's like there's no such chance of the blood going through it to get cleaned. It's got concrete qualities. But the 3 months helped it a little, right?

Frequently, Carl told stories to diffuse direct confrontations. He didn't want to waste his energy on direct confrontation if the system had no real hope of change. He would try to raise the anxiety level a bit through visual images, but if denial was high, he didn't fight it. He left that to the family.

By sharing fantasies, visual images, and metaphors, the therapist communicates through the language of inference. When the family described the problem,

Carl inferred something else. His fantasies were intended to redirect the family's thinking and shatter their gestalt. When Mom said her daughter and son-in-law had to work their problems out, Carl suggested that they might be more content with their "back-turning." When the farmer's wife described giving up on her distant husband, Carl's bizarre associations pushed the image further out.

These fantasies, visual images, and metaphors illustrate the complex interpersonal dynamics of the family, capturing the family drama, making it more picturesque. The therapist avoids being coopted by the family by using a variety of lenses to point out different aspects of the same drama. The images give the family something they can hold on to, take with them, and struggle with. Since these are the therapist's associations, there is little for the family to fight against. This is one way to bypass their defenses. Typically, the process involves the therapist sharing a spontaneous thought elicited by something the family does or says. Carl shared associations as if they came out of midair. He would then quickly change the subject, leaving the family to make sense of their experience.

TELLING STORIES

Spontaneous storytelling is an art in therapy. The therapist may tell true stories or construct fictional ones about his or her own life or other families previously treated. This creates a metaphor for the family. The therapist presents the story in a way that the family can't refute, because it's just a story. This approach is similar to parallel play, but it involves drawing more of an inference and, as a result, is not as personal.

Carl told stories as yet another way to seed the unconscious. If conversation was unproductive, he often interrupted the family's dialogue midsentence with a story. This changed the direction of communication and shifted the process from content to symbolic. At times, Carl would fragment his own sentences. He might pause midway through a sentence and then take off in a completely different direction, telling a story that was unrelated to what he had started to say. Carl was an artist. In discussing the use of storytelling, Carl stated:

> I think no story ought to be told unless it pops into your head during the interview. Preplanning or having a cue word that makes you tell a particular story makes it sterile, just like any other technical process. But if the story comes out of your own personal life, it can be repeated endlessly because it's always affectedly loaded for you. Like any other good story, it hopefully leaves the patient with a symbolic experience that he doesn't participate in. If he then decides to partake in it, it becomes his rather than yours. If you tell a story about a death in your family, for example, that story sticks with the family forever. They can't refute it because you are not saying something about them. You are sharing your experience. If they identify with the story, it can become a covert, slow burn, seeding of the unconscious that makes therapy most valuable. (Whitaker & Jaffee, 1992)

The following example illustrates Carl's response to a woman who, during the initial stage of therapy, described her history of panic attacks.

Wife: My panic attacks are awful. My heart races so fast. I start sweating and it really feels like I'm going to die. My husband doesn't understand. He thinks I should just be able to snap out of it. He says I use my anxiety to get out of social responsibilities. I wish, for just one day, he could experience what I go through.

Carl: I was suddenly thinking of an experience that I'd forgotten for a long while. When I was 7 or 8 we lived on a big dairy farm. At times, it would be my job to go down to the barn at night to get another pail of milk. I would take off toward the barn and make believe there was a fox or something horrible coming out of the black, and I would run like hell. It dawned on me when I was grown that I was excited about it. I would arrive at the house with my heart pounding and my palms sweating, and I had enjoyed the excitement.

While the anxiety was very real and stressful for this woman, the story implied that perhaps she could use her anxiety for some kind of gain. Carl believed that any experience is an opportunity for growth and development. It is the ride, not the destination, that moves us forward.

Carl felt that it was valuable for families when a therapist told a story coming from a personal experience that was symbolic for the therapist. Stories are one of the best ways of setting up a process that the family can't escape from. It's important for the therapist to draw from his or her own experience when telling stories. These types of stories carry an emotional voltage that deepens the intimacy level of the system. As children, we were all captured by storytelling. Carl told the following story to a family in which the father consistently denied his son's perceptions.

I remember years ago when I was putting one of my children to bed. I was lying on the other side of the dark room, and my daughter was in her crib. She was 2 or 3 at the time. We'd been singing and telling stories. Finally, I said, "For God's sake, go to sleep," and there was this moment of silence. She said, "Daddy, am I sleepy?" If I would have said, "Of course you're sleepy; father knows best," she would have denied her own experience.

This story disarmed the father and his rigid defense without direct confrontation. It opened up the possibility for therapy to proceed. It was okay for a family to disagree with Carl's stories. The association was not discussed. The family could do what they wanted with it. They could discard it, continue to play with the idea, or perhaps accept it at a later time. If they accepted the material later, it became their construct, not something they had taken from him. They could then push the change process further.

The next example illustrates how Carl used storytelling to send a father a message about how his power impeded the growth of his two adolescent sons. The father, mother, their two sons, and the family's therapist were present for the consultation. After conversing with the boys, Carl tells a story about a man with a steel hook for an arm who ran a school for delinquent boys. He said the man never thought that the boys were frightened of him. He had no idea of his power.

Carl: [to son, referring to son's relationship with his father] I had the craziest thought that if you were little and your dad was as big as he is and fell on you, it would be a horrible mess.

Father: I quit wrestling him a long time ago.

Carl: [to son] Do you think he knows how big he is?

Son: I think he's realizing since our therapy, but I don't think he realizes how domineering he is.

Carl: [to son] Do you know how big you are?

Son: Well, I used to feel I was pretty small. Now, I really don't know.

Carl: Do you think you could take him?

Son: Physically?

Carl: How about in another couple of years?

Son: Yes, give me a couple.

Carl: I was suddenly thinking of a guy I saw years and years ago who had a hook. His arm was gone, and he had a steel hook. He was running a school for boys. I saw him and his wife and kids in therapy. It took me 6 months before I could convince him that I was terrified of that thing. He said I shouldn't be afraid and the kids certainly weren't afraid. I said, "A school full of delinquent kids? I bet there isn't a single one of them who hasn't had this fantasy [gestures his curled finger across his throat and makes a slashing sound]." [laughter] He didn't have any concept of it.

Father: There is an issue of my power and my perceptions of that power.

Carl's story inferred that perhaps the father was not aware of how controlling he was and how his authoritative stance affected the boy's development. The father identified with the story and began to talk more openly about his powerful role in the family. The story made it easier for the family to talk about a confrontational issue with a balance of distance and personal investment. It gave them the opportunity to pursue or ignore the topic.

In a continuation of the consultation, Carl speculates that insecurity may be underlying the father's need for power. Again Carl introduces the topic of inadequacy by talking about his own weaknesses. Then he tells a story of a couple he worked with in which the wife was so adequate that the husband was a failure. The story is meant for the wife to absorb by overhearing it through Carl's discussion with the husband. The story implies that perhaps she needs to find a way to defeat her husband through diffusing some of his power in the family. Carl immediately went onedown as another hopeless, befuddled man to minimize any potential insults.

Carl: I think part of it's just being a man. Men are hopeless. I know I'm just befuddled about some things. Like, I can't love as much as I want to. I can't seem to turn the throttle up far enough to satisfy me. I feel pretty inadequate about that. I feel unable to respond to the depth I want to, like that famous crack that no one can tolerate the intimacy he really wants. [laughter followed by silence]

Father: I have a sense that Carl rejoices in being inadequate. [laughter]

Carl: That's a problem I have; you know me. [laughter] I had a case years ago that taught me so much: this husband and wife, and she was so adequate that he was always a total failure. He kept on; finally he solved it by going bankrupt. He proved himself very competent at defeating her by going bankrupt. I don't think he knew it. I was sure we didn't know it. There was this process that was going on between the two of them, but he certainly won his struggle.

Carl often shared universal experiences through stories. His stories made the encounter more personal without imposing intimacy. Following any story, the family chooses the direction of the discussion, to give them the opportunity for a deeper level of intimacy. Stories serve as mirrors for a family. They can reflect or deflect the images being shown, depending on perspective.

Stories become metaphors for the family. They are a bit more elaborate and engaging than free associative quips made by the therapist. Storytelling breaks up rigid defenses and negative, repetitive family processes. When the family intellectualizes or resists dealing with affectively loaded issues, telling a story midstream changes the flow and direction of therapy.

There is a consistency to storytelling. The purpose is to unbalance the system and give the family something to think about. The experience is similar to being tapped on the shoulder, only to turn and find no one in sight.

COMMUNICATING THROUGH THE LANGUAGE OF INFERENCE

By sharing fantasies communicated through the language of inference, Carl challenged families' irrationality and expanded their automatic responses to their experiences. When a husband expressed fear that his wife was suicidal, Carl asked, "Who in the family wants her dead?" The family would often respond to this question with a sense of incredulity or indignation. This gave Carl the occasion to challenge their unspoken assumption that suicidal impulses are a manifestation of individual weakness or pathology. By sharing his conviction that everything that goes on in a family is at least a two-person process and insisting that overt suicidality is fueled by covert homicidality, he initiated a shift in the family's reality, moving them to a territory where they could feel involved and establish a sense of hope.

Similarly, when a husband complained about his mother-in-law, Carl asked, "If your mother-in-law dies, who will you use as a competitor? By the way, how did you arrange to have your wife stay dependent on her mother so you could complain about being left out?" Carl responded to everything the husband said by inferring complicity in an interpersonal process. The inferences created a two-person scapegoat. Carl inferred that it was not only the wife or mother-in-law who caused problems for the husband but that he also participated in the family's distress.

Inferences are a way of seeding the unconscious processes of a family. The language of inferences challenges irrational symbols and rigid family perspectives and expands the focus of therapy.

COMMUNICATING THROUGH THE LANGUAGE OF OPTIONS

Options offer the family several images depicting how they might change. They challenge the family's views and beliefs that there is nothing else they can do. Broadening options conveys that there are other ways to try. These options may be real or absurd depending on the family's level of defensiveness. Some families are so stuck they can't entertain another way of solving a problem. If they have thrown up their hands in despair, it may be better to be absurd so as to interject some humor into the process. We've all been on the search for misplaced keys in our homes. We keep returning to the place we're sure we left them even though we've looked there 10 times already. Somehow we can't believe our eyes! So it is with families; they do more of the same, even though it isn't working. Each of us can continue to trip over our own blind spots!

In the following example, a wife is frustrated at her futile attempts to stop her husband from having affairs. He refuses to participate in counseling, denies he has been unfaithful, and asserts he does not want a divorce. The wife admits to giving up, saying "There's nothing else we can do." Carl symbolically communicated, through a variety of absurd options, that there were many more ways for the wife to try.

Wife: If he's going to have an affair, the only thing I can do is get a divorce.

Carl: Well, you know, that's a possibility, but had you ever thought of inviting all of his girlfriends in for a party and giving them a corsage? Then you could have him come in late, not knowing what's going on, and tell him you're just wanting him to choose which one he's going to take. Tell him you're giving him away and you want everyone to have equal rights. Or you could call his mother and say "You know, I don't understand how you could raise a son who ended up to be like this. I'd like some help understanding that because I don't want my son to grow up like that and I thought maybe you could help me with what not to do." There are still some other options. Like if you decide to hit him in the back of the head with a brick, I'll go to court and defend you. Or you could be the ideal wife and hopefully the S.O.B. will eventually feel guilty and kill himself.

Carl offered a broad range of options. The purpose was to push the limits so far out that 3 weeks later they might begin to catch on and be more alive to their own options. The therapist's job is to set up the symbolic process of going for broke rather than living in a constant state of uncertainty.

The therapist's role in the middle phase of therapy is to tease the family into being creative and nonrational. Options enable a family to think beyond the limits of their common experience. Creative options can actively intervene in the family's symbolic world to reshape family symbols by reframing the context of a problem or challenging an anticipated outcome. During this stage, the therapist might present a wild fantasy of what could be different using a variety of options.

In another classic example, Carl responded with a pointed, tongue-in-cheek suggestion to a wife who complained of her husband's unwillingness to communicate with her. Despite the genuineness of her frustration, there was a sense of hopelessness in her voice. While she continued to complain about how impossible her husband was, she was doing nothing to resolve the problem. It was almost as if her whining was the cue for him to disappear. She was implicitly colluding in the process she found so disturbing.

Wife: I get mad at him a lot of times, but he just walks away. He won't fight! He walks to the back 40 [acres] and I can't find him. I get mad because he won't fight it out. He just walks away.

Carl: Why don't you get a bow and arrow or something?

Daughter: Take the tractor [to chase him].

Carl: Or a shotgun full of rock salt? They used to talk about that when I was a kid.

By giving voice to these "ridiculous" options, Carl hoped to stimulate the mother to be more proactive in her living. The imagery of using a "bow and arrow" or a "shotgun full of rock salt" conveys a sense of urgency. It implies that things aren't actually hopeless, they're just stuck. Increasing the intensity is the untried solution. Carl intended these options, while overtly directed toward the mother, to be noted by her husband. They might give him reason to pause the next time he's tempted to turn his back on his wife.

In another instance, Carl was working with a couple that was very career oriented. They struggled to meet the demands of their jobs, fulfill their responsibilities as parents, and keep their marriage alive. The wife complained that she was not able to get the children to go to bed at night. She stated that the children responded well to discipline at school but that their behavior was quite unruly at home. She felt like a failure as a parent.

Wife: I'm not able to get the kids to bed at night. They listen at school but not at home. I feel terrible about it. I'm really failing as a parent.

Carl: Well, maybe you could soundproof your own room, since it's obvious you're the one who's exhausted. Or you could delegate your maternal responsibilities to your husband and let him feel guilty. If he happens to be successful, you could learn from him. Or you could announce to the kids that you're giving up your role as a mother and tell them they have to be the mother and are responsible for getting you to bed.

Carl felt that therapists could become more and more outlandish in their options as the therapeutic alliance became more and more solid. The goal is to emphasize the silliness of the situation in an effort to help the family transcend their pain and their rationalization as they move into the territory of irrational thinking. Options convey a message about the absurdity of living and give a family permission to live their life however they want.

In comparison with the language of inference, the language of options purposely challenges the family's irrational thinking. The idea is to offer legitimate and absurd images depicting ways in which the family might change. While Carl's suggestions might appear flippant on the surface, he cared deeply for the families he worked with. The understructure of caring increases the family's tolerance for absurdity. Silliness and absurdity amplify the pathology until the symptoms remit, break up, or come crashing down. The language of options moves the family into the nonrational realm of relating, stimulating the family's unconscious creative processes.

CREATING SYMBOLIC EXPERIENCES

Symbolic experiences involve breaking through the normal, practiced ways of perceiving life and beginning to see things from a different point of view. They are experiences that jolt our way of being and disrupt the familiar comfort of the deepening ruts of our everyday living. They contaminate our programmed patterns and move us into new territory.

Dr. Pauline Boss (personal communication, September 1997) recalled an experience with Carl that was symbolic for her, as well as the client. "Carl asked if I would be his co-therapist for a particular case. After my spontaneous 'Yes!' I wondered why he hadn't asked one of the male residents. When I arrived for the first session, I understood why. The woman who came to Carl for therapy had had affairs with three previous therapists. Angry at seeing me, she asked, 'What the hell is she doing here?' Carl answered, as usual, in symbolic language. 'We're thinking about getting married.' Symbolically, he reassured her that she would be safe in this therapy." He was letting her know that he was already invested in another relationship and that he was not available.

Dr. Milt Miller was responsible for hiring Carl at the University of Wisconsin. It was common for Milt to invite Carl to consult with him regarding his long-term patients. One particular consultation hour stands out as a powerful example of a symbolic experience. The following is Dr. Miller's description of the experience (personal communication, September 1997).

My patient, Sarah, said it all the time, "You're a lousy doctor so I feel lousy!" Sometimes she'd say it to others, briefly quit her six-year therapy and seek outside consultation with three or four of my closest colleagues. There she would complain bitterly about mistakes I'd made, the wrong interpretations, the time I'd forgotten an appointment, etc. After three or four weeks of peace in my life, she'd call sweetly, say she realized I'd been trying to help her and ask to return to our weekly meetings.

She had plenty of symptoms. At 37, when she had come to see me, she was contemplating suicide and had made two serious attempts, rat poison and hanging. Her mother had passed away when she was seven and her father had remarried several times. She was his only child. He was a colorful, apparently successful and charismatic business executive, busy and away most of the time. Sarah had a bitter resentment towards him. She fought with him whenever they were together, often coming to blows. No other man stirred her as he did.

Sarah's life was chaotic. She drank to excess and used street drugs. She fell in love only with married men who were alcoholic and suicidal. When angry, she was noisy enough to attract early morning police visits. She was on bad terms with her apartment neighbors who had also complained that her two year old daughter was not well cared for. Her daughter was conceived with an unnamed father (she would never talk about him and he had no contact with the baby). She realized later that her decision to have a baby had a lot to do with wanting to provide her father with a grandchild as any good daughter would do. As it turned out he had little interest in the next generation.

Sarah hungered both for mother and father. I saw her behavior as self-inflicted punishment for the unworthy child she felt herself to be (since her mother disappeared and her father didn't love her much). I thought that her daughter, as an extension of herself, would also be at risk of feeling like an unworthy child. She was not an easy person to befriend, had no female friends and her friendships with men were brief, tempestuous, full of accusations and total dependency. With boyfriends, she was so full of fear of rejection that she would provoke rejection before they could take the initiative: you can't fire me, I quit! I felt that I was providing supportive care, a certain stability, advice sometimes, and after one year of psychotherapy, I put her on the antidepression medication, Tofranil. I had kept her on a moderately low dose for five years. I saw her once a week. Occasionally she came in for an emergency appointment. Sometimes, when drinking, she'd call my home at 3:00 a.m. and hang up.

Sarah had been full of suspicion when I asked permission to bring Carl Whitaker in to consult with us. She assumed I was trying to dump her as a patient. And, as she did sometimes, she had some paranoid ideas that maybe Whitaker had been sent by her father, perhaps to take her daughter away. "No such luck, my dear," I'd told her. "Dad has other important things to do. No time to mess with you. But keep dreaming." She gave Whitaker an earful. What a lousy waste of time her therapy had been. What a cold and uncaring man I was. Would he like to accept her as a patient since he must be better than I was or why would I ask his advice. All men are bastards. No one had ever loved her. She'd stopped drinking for me and I didn't appreciate it. She was sure I had much more interest in my other patients. But that didn't bother her. She didn't give a damn about me. She'd been thinking of switching to a massage therapist. At least there, you got something for your money. After awhile he interrupted her.

"Sarah," he spoke softly to her. "Why don't you get up out of your chair and go over and sit on Milt's lap, give him a good wet kiss and see if you can turn him on? No point in waiting another six years to find out."

"You're kidding," she said. "Stop stalling," he told her. "This is it, Sarah. Six years! Now or never. What have you got to lose?" She turned to me for help, I smiled weakly and found that I was clutching the bottom of my chair. She got up from her chair, walked toward me, came within a foot of me, stopped, looked at me, then turned to him and said, "He doesn't want me and I don't want him. That's the one good thing about this relationship and you want to fuck that up!" She walked in front of him. I thought she was going to hit him. "Did my father send you here, you son-of-a-bitch?"

Carl was nonchalant, relaxed, looked up at her and said, "Why would he send me here when you carry him with you wherever you go? You've got a lot of nerve Sarah, calling me a son-of-a-bitch. Your father's the son-of-a-bitch. Don't confuse us. And don't change the subject, Sarah. Do you want Milt or not? Let's settle it right now. The biggest waste of time in the world is to use a good psychiatrist as a fantasy lover." "You are a smart son-of-a-bitch" she told him. And all of a sudden, she started to laugh. She told Whitaker, "I'm glad you came today and I hope you never come again."

I continued to smile weakly, still clutching the bottom of my chair.

This single hour contaminated the relational set that had become a pattern. The therapist-patient relationship could now move forward, unfettered by the paralyzing impact of a covert seduction fantasy. That pattern, once exposed, never regained its former power.

A more mundane example of a symbolic experience occurred during a session with a young mother and her 4-year-old son. Mrs. L brought Josh to therapy because of his wild and exhausting temper tantrums. The normal course of events went something like the following. Josh would be playing in a manner that his mother felt was risky or inappropriate. When she attempted to correct him, he became loud and defiant. Mrs. L would then back off, deciding the specific issue wasn't worth the struggle. Josh prevailed. The pattern was clear, the rut deep. During their sixth session, the typical pattern repeated. Mrs. L told Josh to take his Power Ranger out of his mouth. He ignored her request. The following exchange occurred.

Mom: Take that out of your mouth this minute or I'll take it away from you.

Josh: [looks his mother directly in the eye and growls defiantly] It's mine and you can't have it. I'm a Power Ranger. You're just a mommy.

Mom: [in her frustration and embarrassment, she begins to plead with Josh] Please take it out of your mouth, honey. Be a good boy and Mommy will take you out for an ice cream on the way home.

Therapist: [to Mom] How do you think a Power Ranger mommy would handle this?

Mom: [pauses] I've never thought of that. You know, I bet she'd say it one time and if the little Power Ranger didn't respond she'd just walk over and make him do it.

Therapist: Maybe your name could be Paula, Paula Power Ranger, mother of Josh.
[Josh listens intently; he actually removes the Power Ranger from his mouth to object to his mom's new identity]

Josh: You're not Paula. You're Mommy.

Mom: Okay, Josh. I'll be Mommy now. When I want you to do something and you refuse I'll be Paula Power Ranger.

Josh: No. I'm putting my Power Ranger back in my mouth.
[Mom looks at the therapist]

Therapist: So, Paula, what's next?

Mom: Josh, give me that Power Ranger now.

Josh: No! It's mine!
[Mom walks over to Josh, takes the Power Ranger, and returns to her chair; oddly, Josh fails to resist]

Mom: Well, that was easy enough. What happened?

Therapist: I don't know, Paula.

Mom: This Paula the Power Ranger mommy is a good idea. I might even make a cape for myself.

Therapist: Sure. You could make one for Josh too, only smaller.

This playful, make-believe experience flipped the mother into a mind-set of being more comfortable with the idea of using her personal power. She had an experience that worked. She could see it was easier for her and actually better for Josh too. While the normal struggles continued, the intensity that made them so destructive diminished. Their struggles were now workable. Josh was no longer framed as an impossible child.

The following vignettes are excerpts from Carl and cotherapist David Keith's work with a schizophrenic family. Schizophrenic families are often most comfortable when engaged in intellectual discussions. They tend to feel awkward socially and are uncomfortable giving and receiving physical kinds of contact such as a pat on the back, a hug, and so forth. Intimacy can be a struggle. In the first vignette, Carl and David repeatedly challenge the family to risk being more intimate with each other. They created experiences in a variety of ways. They wrestled with the identified patient and the siblings. They teased the family about its fear of touch. They encouraged members to be more open in their discussions and made suggestions regarding how the family could practice being more affectionate with one another. The example to follow illustrates how Carl introduced the theme of intimacy versus distance in the family.

Son: How do you want to change the relationship between me and my parents and brother and sister?

Carl: Any way we can. I think any change is better than the way it is. It increases the flexibility, you know?

Son: Well, how am I inflexible? What do you mean?

Carl: The inflexibility of distance. You keep everyone at a distance. You don't let anyone in. The question is whether you can get any closer or any further away. Whether you can loosen up and get any closer or tighten up more and move even further away. Any change in distance might help.

Son: I suppose it would be good for clinically diagnostic purposes.

Mother: Why don't you talk in regular English?

Carl: Anyone can talk in regular English. When you're that important you have to talk in special phraseology.

As the session continued, the discussion shifted from merely talking about closeness and distance to actually pushing the family to take a chance. In response to the son's apparent inability to process the idea of changing proximity, Carl shifted to a concrete "suggestion" that carried tremendous symbolic significance.

Son: I can't see it. I am baffled by how you want me to change the relationship between me and my parents.

Father: To make the distance between us greater or closer.

Son: You said any change could be better. I just don't know about getting closer to my parents. I need to have some incentive to get closer to my parents. You need to tell me how it's going to do me any good to get closer to them.

Carl: I don't know, maybe if you went over and sat on your father's lap it might do a tremendous amount of good for you.

Son: I can't. No. I just can't.

Carl: It would change your whole future.

Dad: Come on over and try it. What have you got to lose? Your future looks pretty bleak now.

While the actual event of the son sitting on his dad's lap didn't occur in the moment, the seeds were sown. More significant was the fact that the father picked up on the theme and made it his own. He was more actively invested. At some level, his son felt the shift.

In the next example, Carl uses himself to facilitate movement in the family. Carl spontaneously gets up and sits on the son's lap. He then begins to wrestle with him, which results in the family's participation. Carl creates a context in which the family can experience more intimacy.

Sister: I was wondering if Tom ever craves personal contact.

Father: I'm sure he does, but it's hard to find ways of giving him personal, physical contact.

Sister: He always moves away.

Father: That's the reason I tousle his hair occasionally. It's the only way I can make contact without getting pushed away.

Carl: You could go over and sit on his lap when he's in a corner like he is now.

Father: It's very difficult. Go over and try it.
[Carl quickly hops up, crosses the room, and sits on Tom's lap. Tom initially curls up into a fetal position to fend Carl off. When that fails, he struggles to free himself from Carl's cuddling. The session has suddenly come to life. The level of affect is rapidly escalating.]

Carl: See, you can just sit on his lap when he's in the corner, like now.

Sister: Tickle him. [Carl obliges and begins tickling Tom]

Son: No. Don't tickle me, damn it.

Carl: I was just trying to help out, like your father said. This is the kind of cuddling you need.
[With Tom unable to free himself from Carl's cuddling, Mom expresses her concern, perhaps jealousy]

Mother: Maybe we ought to help him.
[Following Mom's cue, the full family comes to Tom's rescue. For the next several minutes, they roll on the floor and grapple on the couch. Arms and legs are everywhere. There are squeals of delight, groans of struggle, and ultimately the panting of exhaustion. Tom finally breaks free and moves away from the family knot. With Tom extricated, the intensity lessens. Order is restored, with only Carl and Tom's younger brother remaining on the floor. Their wrestling has shifted into a warmer, more relaxed sort of resting.]

Son: [as Tom warily circles the group hoping the session will end, he finally speaks] What time is it?

Carl: They came to rescue you, but you won't come rescue your brother.

Son: [Tom continues to pace the room] I don't want to get involved.

Carl: The family that doesn't want to get involved.

Carl punctuates the family interaction by describing them as "the family that doesn't want to get involved." The wrestling match, the physical experience of grappling together and moving beyond the limitations of words was a significant experience for the family, as well as for the therapists. The opening anxiety and vulnerability culminated in a clear sense of intimacy. The family made contact and played together, if only for a few moments. While Tom pulled out at the first opportunity, the fact of the encounter was irrefutable. There was an experience of being one body. These 5 minutes of "craziness" became a symbolic experience, serving as a reference for future relating.

Several months later, Carl was able to sit on the sidelines and coach Tom, instructing him on how to put his arms around his mother and sister to give them a hug. When Tom made rigid attempts to do so, Carl provided encouragement, saying "That's very good. The three of you could really have a good hug and it would make a hell of a lot of difference to all of you."

Carl: [to Tom] Put your arms around your mother and sister, for God's sake.

Son: I know, but it hurts too much.

Mother: We won't hurt you. You can practice on us.

Son: This is too embarrassing. I'm not that type anyway.

Carl: There will be no sexual intercourse in this room. You can relax.

David: We are very much against that. In fact, we'd have to report it and we wouldn't want to be put in that position.
[Mother and sister try to put their arms around Tom]

Mother: Well, he's pretty nice. Even your grandmother thinks so. Maybe we can get her to come along and hug you.

Carl: Sure.
[David hands the family a wooden massage tool]

Mother: What is it?

Son: This is for a massage. They use it to get me to relax, you know. [Tom shows his mother how it works by rubbing it on her back]

Mother: Does it help you relax?

Son: Maybe. [laughter]

Carl: I am very serious. I think you ought to make contact with these gals and learn how to be a human being, instead of being an isolate. I think it's ridiculous if you waste the next 4 years sitting off in the corner.

Son: Just tell me what I need to do to gain a more respectable image. Are you saying their massaging me will affect me? Will I have to massage them or what?

Carl: That's a very good idea. The three of you could really have a good day and it would make a hell of a lot of difference. What do you want, a family that lives in cubicles by themselves, rather than having to deal with each other? Put your arm around her, for God's sake. Stop isolating yourself from your mother and sister. You're ridiculous!
[The mother and sister put their arms around Tom]

Carl: Put your arm around them. Don't make it so onesided.

Son: That's ridiculous. I feel so stupid.

Carl: Put your arm around both of them and give 'em a big hug.
[Tom hugs them]

Mother: There, you did it!

Carl: Forget your image, love your family.

Carl wanted to reorganize the infrastructure of the family. The segments illustrate how he tried to rupture and restructure the family process. While Carl helped the family reintegrate, he recognized that each family was part of a unique culture that he did not belong to. He cautioned therapists not to try to remake the family but instead help them perfect their own process of living.

When describing the therapist's role in facilitating the reorganization of family patterns, Carl told the story of what happened to him when he was taking tennis lessons. The pro said, "Well, your natural pattern is pretty bad. If I tried to teach you how to really play tennis, I would have to destroy your usual way of service and then reteach you all over again. I think it would be wiser to just try to perfect the technique you've already developed, even though it's distorted" (Whitaker & Connell, 1990). Rather than contaminating a family's natural culture, Carl reempowered the family to improve their functioning through perfecting their own unique style.

USING ROLES

Carl participated in the "as if" symbolic world of therapy by taking on various roles. He created symbolic experiences by taking on the role of mother, father, grandfather, boyfriend, or husband, depending on what the family needed. Carl shifted into a role to provide an experience for the family and then quickly moved out. For example, in one session, when the oldest daughter expressed her pain related to a recent breakup with her boyfriend, her father presented himself as insensitive and peripheral to the system. Carl decided to replicate the role of father by engaging the father in irrelevant conversation. By doing this, Carl was also presenting himself as insensitive and peripheral to the family system. The youngest daughter responded by screaming at Carl, "I don't want to talk about that. I want to hear what my sister has to say!" Carl became the symbolic father. The daughter could not take on her own father directly but was very capable of expressing her feelings about Carl's insensitivity.

Likewise, the family had not been able to express anger toward the father directly. However, they did express anger toward Carl, whose actions symbolized those of the father. The father was then able to experience the family's anger indirectly. He was able to get a better sense of how his insensitivity affected the family. The father gradually became more involved with the family, and he began to invest more of himself in the treatment process. As a family experiences the father as more caring, the symbolic meaning of "father" may change.

By temporarily enacting the role of father, Carl was investing himself in the family's symbolic world with the goal of creating change in the family's infrastructure. Because Carl's enactment of the father's role represented more than the interactional process itself, the family evolved this encounter into a symbolic experience. If the family's symbolic meaning of "father" changed, their perception of the father and their perceptions of the family might change as well. As the father continued to respond to family members in a caring manner, the new symbol was further solidified.

When describing the process of role flipping, Carl said, "I think in family therapy you play with various introjects that are there. You can help the family change the introject they have for each other by being a part of the introject yourself. Each time you play with the introject, the child as the mother or father, or the introject the parents have of the child, you flip it, you cut it off." Carl emphasized that "it's an as if world. You're playing as if you are the mother or father. But you're not really the mother or father or the introject. You're acting out a part to help the family find more of itself" (personal communication, 1990).

Carl changed and reversed roles throughout the course of therapy. He believed that, by enacting a role, the client or family was free to just be. In the previous example, when Carl enacted the role of father by being insensitive to the daughter's pain, the father was then free to move out of his role. He responded by becoming more emotionally involved in the session. During the midphase of treatment, Carl and Gus Napier, a co-therapist, highlighted an important therapeutic moment that they believed facilitated a deeper level of change in the family. They described an incident in which a 10-year-old struck out at Carl. The authors wrote: "It was a complex moment. On one level, Carl usurped a parental role in the Brice family. Don, the son, had defied Carl in the way he defied his own parents and Carl took over for the parents. For a while Don became his child, he Don's father" (Napier & Whitaker, 1978, p. 185). Carl wrestled with the son, providing a model for the family of being forceful yet caring. In the subsequent weeks, Don's father replicated the process and symbolically communicated that he was more powerful than his son. According to the authors, "The therapeutic moment is highly variable and it is difficult to generalize, except that the therapist finds something extremely significant in what is happening in the family and reacts strongly, personally. The moment may be loving, humorous or angry, but is always deeply felt. The therapist's contribution comes primarily out of his own person, not out of his professional skill. He or she is pushing for change'' (Napier & Whitaker, 1978, p. 186). Carl had temporarily enacted the role of father to offer the father a model for how he might deal with his son.

The goal of this approach is to not merely induce understanding but to create an experience for the family. The therapist struggles with the dilemma of how to make the therapy a symbolic experience. Symbolic experiences are significant moments that somehow become imprinted in memory and challenge our perception of ourselves and/or our family life in some way. Carl created symbolic experiences in a multitude of ways. Whether coaching a schizophrenic on how to give a hug, wrestling with an unruly adolescent, or temporarily shifting into the role of an insensitive father, he completely invested himself in the process. He used himself to push for change. When there was movement, he got out of the way. He reassured the family that if they were willing to battle the storm, they had the power to creatively reorganize in a healthier way.

SUMMARY

This is the most crucial phase of the therapy process. Associative language is used to access the family's infrastructure, seed unconscious processes, and challenge the family's perspective. Rather than responding on a literal level to the family's pain by offering concrete solutions, our intent is to facilitate the development of a more intimate metaphorical language. We believe this language evolves through the sharing of free associative fantasies and mutual storytelling.

On the surface, Carl's work may appear outlandish, whimsical, and perhaps even crass. However, when closely tracking the core processes underlying the approach, it becomes evident that there was a method to his madness and a consistency to his interventions. Carl's free associative sharing accessed the rich world of fantasy that bubbles under the surface of all human existence. He did more than talk to families about their world or help them understand it. He wanted to find a way in, to make therapy a symbolic experience. This required a tremendous amount of personal investment. He was remarkably skilled at immersing himself in the process, offering his person as a catalyst for change while simultaneously remaining outside the system. He saluted the family in their endeavors and believed in their ability to carry on, realizing he was not part of them and would never be. His respect for families was enormous!

Chapter 10

Termination: Moving Out and Moving On

Now don't forget, when you go outside the door, your life is yours.—Carl Whitaker

In the naturally paradoxical way that endings represent new beginnings, the termination of therapy is the threshold to a new phase of living for the family. The family sought therapy in the despair of an impasse, at the pinnacle of their collective self-doubt. They felt helpless and in need of an expert. As they now contemplate leaving, there's a newfound sense of competence. They're no longer so afraid, no longer so cautious. They see the path more clearly and have accepted the fact that it's their journey to take, their hill to climb.

Termination is an integral part of the therapy process. It's the natural conclusion, the unstated goal of the therapeutic relationship. The therapeutic connection is, by definition, time limited. The therapeutic role and our professional boundaries are the conditions of the contract. Despite the family's investment and our caring, the end is in sight from the beginning.

As momentous as the decision to begin therapy can be, the family's decision to end treatment is often equally profound. Entering therapy can signify the end of the family's total reliance on self-sufficiency, as well as the end of denial. The family consciously acknowledges their limitations. This opens a new world of possibilities and implies an increasing flexibility. The ending of therapy, by contrast, connotes a readiness to face life as it is. It reflects their decision to handle adversity as it comes and to do so without the security of a coach. It's a coming of age that typically represents an increased self-confidence and a higher level of trust in one another. The termination of therapy is analogous to the day a child removes the training wheels from his or her bike and ventures onto the sidewalk.

PROCESS OF TERMINATION

While the previous five phases of the therapy process build upon each other and are more or less sequential, the termination phase can occur at any time. It is not contingent on completing the earlier phases or even on having made any discernible progress. Termination is a pure process phase. The process involves the family's readiness to take charge of and responsibility for their own living. Since it's a direct function of the family's decision-making process, it can emerge at any time and can take a multitude of shapes.

The family's level of investment in struggling together decreases as the beginning of the termination approaches. Their sense of urgency has faded. The anxiety that once fueled the sessions has diminished. In effect, they're saying they've gone as far as they're ready to go, pushed as hard as they're willing to push. It's time to stop.

While the family's diminished investment in the therapy experience is common to all endings, the actual process of termination can wear many faces. In some situations, the family decides to stop without informing the therapist. They may attend one session, decide it's not for them, and never return. The decision to end treatment can occur after or, for that matter, during any session. This type of ending, with the family opting to flex its muscles and act unilaterally, tends to be more characteristic of early-phase terminations. It's indicative of ending before really starting, stopping prior to developing a real therapeutic alliance. It's important to recognize the family's right to make this call. It is often upsetting to the therapist, who may not understand the family's reasoning and consequently feels inadequate.

More commonly, the termination pattern emerges after a longer period of interaction between the family and the therapist. While the family occasionally initiates this issue, it typically emerges more indirectly. For example, seemingly innocuous comments by any family member might trigger a termination discussion. A father might say, "You know, it doesn't feel like we're getting anywhere lately." One of the kids might say, "I'm mad I had to miss basketball practice today," or the mother might report, "We had a wonderful week." The therapist, on hearing these comments, would skip a step or two ahead and respond overtly to the covert implication. The comment might be "Maybe this is as good as it gets" or "Did you think about canceling?" These comments, rather than being indicative of the therapist's desire to end therapy, are aimed at stimulating the family to face and discuss their feelings about continuing or ending. It's a way of getting them to take themselves more seriously. The therapist's job is to help the family grapple with the issue of making a decision.

This pathway into the topic of termination is notable in that it represents a true partnership between the family and the therapist. In voicing their complaints, upsets, or satisfactions, the family is opening the door to a discussion of the status of therapy. When tinged with an undercurrent of declining interest, this discussion may represent a foreshadowing of the termination process. It's the therapist's capacity to sense the family's waning investment and to feed it back to them that triggers the actual discussion.

Central to this process is the therapist's level of awareness of personal reactions to the family's presence. When the therapist begins feeling bored or disinterested, the family needs to know. Similarly, the therapist's sense of increasing responsibility for the sessions often reflects the family's abdication of responsibility. When the therapist feels overly responsible for improving communication or for energizing the session, it may be a sign that the family has stopped rowing and is just along for the ride. As therapists become aware of their inner reactions, it's their responsibility to feed them back to the family. Our belief is that the therapist's internal feelings are not only a product of, but actually belong to, the therapy process. Initiating a conversation with the family about these internal feelings highlights the issue of continuing or terminating.

Comments from the therapist such as "You know, I don't get the feeling you're really here today," "I'm having a hard time paying attention, are you sure you want to be here?" or even "I just had the fantasy you were bored and reading from an old script; do you have anything more current?" can focus a session. Everyone becomes focused on the present, with attention clearly directed at the issue of "Why are we here today?"

While the family's decision to end therapy often generates strong feelings in the therapist, it is critical that the therapist remain respectful of the family's right to make this decision. It is a continuation of the cycle of joining and separating that not only is the core of the therapy process but is at the center of all human relationships. Whether sad or relieved, disappointed or pleased, it's the therapist's job to stand by the family as they embark into the future.

When a family actually ended therapy, Carl congratulated them on their decision to live their own life and reassured them that they could call if things did not work out. He did this even when no progress was apparent. Carl believed that if they decided to return at a later date, they would begin with a higher level of investment. They would face each other more honestly in the bounds of a more naturally intimate experience.

TIMING OF TERMINATION

The issue of timing is difficult to resolve. At a very basic level, therapy should end the moment the family decides to accept full responsibility for their living. When they embrace the fact of their process and the necessity of carving their own path, the therapist becomes irrelevant. In the symbolic-experiential model, termination is almost anticlimactic. The process is about the family getting to the point of deciding to live their life without the presence of a therapist. Central to this orientation is the conviction that the therapist doesn't have a vote in the matter. In a sense, it's not the therapist's concern. When the family leaves the office, they live their life and, it is hoped, the therapist does likewise.

Premature Termination

As a profession, we've complicated what should be a simple, straightforward process by inferring that the therapist should have a voice in the family's decision to terminate, or at least should sanction that decision. We fail to see that the very idea of the therapist casting a vote interferes with the family taking full responsibility for their actions. The therapist's vote dismisses the family's capacity to make this critical decision.

The commonly used phrase *premature termination* is an odd way of thinking about the ending of therapy. It suggests the family is unprepared for their future. It's actually a misnomer to think of this term as having anything to do with the family at all. It's more reflective of the therapist's feelings about the family, of the therapist's expectations of them. The concept of premature termination confuses the issue of whose experience is relevant to the decision to end. This confusion brings to mind the story of a young newlywed couple making an early visit to a sex therapist.:

Wife: [sheepishly] Well, Doctor, this is hard to talk about, but we really need help. We've been married 2 weeks now and our sex life is really frustrating.

Therapist: Okay, so tell me a bit more. Try to be more specific.
[Wife nervously glances at husband before resuming]

Wife: Well, Doctor, I'm sure you're familiar with this problem. My husband has a problem with premature ejaculation.
[Therapist glances at the husband, who appears unusually calm; there's no evidence of the typical degree of upset or embarrassment]

Therapist: So Joe, tell me about your sexual frustration.

Husband: I'm not sexually frustrated.

Therapist: Well, okay, but what about your problem?

Husband: What problem? I don't have a problem.

Therapist: You know, your premature ejaculation? Having orgasms too soon.

Husband: Premature for who? I rather enjoy them.

Here the politely frustrated young wife and the self-centered young husband beautifully portray the confusion that emerges when there's a lack of clarity about who's responsible for whose experience. His sexual response time, while frustrating to his wife, causes no distress for Joe. The premature ejaculation may indeed be a problem, but it's a problem for her, not for him.

"Premature for whom?" is also the question we must ponder. The family may be well satisfied with their current experience of living. They may be quite comfortable with their decision to end the therapy. They don't necessarily share our fears, worries, or concerns about their future functioning.

Abrupt Endings

For the symbolic-experiential therapist, the descriptive term *abrupt ending* replaces the phrase premature termination. No matter how quickly therapy may end, no matter how precipitous it may seem, the therapist must trust the family's wisdom. To assume that the experience was a failure, had no impact, or was simply a waste of time may be inaccurate.

Carl often told the story of a young man who wandered into his office one day, sat in a chair directly across from him, and, with his legs crossed, silently stared at him. As the session progressed, the young man began to swing his right leg. Carl looked him in the eye and said, "Listen, if you want to kick me, then kick me. Don't just sit there pretending." With that, the young man kicked Carl solidly in the shin. Without hesitating, Carl returned the favor, but with a bit more emphasis. After another 10 minutes of silence, they repeated their rather unorthodox way of connecting. The pattern repeated two more times before the session ended. As the young man got up to leave, Carl asked if he would like to meet again. The young man smiled, saying "That won't be necessary. You've helped me quite enough already." Despite the unconventional nature of their contact and the impossibility of actually verifying the long-term impact of this encounter, Carl felt good about the session. He believed that the experience had been real and that if the client had needed more contact, he would have returned.

In a similar vein, a therapist once worked with a couple consisting of a meek, unhappy woman and her cynical bully of a husband. The woman stormed out of the office after the therapist asked if she had any sense of how her passivity fed her husband's tendency to push her around. She was angry enough to knock the pictures from the wall. She failed to schedule any additional sessions and gave up trying to convince her spouse to seek individual therapy. Two years later, the therapist ran into her in the hospital elevator. She made a point of thanking him for providing the opportunity to finally stand up to her husband. She realized something about her own power after having the courage to walk out of therapy. Within 2 months, she had left her abusive husband. The divorce was finalized 6 months later. While the therapist obviously could not know the ultimate impact of that experience, it was a turning point in the woman's life.

A central component of this sort of experience is the therapist's confidence that the family will handle the stress and make the decisions they need to make. If the therapist in the previous example had tried to stop the woman from leaving, talk her into resuming the session, or call her to reschedule, it would have sabotaged her newfound determination to take charge of her own living.

Prolonged Endings

Some families, having engaged in and benefited from the treatment process, are reluctant to leave. They resist ending not because of the current depth of their pain but because they fear falling back into the old ruts. While they're clearly more competent and able to handle life as it unfolds, they're not confident of their abilities.

A therapist recently worked with a couple who had just passed their 25th anniversary. The relationship was marked by rather dramatic ups and downs. It was stable in the sense that their struggles weren't relationship threatening. They mentioned divorce when they were angry but never in a serious fashion. Although they were able to recognize the fact of their mutual caring, they weren't having much fun together. Despite the fact that they both were aware of an undercurrent of love in their relationship, this love wasn't apparent in their day-to-day living. They feared that they were growing apart.

After 6 months of fairly regular therapy, their communication had improved. They had finally come together on how to handle their three challenging teenagers and established more comfortable boundaries with their extended family. They rebounded from fights much more quickly. Sex was once again part of their relationship. Despite these changes, they remained dissatisfied with the quality of their connection. They were reluctant to end treatment.

In their sessions, which occurred every 2 or 3 weeks, discussion steadfastly focused on why they weren't actually doing what they said they wanted to do. In the prior 6 months, they had moved from believing that they no longer had much in common to enjoying fantasies of a return to their dating days. They spoke of the passion they shared for music, movies, and the outdoors during their college days. During sessions they would commit to blocking out time to spend together, to making their personal relationship a priority. Yet 3 weeks later they would return, saying "Well, once again, we didn't do anything together." Nancy had to work overtime or Mike's home repair project got out of hand. This became the pattern. While the "reasons" for their lack of personal time together changed, the fact remained resolute.

As Mike and Nancy began another session with their all-too-familiar report, a visual image of Grant Wood's classic painting, *American Gothic*, flashed through the therapist's mind. As he shared this vision, the tone changed.

Therapist: You know, when you began reporting another 3 weeks without change I suddenly saw that famous picture, *American Gothic*. You know, the husband and wife, side by side, pitchfork and all. But this time, it had your faces on it. Wow! You guys are good for me. I had always assumed they were miserable in their stoicism. It just occurred to me that maybe they were happy, or at least content together. It no longer seems so gruesome.
[Pause]

Mike: You know, you might be right. I don't think we're really so unhappy with each other. We're a lot more comfortable together than we were 6 months ago. Divorce is no longer even mentioned.

Nancy: That's true. We're just so busy that it's hard to find time to relax together. Life is just too hectic. I think we're afraid of losing touch again and going back to those miserable fights we used to have. It helps to know that we've got an appointment scheduled. We know we won't drift too far before facing it.

Therapist: I've got an idea. Rather than keeping your scheduled session in 3 weeks, why not take that time and go shopping for a poster of *American Gothic*? When you get home with it, put your faces on it and hang it above your bed. On some days it might help you relax and appreciate your undercurrent connection. On others the pitchfork might get you to goose each other a little more.

Nine weeks later, Mike and Nancy returned for what turned out to be their final session. They were wearing matching *American Gothic* T-shirts with smiles superimposed over the original stoicism.

One of the interesting aspects of this case was the covert collusion between the couple and the therapist to continue the therapy beyond its real usefulness. Until the therapist reported the image of the painting, he too was unsure of the couple's readiness to fend for themselves. Once the symbolism of the painting changed, the anxiety lessened, and they were all more free to move ahead.

Are "Endings" Ever Final?

The decision to end a particular course of therapy does not convey an objective finality; rather, it reflects a sense of readiness to move ahead with the process of living. The family moves on to the next chapter in their story, this time without a guide accompanying them. The therapist lets go and supports their move, without abandoning them. The therapist respects the family's right to decide to end the treatment, conveying a sense of respect for their right to decide to return if they so desire.

Perhaps an even more profound aspect of the formal ending of therapy is the bilateral internalization of each other that often occurs between the therapist and the family. If the experience has been fruitful—that is, if there has been a real investment in the therapeutic process and in one another—all of the participants internalize ideas, feelings, and voices that are part of the therapeutic "we." These internalizations are available when needed. Family members are free to call them up for comfort.

TERMINATION PHASE TECHNIQUES

Four techniques used to facilitate the termination process are (a) making the covert overt, (b) highlighting changes and competencies, (c) reversing roles, and (d) letting the family know you'll survive.

Making the Covert Overt

Carl moved in on any family members not invested in the therapy. Rather than arguing with them, interpreting it as resistance, or engaging in an adversarial dance about the value of therapy, he simply followed their lead and went a step further. He overtly voiced the issue of termination. He activated the entire family by clearly underscoring this topic. It forced them to face the decision. They either concluded that it was time to end or resumed the process with renewed vigor.

Carl interpreted such comments as "We really don't have anything to talk about" or "We're getting so busy" as a family's desire to tackle their world on their own. He described this as the family's "flight into health" (Napier & Whitaker, 1978). Carl took termination statements seriously as an acknowledgment of family strength. He respected a family's suggestion that perhaps it was time to stop. It was part of Carl's belief that when a family realizes they can live their life on their own, without a coach, the therapy has been successful.

The following vignette highlights this technique with a couple early in the therapy process. During this phase, prior to fully establishing a solid therapeutic relationship, the therapist may seem abrupt or even disinterested. The therapist addresses the issue of continuing therapy, although not fully connected with the couple. They must actively decide whether to proceed or not.

In the fourth session with a couple at an impasse, Pete, the 38-year-old attorney husband, arrived 25 minutes late. Pete was obviously agitated as he settled in. He loosened his tie, paced a bit, and scowled at Linda, his wife of 10 years, before taking a seat at the far end of the couch.

Pete: Hey, can we start any later? I'm losing too much time at work. This is costing us money.

Therapist: So, how did you decide to even come today?

Pete: Well, I thought of not coming. The damn stuff isn't helping anyway.

Therapist: You know, if you left right now you might make it back to the office in time to do another billable hour or two. You'd only lose an hour or so.

Pete: No. I'm here now. I'll stay until the end of the hour.

Therapist: You know you don't have to. Of course, I'd charge you anyway. That's just business.

Pete: Since I came, I might as well stay.

Therapist: Well, I'm not so sure. Linda, is it okay with you if we stop?

Linda: We're just getting started.

Therapist: I know, but it's a shame for Pete to lose all that time at work. Money's important.

Linda: I'm sick of all this talk about work. Work and money are all he ever thinks about. Listen, Pete, we're here for a reason. I'm not going to put up with this anymore.

Following this brief exchange, the session continued with a renewed intensity. Having consciously faced the possibility of ending without accomplishing anything, Linda's participation and level of investment accelerated. She wanted to face issues previously masked. She was no longer waiting for the therapist to figure them out and provide a cure. As she took the initiative, their undercurrent alienation and the profound pain of their impersonal sex life came to the fore.

Carl often gave voice to the philosophical posture "It's better to fail to start than to start and fail." This was true not only at the onset of therapy but at every step along the way. The preceding example illustrated how Carl immediately began to pull out in response to the husband's lack of investment. Someone in the family must provide the real impetus to change. The therapist can facilitate the process but can't fuel it.

There are times when the therapist puts words to an undercurrent feeling of boredom or indifference, even though the family makes no reference to it. This is often the case with families who have mistakenly associated the real progress they've made with the physical reality of sitting in the therapist's office. They've become dependent on being "in therapy," even though they're handling life quite competently. They no longer need training wheels but are reluctant to remove them.

The intervention is more personal when it is used with couples who have actually engaged in the therapy process and worked through the various phases of therapy. It emerges out of the therapeutic connection and is specific to particular couples. In the case that follows, Carl's connection with the couple led to a free associative picture that opened the territory for them to discuss termination.

The sessions had lost their zip after nearly a year of productive work with a delightful young couple, both products of wildly dysfunctional families. They were invested in one another and committed to having a "healthy" relationship. Their dedication led them to commute more than an hour each way to attend sessions. Following the sessions, they typically stopped for dinner before the drive home. Midway through a particularly pleasant but uneventful hour, the following exchange occurred.

Therapist: You know, I just had a vivid image of the two of you dancing together. When's the last time you hit the dance floor?

Wife: Wow, I don't know! We used to love to go out, and Jack is a great dancer. I guess we just haven't made the time for it lately.

Therapist: How about it, Jack? Do you remember?

Husband: No, but we did used to really love it. We'd dance all night. Close the place down. We just don't have the time anymore.

Therapist: Well, that sounds crazy to me. Sounds like what happened to your folks. They got so busy they forgot about living. [pauses] Hey, I know how to fix the time problem. Why not skip your therapy the next 2 weeks and spend it on the dance floor?

Wife: I'd love to. I like that idea.

Husband: I do too, but remember we promised to continue to work on our relationship. Therapy is a priority. We don't want to fall back to where we felt like strangers. We need to continue to communicate.

Therapist: Well, I'm all for that. But for next week, why not let your bodies do the communicating on the dance floor? You might have more fun, and the cover charge is a lot less expensive than it is here.

Further conversation revealed that while the couple was fearful of falling back into the old pattern of not communicating, they had secretly begun to wonder if they weren't ready to handle it on their own. The formality of a regularly scheduled appointment was reassuring. It gave them a sense of confidence that they wouldn't regress. When the therapist suggested another way of being together, they were open to the idea.

Linda and Jack did go dancing and recaptured some of the liveliness of their dating years. They also continued in therapy but at a less frequent rate. Over the next 6 months, sessions went from weekly, to bimonthly, to monthly. At that point, treatment was terminated with the option of the couple resuming if they ever felt they were losing the rhythm.

Highlighting Changes and Competencies

As families approach the end of therapy, it's important that they recognize and consolidate the real investment they've made and the real progress they've achieved. One method for facilitating this is to highlight the interactive processes that reflect change. Through support of their efforts to solve their own problems and resolve their own impasses, the family becomes even more courageous. The therapist can engender a sense of empowerment by reminding the family of the skills they've demonstrated and the successes they've achieved. Simply underscoring their actual competencies can create a symbolic frame that transforms a single experience into a family fable that can guide their living.

For example, one family with unruly adolescent sons had great difficulty setting and enforcing limits with them. On one particular evening, the father was tired of the old pattern of arguing about curfew. He said to his argumentative son, "You know, I'm tired of this. From now on, when you argue with me about curfew, you'll have to come home one-half hour earlier." The son began his usual tirade of reasons why midnight was too early. His father said emphatically, "Now you'll be home at 11:30; would you be interested in making it 11:00? It really doesn't matter to me!" The son realized he was in a losing battle and dropped the topic. The therapist was enthusiastic with congratulations and said, "Oh my, I might be out of a job if you get too good at this! Good for you!" This helped the father recognize he was not powerless to deal with his son but, rather, needed to be clearer and firmer with his expectations. Shortly after this encounter, the family terminated. Despite their protests, adolescents need to know their parents are in charge. They can always break the limits but need consequences for infractions. Carl believed a therapist should applaud any attempt a family member makes to be different in the final stages of therapy.

In addition to the more dramatic changes in a family's style of interacting, a multitude of subtle, almost imperceptible shifts can be of great significance. Carl and co-therapist Dr. Gus Napier described what they perceived to be change in one couple: "We began to see highly significant little things; they glanced at each other more often; they sat together; occasionally their hands touched. They did not do anything dramatically different, they were different. It was as though somewhere the sun had come out and the room gradually lightened" (Napier & Whitaker, 1978, p. 265). Similarly, Carl and co-therapist Dr. David Keith wrote about another client. "Bill left the interview room in a different way. It was our sense that he had been hooked that day. He parted with a warm handshake. Bill never allowed himself to be touched before, let alone offering his hand. It was the offering of his hand and the warmth in his eyes that was suggestive of change" (Keith & Whitaker, 1980, p. 51).

Through comments on these less obvious shifts in behavior, family members typically learn to pay more attention to overlooked personal aspects of their relationships. Their capacity to connect is enhanced, and they can become more appreciative of one another.

Reversing Roles

Another technique for facilitating the termination process and empowering the family is to engage in a role reversal of sorts by asking the family for feedback about how you functioned as their therapist. Through asking the family to consciously focus on and discuss their views of how well or how poorly you worked with them, their residual transference fantasies are contaminated. They have the opportunity to comment not only on your role function but also on their experience of your mistakes and limitations.

In the later stages of therapy, Carl would ask questions such as the following: "Could you give me some idea of how I could have done a better job?" "Can you tell me about how I've failed in working with you, even though we are now advancing?" "Was I too harsh in the early days?" "Was I too soft in the later days?" and "Did you sense my own hunger for help?" Carl believed the family's capacity to provide corrective feedback to the therapist was evidence of their increased capacity for autonomous functioning. They were feeling competent enough to release the therapist as guru and revel in their perceptions of his humanness. In a sense, the therapist becomes a patient to the family.

Carl compared this phase with the empty nest in normal family life. When parents are preparing to launch their children and the responsibility of parenthood begins to fade, the adolescent should be given the opportunity to look her or his parents in the eye and give them direct feedback about their efforts. This often serves as a coming of age experience for the adolescent. She or he has the sense of being treated as an authority and being able to offer helpful advice to the older generation. This experience of being "a parent to your own parents" often helps adolescents take more responsibility for their own living.

Carl recalled the "going away gift of correctiveness" his own son gave him prior to leaving home. In response to Carl's request for some feedback about where he had failed as a father, his son replied, "You know, one of the problems in our living was that you would give me a project, and, as I got towards the end of it, you couldn't stand the suspense and you'd take it over. At first I worried that I was incompetent to finish the job. Later on I realized it had more to do with you than with me. That made it easier to take." This brings to mind the old saying "Be careful what you ask for, you just might get it." Parenting is a humbling experience. Fortunately, humbling experiences make one more human.

When anxious and in need of relief, therapists, much like concerned parents, have a hard time truly letting go. Rather than trusting that the family is ready to test their wings, the therapist may become protective. The temptation is to say "Why don't you stay a bit longer so I can correct your table manners?" or "Your preparation would be so much more complete if you would just slow down a little and leave at a more appropriate time." While typically well intended, such maneuvers constitute a misuse of power, taking advantage of transference to set up some kind of control system. During the last phase of therapy, the goal is to move away from this dependency. Carl would say "Now, don't forget when you go outside the door, your life is yours. I would be glad to be part of it if you come back, if you want me to. But don't expect to live up to what I say. You make up your own life."

Letting the Family Know You'll Survive

Finally, Carl stressed the need to inform the family that you will not be a "lonesome mother." The family needs to know that the therapist has other patients and a life separate from the family; they don't need to panic about leaving the therapist alone. Otherwise, the family may prolong termination because they think the therapist wants them to continue. Carl would introduce "bits of his real world" by talking about new projects he was working on, a trip he was planning with his family, or an encounter with another family. He thanked the family for the opportunity to work with them. He commented on what he had learned from them and wished them well on their journey.

SUMMARY

The objective of family therapy is to open up the family's unconscious processes to new experiences. The therapist views any hint that connotes a slowing or alteration of the family's initiative as a potential way of ending. Stop therapy whenever the family is willing to take a chance on living without a stranger wandering around in their inner world.

In family therapy, all is well if it ends well. Concluding the nuclear processes of family therapy is as significant for the lives of the family as was the beginning. The onset and the ending are natural complements of each other, counterparts that bracket a significant episode in the family's life. The disengaging of a family ideally includes a thoughtful retrospective of remembrances, an attempt to understand the powerful events that have swept through the family. It is difficult to express anger; it is even more difficult to express love. This openness is particularly powerful in the final stage of the therapy process. It should be clear, however, that for every future challenge and pitfall, there is the possibility of exciting growth for the therapist as well as for the family.

Chapter 11

Consultation

Over the years, I have become more impressed, at times awed, by the power of a consultant, whom I affectionately call foster father.—Carl Whitaker

Consultation is a technique used, since the early 1940s, to evaluate the therapeutic alliance and resolve therapeutic impasses. The consultant, as an outsider, experiences the complexities of a system that are rarely encountered by the participants. Consultation is not therapy, although it may be therapeutically useful. Therapy offers concerns and security to help the family resolve ambivalence with their own assertive competence. Consultation adds "indifference" to the therapy process, the ability to act as an advisor rather than a caretaker. Consultation is an effort to intensify a therapy system's organization and competence. One of the goals of consultation is to modify the emotional currents that contribute to impasses. Another goal is to remove obstacles that impede the system's growth (Connell & Russell, 1986; Connell, Whitaker, Garfield, & Connell, 1990; Whitaker, 1986). The focus of a consultation is therefore on the therapeutic system. The consultation is never a critique of the therapist's work; rather, it is a review of the therapy process.

Family therapy presents a series of challenges to the intelligence, maturity, and humanness of any therapist who risks trying it. The simple truth is that a therapist must use power and considerable effort with the family in order to keep the family moving in its growth. At a natural point of diminishing movement or in the presence of a growing impasse, an outsider's perceptions and contributions can create a new force, "raising the temperature" of the therapeutic group. As the family therapist listens to the consultant's interaction, new information is generated to expand his or her experience. The therapist is free to transcend

We wish to acknowledge Dr. David Keith for providing the case consultation used in this chapter, and we thank him for his helpful process comments.

routinized patterns of relating to the family and learn from the consultant new ways to respond to the family's usual ploys.

A consultation interview often reveals information previously unknown. This is not because of the therapist's inadequacy, but because the therapist's caring interferes with his or her freedom to stimulate anxiety. Consultants can intrusively disrupt the power that families have to co-opt therapists by making them members of the family or by excluding them. Having a consultation means that the consultant will always be present in the mind of the family and on call should the situation become uncomfortable or ineffective. As the therapist dares to be vulnerable by deliberately going ''one-down'' to talk about concerns that he or she is not as effective as he or she would like to be, the therapist models for the family the hope that they too can be vulnerable without being destroyed.

This chapter describes a consultation in a case in which an impasse complicates ongoing family therapy. An impasse involves a deterioration in the therapeutic relationship and, as such, reflects a slowing of the therapy process. The family and the therapist withdraw involvement in the change process, preferring to maintain the status quo. An impasse is always a bilateral failure to expand the range of the therapeutic alliance. Both the family and therapist are a factor. Every impasse involves a lack of collaboration as the larger family-plus-therapist system becomes stuck in rigid and recurring patterns. The impasse may be explicit or implicit, displaced or direct, conscious or unconscious. The most common impasse is when the therapist cares too much and, in that caring, assumes too much responsibility for the family in the real world.

The consultation described here is based on the conceptual framework of symbolic-experiential family therapy. Although consultation is not therapy, techniques used in this consultation are congruent with the dynamic principles of the therapy process outlined in previous chapters. A consultation routinely lasts 90 minutes. The remainder of this chapter identifies critical states in the consultation process and expands the principal ingredients of the procedure. We hope that the presentation of much of a single consultation, as well as our process comments, will provide a slightly different benchmark of how to integrate a symbolic-experiential perspective into your work with families. The family described here consisted of a grandmother (Patty, 68 years of age), mother (Kay, 42), and daughter (Sara, 16).

ENTRY

Gaining entry into the therapy system is a critical dimension of the consultation. As an outsider, the consultant is an invader in the ongoing therapy relationship (Whitaker, 1986). Consultation is a triangle of competing alliances: the therapist's alliance with the family, the alliance of therapist and consultant, and the alliance of the therapy system and the consultant. The consultant gains permission to join with the system based on her or his relationship with the therapist. We recommend bringing in a peer who knows you and your style of therapy.

It is best if the consultant comes into the session without prior briefing and knows nothing of the family before the interview. Prior information may interfere with the consultant's experiencing the system in the "here and now." The introduction should be simple and brief and move quickly into a review of the family's history and the course of the therapy to date. The therapist presents the history in a simple and direct fashion without sounding overly psychological. The consultant needs to hear the shared beliefs of family members, gather information about roles and status, and hear about the family's painful experiences.

Consultant: I thought we could just say a word about what we're up to. This interview is intended to provide some help to your therapist in working with you and you in working with each other. I hope you have a useful experience. [looks to the therapist] Why don't you start by giving me a brief review of this family and your time together.

Therapist: Let's start out by saying Patty has had the opportunity to get to know her grandchildren, Sara and her older brother Thomas, because they have lived with her for a long time. Thomas couldn't be with us today. Since the children were young, they stayed with their grandmother most of the time, while Kay worked. This allowed Kay to support herself and her family and also put herself through a beautician training program. Sara is in her sophomore year of high school and is making decisions about what's important to her and how hard to work. She is also making some discoveries that she'd like to spend more time with her mom. This coincides with a time that Kay is very busy with her own goals but is also wanting to be with her daughter. Kay and Patty have been working together to parent two teenagers. It hasn't been without its challenges. I think that's really where we were when we got started 9 months ago.

Consultant: Right after Christmas? Around January.

Therapist: Yes. The main focus at that time was to work out some arrangements whereby Patty and Kay were clear about who was going to do what in the family. Kay was working and going to school. The children were living with Patty. That still remains the case. Right now Kay and Patty are doing fairly well. There have been some changes.

The therapist's introduction may be too accepting of all that is going on in this family. She accepts that Thomas "couldn't be with us today." We believe he could have been with them if it were clear that it was important. His absence might reflect a symbolic struggle for this family around issues of belonging.

It is best if the therapist finishes describing the family before they are brought into the discussion. The family has the opportunity to hear the therapist talking about them. Hearing about life is different than living it. What matters is the family's access to the therapist's perceptions and their willingness to listen. The consultant's approach in the first few minutes can either ease or heighten their anxiety and can set the tone of the interview. The consultant starts the session wanting to be helpful. If the family initially feels understood and respected, the system may respond with increased openness and engage in a reciprocal give and take later in the consultation. The purpose is clearly to enrich the therapy project and facilitate movement of the process.

STRUCTURING

The consultant's next task includes an assessment of the perceptions of the problems that brought the family to therapy and the agreed-upon methods of operation for ongoing therapy. The best situation for therapeutic effectiveness occurs when perceptions of stresses, goals, and methods of operation are congruent. Structuring involves the clarification of what members of the therapeutic system want from each other and what stresses are driving the family in treatment. It includes an assessment of how well the therapy system has expanded the symptom into an interpersonal framework. At this stage, the consultation focuses as much (or more) on process and feeling as on content and thinking.

Consultant: Was there a crisis that started your working with them?

Therapist: The original problem was Sara's school performance. Her grandmother and mother were concerned that she really didn't care about school. What we worked on initially was who was going to do what part of the parenting.

Consultant: So Sara was having trouble in school. Another part of the problem was how the parent responsibility was balanced. Has Sara's brother been part of the therapy process?

Therapist: Thomas has not been part of the process. He's been able to maintain a more independent lifestyle.

Consultant: Do you think that has something to do with why they came to see you? That he left and knocked things out of balance?

Therapist: That's an interesting thought. I don't know whether he did.

Consultant: How about the kids' father? Where is he?

Therapist: Sara does not have contact with or know her father. That is also true with Thomas.

Consultant: How about a grandfather?

Grandmother: He's been dead 13 years, Sara barely knew him. She was 3.

Consultant: So there aren't many men around in the family?

Therapist: No, not too many men.

Consultant: I hear that's what it's going to be like in about five generations. The men will almost be extinct.

The consultant quickly focuses on the crucial question of what happened that made the family decide to seek help. For the most part, the consultant leaves the identified patient alone. Instead he continues to ask questions concerning where the rest of the family is. The consultant's focus is to expand the symptom by exploring what the rest of the family does to contribute to their trouble. The consultant expands the symptom to include not only the first but the second generation.

The male consultant handles structuring with finesse. He uses self-mocking irony in suggesting that men will be fading out from sheer uselessness. The use of humor is a way to join with the family. It increases the freedom to be playful and imaginative. The consultant attempts to establish the message that nothing is sacred in relation to him.

ACTIVATING STRESS

The next task for the consultant is to gently activate group stress by asking for feedback from the family concerning how therapy has gone. This is a major point of the consultation, to determine whether the therapy is working. The family has the opportunity to comment on its usefulness. The consultation is lively because of the flavor of uncertainty. The consultant now takes over the interview. He or she may address particular issues in the family or in the therapeutic relationship. The consultant wants to talk not only about the family's life but about how therapy contributes to their living.

Consultant: So, Grandmother, do you want to start off by saying how the therapy has gone or how you're working?

Grandmother: Their mother always says that I'm a Gestapo and that she's more easygoing. She thinks I'm doing what I did when I raised her and says it doesn't work today.

Consultant: You mean being a Gestapo in the old days worked better than it does now?

Grandmother: I didn't have any trouble with either one. I had a boy and a girl. I've had no trouble with Thomas either, but Sara doesn't like the Gestapo type.

Consultant: So, how have you managed to change? Grandmothers are supposed to be impossible, you know!

Grandmother: Well, I talk to Kay if we have a problem. I call her up and she tells me to ease off.

Consultant: Did you find it hard to shift?

Grandmother: After raising my own kids, it's hard to raise grandkids.

Consultant: Yeah, I would think that it would be tough to go back to being full-time again.

Grandmother: They don't understand.

Consultant: You mean you enjoy being a Gestapo, because her mother is a softy?

Mother: No. I don't think she enjoys it, no.

Consultant: How about it, Sara? What have you noticed about this therapy experience you've had?

Daughter: [looks at the grandmother] She's lightened up a little bit, not much, but a little bit. She's getting there. It may take a while.

Consultant: What else has gone on besides Grandmother changing? Do you think the main reason you came to therapy was to help your mother get her mother straightened out? That would be an undercover job.

Mother: Sara straightened out her ''no's.'' She defies being told no.

Daughter: I hate being told what to do.

The consultant has followed a consistent pattern for speaking within the therapy system. He speaks first to the therapist and follows that interaction by involving other family members, starting with the grandmother. The Gestapo, of course, was Hitler's secret police. She is using a metaphorical word to describe herself. Like the consultant, she is also being self-mocking and ironic. It suggests she has some capacity to play with her world. This ability to play is a sign of health.

The consultant adopts the grandmother's language and uses a word that has caught his attention to gain access to some of the underlying family struggles. He plays with the picture image of a Gestapo to communicate on a symbolic level. It allows the grandmother to explore nondefensively whether her methods are out of date. She acknowledges the difficulty of going back to being a mother. Comebacks in family living, as in professional sports, are tempting but can be difficult. The consultant also stresses the interpersonal aspect of this struggle. He suggests that perhaps grandmother is tough with the kids not so much in response to them and their needs but because she is giving her daughter lessons in how to parent.

Finally, Sara, the ''problem,'' is invited to share her experience of the therapy. In being asked to comment on her experience, she has the opportunity to diagnose other dyads, triads, and subgroups of the system. Sara's comments suggest that the grandmother is the patient in need of help or healing. The consultant further disrupts the family's tendency to focus on Sara as the scapegoat. He suggests she is doing an ''undercover job'' in an attempt to straighten out the preceding generational struggles between her mother and grandmother.

CREATIVE CONFUSION

Once a consultation has begun, the therapy system, consisting of family and therapist, usually reverts to its earlier condition. Thus, the consultant attempts to penetrate the therapy relationship so deeply that underlying patterns are unsustainable. The consultant becomes a deliberate stress activator. The resulting confusion contributes to the fluctuation in process necessary for the system to remain flexible. Creating confusion forces the system in new and unexpected directions. To create confusion, the consultant may use confrontation to say what is on his or her mind. He or she is not bound by the rules of the therapy system, because there is no contract to provide ongoing care. The consultant's role should be directed toward the facilitation of active participation among therapy system members. The consultant should use language containing several levels of meaning. Deviation amplification and double meaning create opportunities to redefine relationships and experiences. A "tongue-in-cheek" quality helps the system tolerate its anxiety.

Mother: If you tell Sara not to do something, she'll do it.

Consultant: [to Mom] Do you ever get tricky and work it the other way? Tell her to do the opposite? You know, like stay out till 3 a.m. so she gets in by 10:30? [to daughter] You should take your grandmother along sometime. She could find out what you do and probably wouldn't have to worry so much.

Mother: We find out a lot of stuff she does. We catch her in lies. She thinks we're dumb. She pulls some dumb things.

Consultant: Well, that's your job, Sara. You know, to make the older generation feel dumb! That's what you're supposed to do when you're a teenager.

Mother: She keeps trying it out and gets caught every time.

Consultant: What's gone wrong? Did you lose your touch?

Daughter: I don't know.

Consultant: The game's just not as interesting anymore?

Mother: She tried a good one yesterday. She told me there wasn't any school, that it was an in-service day. So, I called the school and caught her.

Consultant: It sounds like one of the problems is that your mother and grandmother are getting smarter.

Therapist: I was really curious about your losing your touch. I hadn't thought of it quite like that before.

Consultant: Maybe she's just losing her dedication.

Grandmother: Last week she missed Monday. She was sick. Tuesday her mother couldn't get her up. She told me her mother had said she could spend the day with her.

Daughter: That's the only chance I get. She's at work all the time or else she's with you.

In this segment, the consultant immediately moves to a language of options to offer some ways Mother and Grandmother could become more playful in their roles. The suggestions are absurd in order to challenge their rigid way of thinking. The consultant emphasizes that there are many options in life. When he tells Sara she is only being a teenager who is losing her touch, he redefines and normalizes the pathology. The goal is to challenge a rigid belief system and create a shift in thinking about Sara's behavior.

As the consultation process continues, emotions begin to heat up, and the obstacles to therapy begin to reemerge. The primary purpose of the consultation is to help the family remain engaged with one another and more effective in their use of feelings. Generally, the therapist's lack of sensitivity or dynamic force will be involved in the reintroduction of the impasse. In order to reinstate the therapeutic process, the consultant fights against factors that contribute to the therapist becoming an introjected member of the family. In a continuation of the previous discussion, the grandmother questions Sara's statement.

Grandmother: That's not true. You could spend time with your mother on weekends, but you chose to spend your time with your friends.

Daughter: I still wouldn't have time alone with her on weekends. She's here with you.

Grandmother: Well, I'm not the problem. You choose Elizabeth over your mother and me.

Therapist: Sara has more choices than she's taking advantage of. It makes me wonder if she really wants to spend time with her mom or not. Their time together is very limited. It puts pressure on the family.

Consultant: [to Mom] Do you think you've turned into a workaholic over the last couple of years?

Mother: No, it's always been the same. I don't have any choice. It's just one of those things.

Consultant: You're saying you worked out the parenting arrangement. My idea when she said that was that you were elected mother [to grandmother] and you were elected father [to mother].

Mother: I don't know if I got elected. When I work I make the kids go to my mother's house. When I'm home they're with me, but I work 5 days a week, sometimes 6. Even as teenagers, I think they need supervision. I live in an apartment and if they make too much noise I could get tossed out. The rule was always that when I go to work they go to her house. It's been that way forever. I'm always at work, so they're always at her house.

Grandmother: Unless they go out. Sara gets mad and leaves. She's not supposed to walk the streets at night. One night she went out without permission and when she came back I said, "You're not going out tomorrow." The next day she came home with her girlfriends and said, "I don't want to live here anymore. I'm going to live at my friend's." Another night I told her to stay in because she had skipped school. Well, her mother let her go out to shop for a purse. So I told her she had to stay in the next night. She wrote a letter saying she wanted to die and threatened to take an overdose of Tylenol. Later she said it was dumb. She had a whole bottle but only took one or two.

In this segment, the therapist seems to be pushing Sara back into the role of scapegoat. She is trying to guide Sara and help her make better choices. The therapy stalls because of the way the problem is constructed. The therapist has cornered Sara with her statement, so the consultant disrupts the process by asking the mother whether she has turned into a workaholic. He suspects that Sara is acting out to increase family members' emotional investment in each other.

Mother and Grandmother quickly resist the consultant's attempt to disrupt the process. They prefer to keep the focus on Sara's misbehavior rather than talk about how they contribute to the problem. They up the ante by describing Sara's trump card: her threat of suicide. The therapist did not mention this in her introduction. Suicide is an issue that is always acknowledged and expanded. To ignore or underestimate it is to make it more likely to happen. The consultant's task is to identify and amplify affectively loaded issues that may be unaddressed in the therapy. It is a time to delve into avoided issues. The goal is to stimulate disclosure around neglected issues so as to create opportunities for discussion of these topics.

Consultant: Just like that, you said you were thinking about killing yourself. God, what do you think would happen to these two if you did kill yourself?

Grandmother: Does she just say that because she wants her own way? Do you call her bluff, or what do you do? Well, how can you stop them anyway? Say she decides to take them. She could go out of the home and still take them. There's no way you can stop it.

Consultant: Well, you can raise hell with her about it. Tell her you'd never forgive her if she did. Say you wouldn't buy her a tombstone or you'd have a funeral with a closed casket and nobody could come.

Grandmother: I don't know if other kids go this far to get their way.

Consultant: The sad thing is that some of them make it.

Grandmother: I know, but there's no way you can stop it.

Consultant: What do you think would happen to your mom and grandmother if you did it?

Daughter: I don't know. I have no idea.

Consultant: Do you ever think of one of them as being suicidal? Do they sometimes get so fed up that they wish they were dead?

Daughter: I don't know. I guess everybody does from time to time.

Consultant: Yeah, but how about them specifically? Everybody's different. Do you ever think of your mom being that upset with herself or with you? Do you ever think that maybe your grandmother might be so sad about things that she wants to be with her husband again?

Daughter: No.

Consultant: I hear a lot about how parents worry about kids, but I rarely get a picture of how kids worry about parents. I assume it's always there. When you think about your mom and your grandmother, what do you worry about?

Daughter: I don't know.

Consultant: Do you worry your mom might be lonely or that she works too hard? What do you think? I don't want you to just agree with me.

Daughter: Well, I do think she works too hard.

Consultant: What else do you worry about when you think about your mom?

Daughter: I don't know, what if she got in a car accident.

Consultant: So you worry something might happen to her? What about your grandmother? What do you worry about when you think of her?

Daughter: Old age or death.

Consultant: How old is she?

Daughter: Sixty-eight.

Consultant: Has anything been going on that's increased your worry? You know, like Grandma having chest pain, or Mom seeming too stressed? Here's how I think. When I hear parents worrying about the kids, I assume the kids are worried about the parents the same plus 10%. I think the kids worry about their parents' happiness. [to grandmother] Do you have any idea how much longer you have to live? How old were your parents when they died?

Grandmother: My mother was 84.

Consultant: Oh boy, you're just a kid then. You're just a late teenager.

Grandmother: But you never know.

Consultant: My dad lived to an old age, so I figure I've got at least 30 years left. No need to make my funeral plans yet. [to daughter] Have you ever thought about finding a new husband for your grandma?

Daughter: No.

Consultant: Women do so much better than men after the death of a spouse. Maybe you should think about it.

The consultant pushes the images of the suicide and death in the hope of contaminating the fantasy of any rewards or potential gains, such as getting back at her mother, that Sara might harbor. He suggests some absurd options of ways in which the grandmother might deal with Sara to inadvertently encourage her to fantasize about the events after her death. He presents a haunting image when he suggests that they refuse to buy her a tombstone.

Next, the consultant continues to expand the symptom by suggesting that Mother and Grandmother are also suicidal. The consultant is trying to increase anxiety within the system, in hopes of reorganizing it. He implies that they are all patients and speculates why they might all feel that life is not worth living. While the consultant is empathic, he does not let their anxiety interfere with the discussion. It is necessary to generate sufficient affect to help participants break out of their patterns and develop more constructive ways of living.

SHARING FANTASIES AND FREE ASSOCIATIONS

Consultation moves from reality struggles to personal struggles, symbolic struggles, and finally, it is hoped, warm personal spontaneity. Gaining a new sense of unity in the consultation, the family may become confident enough to share a more personal investment in the process. The consultant participates in this stage actively as a person, sharing many aspects of his or her own life. The interaction and tone of the consultation should be stimulating and creative. The consultant's goal is to reactivate the therapy system. The consultant and family must be willing to take greater risks if the consultation is to have relevance. Freeing the system to use its self-corrective powers becomes the main thrust of the consultation. The major methodology is to encourage the active participation of the system through exaggeration and expansion of the problem.

Consultant: [to mom] I have a feeling, though, that your mother was her own boss even when her husband was alive.

Mother: You took the words right out of my mouth.

Grandmother: That's the Gestapo in me.

Consultant: You've been the Gestapo for years then, huh?

Mother: She's been the boss.

Grandmother: Kay listens to me. I don't have any trouble with her.

Consultant: How did you get started at it? Are you following in your mom's footsteps?

Grandmother: No, it goes back to a time when my sister and her kids were over for a birthday party. Her son was sneaking cookies off the table. My mother yelled at him and he ran off. My sister chased him, but she couldn't catch him. I said to myself, "If I ever have children, they are going to listen. I won't chase after them like that." It was so humiliating for my sister.

Consultant: How old were you then?

Grandmother: I'm not sure, maybe 20.

Consultant: When you're talking to Sara and thinking about you as a kid, what do you remember about you at age 16? What were you like back then? How did you fight with your mother?

Grandmother: I was quiet. I'm the youngest of four girls. We were all easygoing.

Consultant: Is that right? You didn't get into any special kind of trouble?

Grandmother: No.

Consultant: Was your mom a Gestapo?

Grandmother: No, we had to mind.

Consultant: That's your daughter's idea? Calling you the Gestapo?

Mother: She was strict with me, very strict.

Consultant: How did you make it through?

Mother: I listened because she scared me to death. I had the fear of God in me. I don't even remember doing anything wrong when I was a teenager. I went to school, never skipped class, and did my homework when I got home. She scared me so much that I minded.

Grandmother: The kids that you went with were all nice kids.

Mother: If she said, "Do this, don't do that," I just went along with it. I didn't say anything. She just put the fear of God in me. I was afraid to do anything wrong.

Consultant: When did you finally get the courage to do something wrong?

Mother: I was probably 20 or 21 before I decided that maybe I could do something wrong and not get killed! It took me a long time. All through school I behaved myself. I don't remember doing much of anything wrong.

Consultant: Do you still struggle with it?

Mother: About doing things wrong? No.

Consultant: How'd you get over it?

Mother: I don't know.

Consultant: Did getting divorced help?

Mother: No, I don't think so. I don't try to do things wrong but when I do, I don't feel as bad about it as when I was a kid. Then I was too scared. I didn't like staying in and doing my homework, but I really didn't feel rebellious about it. I just knew that's the way it was. I could take the word ''no'' with no problem. She said no, I said okay. When I got older, I made up my own mind about what to do. Sometimes I made mistakes, but I never set out to do something wrong. It just turned out to be wrong later.

Therapist: I think some of her struggle now is to do the right thing. She says she knows what is ''right'' but still struggles with it.

Consultant: It's going on right now, you mean?

Therapist: Yes. Kay still struggles inside.

Consultant: [to therapist] What's it like for you? How do you see it?

Therapist: Kay's working real hard. She is more confident about her feelings, but acting on them is difficult.

Consultant: What do you think of how your daughter's doing now, Grandma?

Grandmother: She does all right. I never had any complaints about the job she does.

Consultant: How about the other side? Do you ever feel proud of her or sometimes wish you could be her?

Grandmother: No.

Consultant: Maybe part of the struggle for Kay is not wanting to put her mom out of a job. Mom's been real busy for a long time.

Grandmother: How would I get out of a job?

Consultant: You're ready to retire?

During this stage of the consultation, the consultant shifts from topic to topic based on the family's lead. He wants to avoid repetitive conversations and stimulate more personal responses. He shares his own fantasies and free associations in hopes that the family will feel freer to share theirs. He does not press them on any particular topic, because he does not want to give them the opportunity to reject anything. He shares images and metaphors and then quickly changes the subject to bypass their defenses. He asks questions to get them to think more about themselves and what their life has been like.

The consultant identifies repeated cross-generational and intergenerational patterns. There is a theme of Grandmother parenting in a way that corrects her mother and, reciprocally, Mom parenting in a way that corrects Grandmother's strictness. Sara's rebelliousness can be viewed as the first step toward individuation. The presenting problem is a metaphorical statement of the dysfunctional process of family interaction across generations. The symptom can be redefined in an effort to facilitate the family's growth.

At this stage, the therapist comes back into the consultation. The consultant invites her to go a little further with her insights regarding the more covert dynamics of the family. Together, the consultant and therapist talk about the family while they listen.

Quickly, the therapist slides back into being oversupportive of the mother as she talks about Mom working hard. As we work with families, we often become seduced by the system. The therapist's overprotectiveness illustrates how she has become part of the system in maintaining the status quo.

Finally, the consultant again identifies the underlying theme that the daughter and mother are trying to help the grandmother by postponing her retirement. Grandmother needs to work to decrease her anxiety and despair. It keeps her from wondering about herself. It again expands the symptom by inferring that Grandmother is also a patient. Can she face the question of her own humanity and where her life is headed? As the consultant presses Grandmother, she again refocuses on the identified patient and the problem.

Grandmother: Everything with Sara is rebellion. She won't do homework. She doesn't like school.

Consultant: You know, maybe she's keeping you young, keeping you excited. Maybe she's afraid of what would happen to you if you had to give up being a mother. What will happen to you when Sara's grown up? What are you going to do when you're 70? You'll have to retire for a second time.

Grandmother: It will be great.

Consultant: Well, what's next, do you have any idea?

Grandmother: Maybe Thomas will be married and he'll have a baby I can watch.

Consultant: So you really do kind of like this?

Grandmother: It's all right, but when they get to be Sara's age and get defiant it's not good. Thomas was never that bad. He's sassy, but he's good in school.

Mother: He's not really rebellious, just sassy. He's intelligent and needs to have the last word, but he's not rebellious. Sara grew up in his shadow. Her teachers would say, "Oh, Thomas was such a good student," and it was hard on Sara. No one likes feeling compared. She resents him for being the favorite and getting to do everything first. They don't get along real well. I feel bad for Sara. I wish I could have been home all these years, to be a real mother. To cook and be there when the kids got home from school. It just didn't work out that way. Sara doesn't like the fact that she's not with me. Thomas didn't like it either, but he got over that when he was younger. Now he has his own friends and he's in college. It's not as important to him.

Consultant: [to daughter] Maybe you and Mom could go to beauty school and then work together. You could then get married, have a baby, give the baby to your grandmother, work with your mom.

Grandmother: Give me a rest for a while!

Consultant: I don't think you could stand it. You don't look like you go for resting.

Mother: Don't listen to her. I'm telling you she likes to have somebody around to tell them what to do.

Grandmother: She picks up after them when they go home. She hangs up their coats. I won't do that. They're old enough to do it on their own.

Consultant: It sounds like Kay feels guilty for not being there.

Grandmother: Well, I'm just the opposite. I want them to make their own beds.

Mother: When Mom comes to the house, she's just looking for something to holler about. She'll look until she finds something.

Grandmother: No, I don't.

Mother: Yes, you do.

Consultant: You know, I think it's good for the kids to have it both ways so they can learn what it's like to be with somebody who's tough and they learn what it's like to be with somebody who's soft.

Mother: I never make them do anything. I feel guilty that I can't be a regular mother and I couldn't be there. So when they are home, I don't make them do anything. I do it all because I'm trying to be the mother.

The consultant shifts the content to the symbolic by inquiring what the grandmother will do when she is 70. Following this interaction, there is more directness and personal investment in the consultation process. The mother offers a detailed description of the family struggle. She identifies with her daughter and challenges the grandmother by saying she likes to have someone to boss around. The grandmother and mother describe different styles of parenting, and each is critical of the other. The mother-daughter fight from the past begins to surface, and it becomes clearer how their conflict relates to Sara's problems. The consultant confirms both styles of parenting as he momentarily takes the role of parent to the family.

The underlying conflict between the mother and grandmother continues to surface. The argument becomes more tense. The mother inspired her children to act out instead of confronting the problem directly. By teasing and making absurd comments, the consultant has opened up affectively loaded issues.

Grandmother: I have enough to do without picking up after them. I do their wash, their ironing.

Mother: I'm not even disputing that. I'm saying she's a nag. She'll go on and on over the same thing. She just won't stop talking. I can understand why the kids get upset about being there. She never quits.

Therapist: Sometimes I get the feeling that Kay is reminded of herself when she was Sara's age. It seems that's what's happening right now.

Mother: Yeah, she says the same thing to me.

Consultant: Well, I've got a question for you. Do you ever find yourself being kind of tickled by Sara taking on your mom?

Mother: Once in a while, but not all the time.

Consultant: I would assume it's there.

Mother: There are other times Sara can stand up and rebel. She can do things I could have never gotten away with.

Consultant: That's what I'm talking about. There's another weird thing about three-generational politics. Have you ever had the feeling that they gang up against you?

Mother: Yeah.

Consultant: The usual thing is that the grandparents and the grandchildren are united by the fact that they have a common enemy, you.

Mother: I don't necessarily feel like the enemy. I just kind of feel like nothing. It's like I'm Sara's sister. My mother has the final say. She says, "When you're in my house I'm the boss. What I say goes." I get lost in the shuffle. She still scares me when she says to do something!

Grandmother: I want Kay to take over parenting Sara. I want her to tell her what to do.

Mother: It's strange to hear this after all these years. She's saying, "Okay, now you can be the mother and you get to be the boss." I'm lost because I wasn't the boss for all these years. She's handing me over this boss role that I never had.

Consultant: Have you ever had it out with each other? Do you ever stand up to your mom?

Mother: Not until she pushes me over the edge. I was raised to respect my parents. I keep it all inside and don't talk back. She really has to make me boil before I lose it. Then I'll fly off the handle.

Consultant: Have you ever won a round against her?

Mother: No, I usually don't win.

Consultant: I had another crazy idea. Maybe if you could take on your mother more successfully, you could also mother Sara more effectively. I bet nobody's bossed Mom around for years.

Mother: My son tries real hard. Oh, he's another one.

Consultant: Your son's so discouraged about it that he didn't even come.

Mother: He's another one that likes to be the boss.

Consultant: Tell him I'm disappointed that he didn't come.

Therapist: I'm sitting here listening to this and I got a crazy idea. Maybe Patty is wanting Kay to take her on and take charge.

Consultant: I had that feeling too.

The therapist makes a good process statement. This is a sign she is disentangling herself from the family's dynamics and moving back to the therapist role. The consultant wants to shake the system up by identifying what keeps the therapeutic process stuck. It appeared that the therapist was overinvolved or absorbed in the system. She may have become fearful of dealing directly with areas of conflict. The consultation created the opportunity for her to dislodge herself from the family's undercurrent. As the consultant worked with the family, the therapist could temporarily take a back seat and view the process from outside the system.

The consultant asks a question at the crux of the problem: "Are you aware of your pleasure in Sara's misbehaving?" The mother gives an honest answer. Now we can see the coalitions starting to shift. Mother and Sara team up to take on Grandmother, and at times Sara and Grandmother team to take on Mom. The mother deals openly with unresolved anger related to how Grandmother parented her. They move to a point at which the grandmother invites the mother to be a grownup. The consultant is careful not to disrupt the process. He is empathic but feels that this is good conflict and insists that the problem be more fully experienced. The therapist also continues to make good process comments by sharing her own "crazy idea." She feels freer to share her own associations.

Grandmother: The other day, Sara didn't go to school because she wanted to spend the day with her mother. Kay told her to tell me that she did go to school.

Mother: That's not true. I said it was up to her. Sara asked what she should say to you. I said, "I wouldn't lie if I were you. It's up to you to tell her that you didn't go to school." I put the responsibility on her.

Grandmother: Well, it didn't work. I knew Sara had skipped school because I asked Thomas. I was waiting for Kay to tell me Sara didn't go to school, but she didn't say anything.

Consultant: You mean your brother ratted on you? He's supposed to stay on your side.

Mother: He's not on her side. They fight like cats and dogs.

Consultant: That's ridiculous! The only way you can defeat your mother and grandmother is if you and your brother team up together.

Mother: He gets upset with her because she doesn't go to school. He thinks she should be more conscientious and go to school. They don't think alike at all.

Consultant: Tell him he's making a mistake. He should side with Sara against you. It will help you learn more about being a mother. Do you think it's true the reason you came in was because she was having trouble in school, or was there more to it?

Mother: There was a lot more to it than bad grades. She had taken a turn for the worse last year. She began getting suspensions and detentions. Until last year, even though she struggled for grades, she tried to do well. Last year was the first evidence of rebelliousness. But there were other things too. She's always felt Thomas was the favorite and tries to live up to him.

Consultant: What was your deepest fear about what was going to happen if you didn't get help?

Mother: I thought she might commit suicide, or get into drugs, or do anything to be rebellious and get noticed. I know that's why people rebel. They do it for attention. Last New Year's Eve I let her stay at my apartment even though I had to work. I don't do this very often, but she called and begged me to let her go home to my apartment after school. I was experimenting, so I said yes. So she called on New Year's and asked me if she could go roller skating and go home to our apartment and stay over with this girl. I felt bad because I had to work New Year's Eve and I thought she should have some kind of fun on New Year's Eve. I told her she could go roller skating as long as this girl's parents took them to the roller rink and picked them up and brought them back to my apartment. I would call her from work to make sure everything was all right.

Well, the whole thing was a lie. There were never plans to go skating, and no parents were involved in driving her from school to my apartment. The kid that dropped them off at the apartment went out and got drunk, then came back to my apartment and wanted to have a party. They let him in and couldn't get him back out again. He finally got in his truck, drove around the yard, ran over the snow fence, and did a lot of damage to the yard. It was a noisy, wild scene. He woke up the neighbors. After talking to the neighbors, I found out what actually happened. Sara did confess. I tried to do her a favor, and it was all a lie. We finally found the kid, got his name, and had him pay for all the damages. That was the first of her rebelliousness.

Grandmother: The kid wanted to bring in beer and she told him no. That's what made him mad.

Mother: So everything got out of hand. One of my rules is that if she ever does stay at home, she's not to let anyone in besides the friend that she's having stay over. If she's having a girlfriend over, that's the only person allowed in. Don't answer the door, and if you answer the phone don't say I'm not there. Well, she disobeyed.

The consultant continues to expand the symptoms as things begin to refocus on Thomas. He is stubborn. Sara has been "double-crossed" by him. It is important that the sibling subgroup remain intact. Mother and Grandmother remain focused on Sara's misbehavior. They are resistant to discussing options or how they contribute to the family struggles. The consultant refocuses on why they came in for the consultation. The mother can be more open now that they have established a relationship and created a playful context. A story unfolds of Sara being described as a naughty, tricky girl, but as Grandmother points out, Sara knew how to draw a line and not let the guy bring in the beer. She got that right. Sara did not get defensive during this period.

TERMINATION

In the final stage of the consultation, the consultant attempts to reempower the members of the system so that they can take control. The consultant restructures the therapy members' fantasy that someone outside can determine how they should proceed with their lives. The goal of termination is to establish a tone that the system is adequate to confront problems independently. The consultant's stance becomes that of an outsider as the therapy system is recognized as independent and ongoing. The ending usually begins with the consultant acknowledging that the therapy time is almost up. If the family has anything more to deal with, now is the time.

Consultant: We're getting near the end; anything else you want to get at? It sounds like they're doing pretty well with no men.

Therapist: I think so.

Consultant: [to Sara] You don't have any sense that Grandmother needs a husband or your mother needs a husband? How about your mother; she wouldn't have any trouble finding a guy?

Daughter: She doesn't like the one she's got now.

Consultant: Maybe you ought to take over.

Daughter: Yeah, I think I should.

Consultant: That's the kids' job, you know, to find a new father.

Daughter: She'll have more troubles then.

Mother: She doesn't like the guy I've been seeing for 12 years. That's another problem.

Grandmother: He is a jerk.

Daughter: It's true.

Mother: We all agree on that.

Consultant: Well, maybe you ought to get rid of him and find another one. Parents are so dumb when it comes to finding someone.

Mother: Get into another relationship? I don't like this relationship. I think I just put up with it because I don't want to go through the whole hassle of starting over. I'm too tired to think about ever starting over.

Consultant: I wonder if that's your worst sin, that you put up with stuff that doesn't add to your life.

Mother: I do that quite often.

Consultant: I know it. I think it can steal your soul if you end up putting up with too many things. Life becomes all compromise. [to Sara] Do you think you'll ever go find your dad?

Grandmother: That's impossible.

Daughter: Yeah, I will never know who my father was.

Consultant: It sounds pretty rough. Is this something you have all talked about?

Mother: This is not a family secret; everyone knows about it. We just do the best we can. That was a long time ago.

Grandmother: That's Sara's other fault. She wants a dad. She picked her girlfriend's dad. She bakes him cakes and everything. She likes him.

Consultant: No luck, though. Sometimes if you pick two or three men, you can use the group like a dad.

Mother: I always thought my son would be the one that wanted a dad. But he hasn't had as big a problem with it as Sara has had.

Grandmother: Yeah, but Thomas knows who his father is.

Mother: But he never wanted to look him up or anything. He didn't have this thing where he had to have a dad.

Consultant: But he could go see his father.

Mother: No. I mean, if he wanted to he could. He could go say, I'm your son. But he has never done that.

Grandmother: It was the other way around. His father never wanted to know him.

Consultant: So at least he knows there's somebody somewhere, but Sara, you don't.

Therapist: I found it interesting, Sara has a small recollection of her grandfather.

Grandmother: Yeah, but you think your grandfather didn't like you. It was because he didn't like Kay because she had a baby and wasn't married. But it wasn't that he didn't like you.

Mother: When Sara was born, I was living with my parents. Since I wasn't married, I wasn't allowed to bring her into the house. I had to put her in a foster home for about 6 months until I could find a job, get an apartment, and be able to take her.

Consultant: Sounds like he was tough too, then?

Mother: He just hated me, he despised me.

Consultant: Was it because of the babies, or was it something else?

Grandmother: It was because she wasn't married.

Mother: Total disgrace, ever since then things went downhill. He never called me by name. I got called everything but a truck driver.

Consultant: Did he ever make up before he died?

Mother: No. I wasn't even allowed to bring Sara into the house. When it came time for me to visit her, I went to the foster mother's house. Well, finally he saw her one day and decided to like her because it wasn't her fault.

Grandmother: She was walking then.

Mother: So she knew him for a short time before he died. He finally gave in and decided it wasn't her fault. Even though he hated me, why should he take it out on her? So for her it can't be a wonderful thing. For some reason Thomas felt so much more wanted. His life started out better. Nobody put him in a foster home. He was the first grandchild, and everybody gave him everything he wanted. If he even whined about something, he got it. Everyone spent time with him. Sara came along and the circumstances behind that weren't the greatest. Then I had to put her in a foster home and work. I got her on her birthday. She was my birthday present. Anyway, she arrived under totally different circumstances.

Consultant: Yeah, it is kind of sad when you hear about it.

Mother: I had to work hard to get her.

Consultant: So maybe that could tell a lot about why she feels the way she feels. It sounds like over these 9 months a lot of things have straightened out.

Mother: We're trying.

Consultant: None of you seem very upset about it, though.

Mother: We are. We may not be upset right at this second. But when things go wrong at home, we're upset.

Consultant: Well, that's life, you know. It's always got ups and downs.

Mother: Oh yeah, well, that's what I keep telling Sara. You've got to just keep going. Every time you think that things can't get worse.... You've got to think of the things you can be thankful for, and not the things that you don't like.

Consultant: Maybe, if you figure out a way to quit putting up with things. Try to get some clear sense of where you think you want to go. It would help Sara.

Grandmother: She puts up with a lot at work and then blows up at home.

Mother: Well, I have to.

Grandmother: Well, the other one tells everybody off.

Mother: Well, I'm not like that. I don't.

Consultant: She's not any good at it, I don't think.

Mother: You know, I'm afraid I'll insult somebody. That's my worst fear, to think I insulted somebody else. I usually just keep it to myself and keep my mouth shut.

Grandmother: That's the Russian in you.

Mother: Oh, it takes a drink for me to open my mouth.

Consultant: Maybe you can just keep coaching her on how to stick up for herself.

Mother: Yeah, I'm getting a little better. For years I never argued with anybody. I bet I was 30 years old, maybe even older before I got in an argument with anybody other than my son.

Consultant: That's what kids are for; they teach you how to stick up for yourself.

Mother: Well, he's the one that go me to argue. He got me so mad I couldn't help it. Before that no one ever made me mad enough to get in an argument. I would just say okay and just keep it inside me.

For all the upset, the consultant reinforces that the family has integrity. The task of the consultant is to invoke a different and perhaps more congruent reality. The family should not alter their course because someone else tells them to change directions. The consultant accomplishes their goal when the family and therapist are free to take or reject whatever they want.

As the consultation draws to a close, the consultant becomes more explicit about earlier inferences. He asks if Sara would like to go find her dad. Then the intimate family struggles come out. Frequently, these painful stories are shared in the final stage of a consultation. The telling of this complex story is sad. The women are upset but seem united in their problems with men and belonging. The consultant shares his emotional response. Intimate disclosures such as rape, suicide, and other traumatic events are not uncommon in consultations. These disclosures are typically presented in two manners. One manner is matter of fact; the family is already aware of this information. The other type of self-disclosure is more emotional and unsettling. These disclosures are unknown to both the therapist and other family members. They require extensive processing during the consultation and in the ongoing therapy.

The consultant continues to challenge the mother's role and coaches her on how to be "a someone." She needs to learn to get past just putting up with things. He instructs Grandmother to keep on coaching, and maybe her daughter can be helpful in teaching her to stick up for herself. Finally, the consultant gives the family one more opportunity before they stop. The consultant must be sensitive to the limits of the experience and back off when those limits have been reached. The important cue is a breakthrough with the system, but within the limits imposed by the allotted time. If the consultant can communicate that he or she does not need to save the family, it may help them break through the impasse.

Consultant: We've got to stop. Do you have any questions you want to ask us before you leave?

Mother: Is there anything I could do to help her do better in school or to have more incentive? She doesn't want to go to school. She doesn't want to try. What do I do in that department?

Consultant: The thing that occurs to me is if you start pressuring more for you getting what you want, it may help her.

Grandmother: Yeah, because I don't say anything about her school work, right? I don't even mention it. I leave that to her mother.

Consultant: Sometimes I wonder if school is really worth it. It seems like kids go to school because people make them. They don't learn anything, and then they get out and figure out what they need to know. Then they learn something, when they need to. If it gets too much of a pain in the neck, you might consider her dropping out, going to beauty school. Then if she decides she wants to go back, she could.

Mother: No, that would be over my dead body, sorry.

Consultant: So, are you suicidal too?

Mother: I guess. I hadn't thought of it that way before.

Consultant: God, I wouldn't die for a kid dropping out of school. It isn't worth it.

Mother: I tell her there are requirements in life.

Consultant: You could blame your mother for her failure.

Grandmother: What's she going to do, bum around all day with somebody else?

Mother: I try to teach her that you're not going to like everything you have to do in life, but there are requirements. There are some things you have to do that you're not going to like. You can't do everything you like. It doesn't work that way. Somehow she hasn't gotten that message.

Consultant: But she's suspicious of you when you say that. I should say, I'm suspicious of you when you say that. It feels like you've been cornered by that but you're trying to figure out a way to defeat it.

Mother: Oh, I haven't liked it, but I had to do a lot of things I didn't want to do. I'm trying to tell her to put up with things.

Consultant: And she knows that you don't really mean it. That you wish it wasn't so. No, I've got all kinds of crazy ideas. How about you, Sara; do you want to ask any questions?

Daughter: Mom, can I quit school?

Mother: No.

Consultant: What would you do if you did?

Daughter: Get a job.

Consultant: Where? You've got to be careful.

Daughter: Probably McDonald's or something.

Grandmother: You'd have to work fast. You're pokey.

Consultant: I think she's a good worker.

Grandmother: She likes to stay in bed until 2:00.

Consultant: Well, the boss wouldn't mind.

Grandmother: During the summer, I get her up about noon. But at home she'll stay there till 2:00 if her mother doesn't wake her up.

Consultant: You know, I've got another idea for you, Sara. There's a friend of mine, we've worked together for years. He has always suggested to kids that they go back and pretend they are 11 for one afternoon a week. So you could do that on the afternoon when your mom's home. You could be 11 and, how old were you when she was born?

Mother: Oh, God, I don't know, 24.

Consultant: Twenty-four, so you'd be 35 and just play house. Then you could get to be cuddled. It really is very nice. It sounds like you both feel cheated by not having had enough of that.

Mother: If I could just win the lottery, that would solve the whole problem! I could stay home, take her shopping and buy her all the things she wants me to. She'd be happy.

Consultant: Good luck.

At the end, the consultant makes another playful suggestion that they could go back in time but this time do things differently. The covert message is that they don't need to give up. There are many ways to try. He leaves them with an image of how they might work things out by cuddling. The consultant then quickly moves out of the system. In ending, the consultant thanks the family for their spontaneity and wishes them well on their journey. The consultant's departure must be firm and definite, leaving the therapist and family free to continue on their own.

SUMMARY

Family therapy frequently takes on the quality of a secret exchange between the family and therapist. The therapist often carries the burden of a difficult case alone, to the detriment of both the family and the therapist. Few therapists can go it alone without undue distress to themselves and some of their client families. The routine use of a consultant in ongoing therapy is one means of helping the system remain personal and involved in the therapy process. The outsider's view of the therapy process complements and supplements the relationship. An effective consultation leads to improvement in and renewal of therapy. It attempts to sample here-and-now experiences of the honest relating of the therapy system by focusing on present-tense interactions.

This chapter has described a method of consultation and how it helps restructure therapy. The use of a consultant to add emotional voltage is important when the therapy system is at an impasse. An impasse often centers on the lack of clarity of the problem, contradictory treatment goals, noncompliance with the treatment structure, or an inability to develop a collaborative relationship. Each consultation is idiosyncratic and contingent on the interview at hand. Procedures for this model, however, are rooted in a symbolic-experiential orientation to working with families. We hope the ideas discussed in this book give substance to our conceptual formulations. We believe that it is valuable to explain the process and hope that family therapists will profit from the help of a consultant.

References

Barrows, S., & Zeig, J. (1981). Interview with Carl Whitaker. *American Journal of Family Therapy, 9*(2), 3–11.

Betz, B., & Whitehorn, J. C. (1975). *Effective psychotherapy with the schizophrenic patient.* New York: Jason Aronson.

Connell, G., Mitten, T., & Whitaker, C. (1993). Reshaping family symbols: A symbolic-experiential perspective. *Journal of Marital and Family Therapy, 19*, 243–251.

Connell, G., Mitten, T., & Whitaker, C. (1995). Les fondements de la therapie symboliqueexperientielle. In M. Elkiam (Ed.), *Panorama des therpaies familiales* (pp. 359–385). Paris: Editions Du Seuil.

Connell, G., & Russell, L. (1986). In-therapy consultation: A supervision and therapy technique of symbolic-experiential family therapy. *American Journal of Family Therapy, 12*, 313–323.

Connell, G., Whitaker, C., Garfield, R., & Connell, L. (1990). The process of in-therapy consultation: A symbolic-experiential perspective. *Journal of Strategic and Systemic Therapies, 9*(1), 32–38.

Haley, J. (1988). Reflections on supervision. In H. S. Liddle, D. C. Breunlin, & R. C. Schwartz (Eds.), *Handbook of family therapy training and supervision.* New York: Guilford Press.

Keith, D. V. (1982). Symbolic-experiential family therapy. In J. R. Neill & D. P. Kniskern (Eds.), *From psyche to system: The evolving therapy of Carl Whitaker.* New York: Guilford Press.

Keith, D. V., & Whitaker, C. A. (1978). Struggling with the impotence impasse: Absurdity and acting in. *Journal of Marriage and Family Counseling, 3,* 69–77.

Keith, D. V., & Whitaker, C. A. (1980). Add craziness and stir: Psychotherapy with a psychoticogenic family. In M. Andolfi & I. Zwerling (Eds.), *Dimensions of family therapy* (pp. 139–160). New York: Guilford Press.

Kopp, S. (1976). *If you meet the buddha on the road kill him.* New York: Bantam Doubleday.

Malone, T. P., Whitaker, C. A., Warkentin, J., & Felder, R. E. (1961). Rational and nonrational psychotherapy—A reply. *American Journal of Psychotherapy, 15*, 212–220.

Minuchin, S. (1982). Foreword. In J. R. Neill & D. P. Kniskern (Eds.), *From psyche to system: The evolving therapy of Carl Whitaker.* New York: Guilford Press.

Napier, A. (1988). *The fragile bond.* New York: Harper & Row. Napier, A. Y., & Whitaker, C. A. (1978). *The family crucible.* New York: Harper & Row.

Neill, J. R., & Kniskern, D. P. (Eds.). (1982). *From psyche to system: The evolving therapy of Carl Whitaker.* New York: Guilford Press.

O'Hanlon, W. H. (1989). Family therapy news. *Family Therapy Networker, 13*(2).

Simon, R. (1985). Take it or leave it: An interview with Carl Whitaker. *Family Therapy Networker, 9*(5), 27–37, 70–75.

Simon, R. (1989). Reaching out to life. *Family Therapy Networker, 13*(1), 37–43.

Sharpsteen, B. (Producer), & Geronini, C., Luski, H., & Jackson, W. (Directors). (1951). *Alice in Wonderland*, An Adaptation of Lewis *Carroll's The Adventures of Alice in Wonderland Through the Looking Glass* [Film]. (Available from Walt Disney Productions)

Spradley, J. P. (1979). *The ethnographic interview*. Chicago: Holt, Rinehart, & Winston.

Warkentin, J., & Valerius, E. (1976). Seasons in the affairs of men. In A. Burton (Ed.), *In what makes behavior change possible?* (pp. 152–176). New York: Brunner/Mazel.

Warkentin, J., & Whitaker, C. A. (1964). *The one-to-one therapeutic relationship in the treatment of schizophrenia*. Paper presented at the Eastern Pennsylvania Psychiatric Institute Conference.

Whitaker, C. A. (1944). The delinquent's first interview. *Probation, 23*(1), 15–20.

Whitaker, C. A. (1946). Ormsby Village: An experiment with forced psychotherapy in the rehabilitation of the delinquent adolescent. *Psychiatry, 9,* 239–250.

Whitaker, C. A. (1958). Psychotherapy with couples. *American Journal of Psychotherapy, 12,* 18–23.

Whitaker, C. A. (1961). The ongoing training of the psychotherapist. In N. P. Dellis & H. K. Stone (Eds.), *The training of psychotherapists: A multidisciplinary approach* (pp. 151–168). Baton Rouge: Louisiana State University Press.

Whitaker, C. A. (1962, July). The use of aggression in group therapy. *Journal of the Los Angeles Group Therapy Association,* pp. 4–14.

Whitaker, C. A. (1965a). Acting out in family psychotherapy. In L. E. Abt & Weissman (Eds.), *Acting out: Theoretical and clinical aspects*. New York: Grune & Stratton.

Whitaker, C. A. (1965b, January). *The psychotherapy of married couples*. Lecture delivered at the Cleveland Institute of Gestalt Therapy, Cleveland, OH.

Whitaker, C. A. (1966). Training for the unreality experience. *Voices, 2,* 43–46.

Whitaker, C. A. (1972). Commentary: A longitudinal view of therapy styles where n=1. *Family Process, 11,* 13–15.

Whitaker, C. A. (1973). My philosophy of psychotherapy. *Journal of Contemporary Psychotherapy, 6,* 49–52.

Whitaker, C. A. (1974). A family therapist looks at marital therapy. In A. S. Gurman & D. G. Rice (Eds.), *Couples in conflict* (pp. 165–174). New York: Jason Aronson.

Whitaker, C. A. (1976). A family is a four-dimensional relationship. In P. J. Guerin, Jr. (Ed.), *Family therapy: Theory and practice*. New York: Gardner Press.

Whitaker, C. A. (1986). Family therapy consultation as invasion. In L. Wynne, S. McDaniel, & T. Weber (Eds.), *Systems consultation: A new perspective for family therapy* (pp. 80–86). New York: Guilford Press.

Whitaker, C. A. (1989). *Midnight musings of a family therapist*. New York: Norton.

Whitaker, C. A., & Abroms, G. M. (1974). New approaches to residency training in psychiatry. In G. Farwell, N. Gamsky, & P. Mathieu-Coughlan (Eds.), *The counselor's handbook*. New York: Intext.

Whitaker, C. A., & Bumberry, W. M. (1988). *Dancing with the family*. New York: Brunner/Mazel.

Whitaker, C., & Connell, G. (1990). Die infrastrukur die familientherapie. *Integrative Therapie,* 358–369.

Whitaker, C. A., Greenberg, A., & Greenberg, M. L. (1979). Existential marital therapy. A synthesis—A subsystem of existential family therapy. *Interaction, 2,* 169–200.

Whitaker, C. A., & Jaffe, R. (1992). *Parallel play: The journey inside*. Learning edge series. AAMFT video.

Whitaker, C. A., & Keith, D. V. (1980). Family therapy as symbolic experience. *International Journal of Family Psychiatry, 1,* 197–208.

Whitaker, C. A., & Keith, D. V. (1981). Symbolic-experiential family therapy. In A. Gurman & D. Kniskern (Eds.), *The handbook of family therapy* (pp. 187–225). New York: Brunner/Mazel.

Whitaker, C. A., & Malone, T. P. (1953). *The roots of psychotherapy*. New York: Blakiston.

Whitaker, C. A., & Malone, T. P. (1963). Psychotherapy of the actingout schizophrenic. *American Journal of Psychotherapy, 17,* 417–426.

Whitaker, C. A., & Warkentin, J. (1965). Process koans. *Voices, 1,* 91–92.

Whitaker, C. A., Warkentin, J., & Johnson, N. (1950). The psychotherapeutic impasse. *Journal of Orthopsychiatry, 20,* 641–647.

Index